Dear friends of the Penn State University Moms + Dads Football family,

We have cherished knowing Dennis and love that he and Tom have continued to stay close.

We thought you might enjoy this attempt to describe the importance of teachers and how they go beyond the "basics" every day. You might recognize the story that starts on page 104. Forgive us for any embellishments on

what we were told was a story that came to Dennis from Dad.
Thanks for all your kindness you gave Tom.

THE PROBLEM ISN'T TEACHERS

Stories and Essays that tell the Truth About the Real Plight of American Education

RAYMOND J. GOLARZ
and
MARION J. GOLARZ

Marion Golarz

authorHOUSE®

AuthorHouse™
1663 Liberty Drive
Bloomington, IN 47403
www.authorhouse.com
Phone: 1-800-839-8640

© 2012 Raymond and Marion Golarz. All rights reserved.

No part of this book may be reproduced, stored in a retrieval system, or transmitted by any means without the written permission of the author.

Published by AuthorHouse 8/14/2012

ISBN: 978-1-4772-5535-3 (hc)
ISBN: 978-1-4772-5536-0 (e)
ISBN: 978-1-4772-5537-7 (sc)

Library of Congress Control Number: 2012914116

Any people depicted in stock imagery provided by Thinkstock are models, and such images are being used for illustrative purposes only.
Certain stock imagery © Thinkstock.

This book is printed on acid-free paper.

Because of the dynamic nature of the Internet, any web addresses or links contained in this book may have changed since publication and may no longer be valid. The views expressed in this work are solely those of the author and do not necessarily reflect the views of the publisher, and the publisher hereby disclaims any responsibility for them.

Table of Contents

Dedication	ix
Acknowledgments	xi
Foreword	xv
Preface	xvii
Author's Preface	xxi
Introduction: Upside Down and Simply Wrong	xxv

SECTION ONE: HERE, THERE, AND BACK AGAIN

Chapter 1.	"America, We Have a Problem"	3
	"Off the Record?"	5
	The Trees Didn't Look Quite So Lovely Anymore	10
	"I Don't Know How Much Longer I Can Do This."	12
	The Rookie	13
	"They Will Here!"	15
Chapter 2.	The Way It Was	26
	Miss Virden	27
	Opening the Treasure Box	31
	New Teacher in Old Cloth	34
Chapter 3.	"Watch CNN. Our School Is on Lockdown!"	47
	Statistics Never Tell the Whole Story.	53

SECTION TWO: PAIN COMES TO SCHOOL

Chapter 4.	Child Abuse	59
	Recurrent Image	59
	A Fragile Decanter	61
Chapter 5.	The Crush of Poverty	64
	The Real World	67
	Shades of Gray	74
	The Parent Center	77
	Old Neighborhoods and Such	79
	A Couple of "Right-On" Articles	81
	Poverty Is No Accident	84
Chapter 6.	Drugs and Schools	88
	Drugs from Hell: Meth Labs	92

SECTION THREE: "AND THE WALLS CAME TUMBLING DOWN"

Chapter 7.	What Ever Happened to Safe and Orderly?	97
	Assistant Principals' Meeting	97
	Order and Sacredness in American Courts of Law	101
Chapter 8.	A Civil and Disciplined Environment	103
	One Teacher's Nightmare	108
Chapter 9.	When Education Became a Right	112
	The Young Boxer	119

SECTION FOUR: THE CRITICAL IMPORTANCE OF GOOD PARENTING

Chapter 10.	The Cycles of Success	129
Chapter 11.	Poverty Cripples Parenting	134

SECTION FIVE: THE WAR OVER PURPOSE

Chapter 12.	Revisiting the Purpose of Public Schools	139
	Confusion over the Role of Public Schools	141
	The Business Agenda	143
	Finding a Scapegoat	144
	The SCANS Report	147
Chapter 13.	A Bus Ride with a Purpose	153

SECTION SIX: THE PRICE OF PREJUDICE

Chapter 14.	A Set of Stories	163
	A Proud Young Navajo	164
	A Trip to the Bus Garage	166
	Dr. Hernandez	167
	Heartland Basketball	169
	"Old Friends That I Haven't Seen for Awhile"	170
	"Oh, Say Can You See"	172
	Knowing Your Audience	173
Chapter 15.	Pebbles into the Water	175
	Words to the Wounded and Abused	178
	A Tree Grows in Chicago	179
	I Met a Nice Man	180

SECTION SEVEN: THE EVOLUTION AND NEED FOR UNIONS

Chapter 16.	Together We Stand	183
	"Sweet Land of Liberty"	184
	"Lift That Bale"	188
	The Growth Years of Teacher Unions	191
	Union Leadership with Courage and Vision	193
	Planting the Beans	194
Chapter 17.	Southern Indiana	195
	A Union Comes Through	199
	Collaborative Bargaining	203
	Language of the Heart	207

SECTION EIGHT: FOR EXTRA CREDIT

Chapter 18.	Thoughts from the Trenches	211
	A Glimpse Inside Our Classrooms	213
Chapter 19.	Good Teacher? Bad Teacher?	219
	Can You Act, Dance, Sing?	225
	Start by Saying Thanks	227
	The Definitive Drucker	229
Chapter 20.	You Don't Really Know Us	231

Epilogue: A War worth Waging	235
Suggested Readings	241
About The Authors	245

Dedication

To Teachers Everywhere

Thank You

Acknowledgments

No matter how often you have written, whether one book, or two, or five, as a writer you are never really sure that you said it right, or wrote it clearly or—God forbid—made a critical omission or included a gross inaccuracy. Therefore, before you publish, you ask a group of people you truly admire to read your manuscript. You might ask them to consider as we did: Was it easy to read? Did we miss the mark? Did we leave anything out?

So, to our readers, we extend a genuine thank you. We needed your help more than you knew and found much wisdom in your remarks: Dr. Lonnie Barber, former teacher and current Superintendent of the Blaine County Schools, Hailey, Idaho; Dr. Tom Evert, former teacher and former Superintendent of the Janesville Public Schools, Janesville, Wisconsin; Mr. William Hays, current teacher in the Monroe County Community Schools in Bloomington, Indiana; Dr. Phedonia Johnson, former teacher and former director of the Chicago Inner City CANAL Project in Chicago, Illinois; Dr. Bette Lang, former teacher and former Superintendent of the Stevens Point Area Public Schools, Stevens Point, Wisconsin; Mr. Pat O'Rourke, former teacher and current president of the Hammond Teachers Federation in Hammond, Indiana; Dr. Gary Phillips, former teacher and current director of the National School Improvement Project, Bainbridge Island, Washington; Mrs. Mary Phillips, former teacher in the Central Kitsap Schools, Silverdale, Washington; Dr. Robert Ranells, former teacher and current Superintendent of Wallace School District, Wallace, Idaho; Dr. Mary Ann Ranells, former teacher and current Superintendent of the Lakeland Schools in Rathdrum, Idaho; Dr. Pam Santesteban, former teacher and former Assistant Superintendent of the Madison Elementary Schools in Phoenix, Arizona; Mrs. Tanya Scherschel, current substitute teacher, O'Fallon, Illinois; Mr. Sam Thomas, current teacher in the Richmond Community Schools, Richmond, Indiana.

The chapter titled "The Critical Importance of Good Parenting" could never have been appropriately written without the assistance and candid personal insights of a group of highly successful young parents. We asked for their involvement, in part, because they are successful by any definition, but we chose them more because, in addition to their obvious success, we had, on many occasions, watched them parent. They are masters. Theirs is the quality of parenting that makes the difference. So, to this group we say, "Thank you." Without your help, this chapter would never have been written with the depth and clarity that it now reflects: Jonathan Broadwell; Hon. Marshelle Dawkins Broadwell; Dr. Aurelian Craiutu; Christina Craiutu; Heather Golarz; Michael Golarz; John Scherschel; Tanya Scherschel; Dr. Mary Smith; and Tim Smith.

Our son, Dan Golarz, teaches calculus in the inner city of L.A. He, like so many teachers, discourages compliments directed his way. We're reasonably sure, therefore, that he will not like us saying this, but we must. He has taught and continues to teach us so much. The writing of this book has his handprints all over it. So, we simply say to him, "Thank you, Dan. Thank you very much."

One late night, Ray was finishing a four-hour session making a number of tweaks and adjustments to the document of this book on the computer. His arm tired from the extended session and rested on a number of keys on the keyboard. Everything went dark. The screen in front of him was blank. A 267 page document was gone. To anyone who has not been there, we can assure you that the total panic, coupled with the rapid spike in body temperature is hard to adequately describe. If you have had the experience, simply mentioning it brings back to you a pain you'd really rather not resurrect.

Ray grabbed the phone and dialed our youngest son Tom who was at that time in Indianapolis with friends. He told him what he had done and then described what happened. Tom said several times in a calm and composed voice, "Dad, don't touch the computer. Don't touch anything." He concluded by saying, "Dad, I'm on my way home. Remember, don't touch anything."

To our son Thomas John Golarz, "Thank you, son, for the countless interruptions to your days and your life as we struggled through this book—a book that would never have been done without you."

A heartfelt thank you to Mr. Pat O'Rourke, who wrote the Foreword for this book, and to Dr. Mary Ann Ranells, author of the book's Preface. Thank you both for assisting us by so eloquently setting the appropriate tone.

Finally we wish to express our profound appreciation to Dr. Bruce M. Smith, former editor-in-chief of the *Phi Delta Kappan*. With his professional experience, superior editorial skills, and thorough understanding of the education landscape, he gave us wise counsel regarding content, appropriate language and the need for clarity. Most importantly he acknowledged our effort to deliver this necessary and long overdue message affirming the dignity of teachers.

Foreword

With over 40 years of experience, Ray and Marion Golarz are uniquely qualified to analyze the state of education in our country. In an environment that has grown increasingly hostile to teachers, these authors take a careful look at the attacks that seem to be coming not just from influential parties, but from ordinary citizens as well. Using carefully crafted essays and poignant stories, they draw on history, experience, research, and common sense to examine the situations, conditions, and beliefs that have led to the extremely negative opinions currently directed at teachers who, with the legitimate help of their unions, are trying their best to cope with the overwhelmingly difficult challenges that come to their classrooms.

Throughout the book we are reminded of the mission given this society by our forefathers. It was their understanding, as our authors point out, that in order to preserve this unique democracy, all citizens need to have an education that would equip them not only to enrich their lives, but would also allow them to engage in the work necessary to fulfill their obligations as citizens of this great nation.

If you are a teacher, *The Problem Isn't Teachers* will inspire you to take pride in what you do and in what your predecessors have done to help people take advantage of the gifts of freedom and opportunity offered to our citizens—gifts and opportunities that are unparalleled in other parts of the world. You will be encouraged to think about the contributions that have been made by those who toiled in the old one-room school houses that dotted our prairies, farms, and villages and by those who still toil in our towns, cities, and mega-cities. You will understand better why your job has never been easy and why the problems you face now sometimes make your job nearly impossible. You will feel good again about your work, knowing that you try to offer caring support to all of your students, including those who are disadvantaged or troubled. You can feel confident that you offer instruction in subjects that allow students to have the choice to lead independent, rewarding, and meaningful lives. You will be gratefully reminded that you and your fellow teachers throughout our history have helped your students to gain the capacity to be active participants in the governance of our American nation.

If you are a parent, a student, or an ordinary citizen, you will, after finishing this book, have a deeper understanding of the challenges that face our educational system and especially those that face classroom teachers every day. Thus, you should have the knowledge and wisdom necessary to confront the negative criticism that in today's world calls for such drastic measures as the unreasonable firing of good teachers or the focused attempt to strip them of their unions.

With care and detail, the authors lament the conditions which continue to lead to the frustration and pain that overwhelm so many teachers. They also state repeatedly that their biggest fear is that the current shortsighted decisions regarding how education should occur in this country may cause us to lose the very democracy that has made it possible for a free people to choose the kind of life they want for themselves and for their children. To change this direction, they offer a set of bold—with a capital B—recommendations. Any move toward implementing these recommendations will go a long way toward ensuring that we are the kind of nation and the kind of citizenry our forefathers envisioned.

Ray and Marion have been my friends and professional colleagues for over four decades now, so I can assure that they write not only of what they have read, but of what they have, with others of this profession, lived.

This is a book you must read.

> Mr. Patrick O'Rourke, President
> The Hammond Teachers Federation
>
> Founding Appointee of the United States National Board of Professional Teaching Standards
>
> 20 Year Member of the American Federation Of Teachers K-12 Program and Policies Committee

Preface

This is not an easy book to read. For those who love children, have devoted their lives to their well-being, and believe public schools keep our country strong, *The Problem Isn't Teachers* will inspire you, make you laugh out loud, make you weep, and anger you. You will not find answers. You will not find hope. You will, however, become transfixed within the stories and characters as the authors take you on an emotional, thought-provoking journey through the complex issues thwarting the possibilities of greatness in our public school system.

For critics of public education, you will be disturbed by the raw emotions juxtaposed to the unceasing damage caused by ill-fated legislative fixes that ultimately confuse the ends with the means and make futile attempts to correct societal ills by placing blame on the very institution that keeps the tapestry of our nation from unraveling.

The stories in this book portray the urgent need for all—proponents and critics alike—to join together to confront the issues that could finally transform education to meet its undeniable purpose—teaching and learning for all. The authors weave the tapestry revealing the values critical to civility. Beginning with a brutal portrait of the current challenges confronting our schools, the authors move on to a series of revealing snapshots of classrooms in days gone by. It is a nostalgic reminiscence of a stronger nation, a deeper conscience, and a reliance on values embedded in threads of gold and silver forming the borders of the tapestry. From there the threads take on darker colors with a coarser texture. Each chapter weaves an iconic symbol ranging from the effects of poverty, to child and drug abuse, the feeling of helplessness in the schools to maintain discipline. The examination of court decisions and legislation through narrative will shock you and knock you to your knees. The patterns in the tapestry reflect an array of ever changing hues as confusion reigns regarding the purpose of education brought about by outsider influence, misguided business models that have no place in a world of children, and political insanity.

An examination of the variables surrounding the labels of "good" teacher or "bad" teacher makes you laugh and cry, but, in the end, the burning question remains, "Do you love what you teach and do you love those you teach?" It's what keeps you coming back every day.

An examination of the importance and need for unions shatters misperceptions and hateful criticisms. There is no fight when we do it right. There is great debate—a debate of ideas, not people. And the tapestry has a river of red running through it.

The book concludes with a return to what we want for all children—to leave a legacy that will serve our children for the generations to come:

> We bequeath to our descendants a better, safer world than the one in which we live today: a world in which people will be free from the terrors of war and oppression; free from the handicaps of ignorance and poverty; and free to realize their own talents and fulfill their own destinies. (anonymous)

Everyone should read this book to better understand the complexities of improving our nation. Blaming the public school system is not the answer.

With heartfelt admiration and appreciation to Dr. Raymond and Marion Golarz, I hope you will be committed to joining the "fray." There is no better calling; there is no cause more deserving.

Mary Ann Ranells, Ph.D.
Superintendent, Lakeland School District, Idaho
President, Idaho School Superintendents Association

Note to the Reader:

In this book we have included true stories and anecdotes which are intended to illustrate in a vivid way the significance of the issues we raise in our discussions. Where these are drawn from the professional and personal experience of Ray Golarz, they are narrated by him in his own voice. The essays, opinions, and recommendations presented herein represent what we both understand to be our nation's history and the current problems it now faces, along with our view of what must now take place in order to best prepare our young people to lead full lives while they strive to ensure the preservation of our democracy.

In order to protect some identities, we have occasionally changed or withheld names.

Author's Preface

An Unfair Fight

Because American teachers today seem to have so many formidable opponents, it seemed natural to incorporate within the text of this book a boxing metaphor. You will find the boxing metaphor used in this Author's Preface, in the chapter dealing specifically with Supreme Court decisions, and in the Epilogue. In each case our champion is the American school teacher. The opponents vary.

When I was a young kid, I was taught to box. From the men who taught me, from the older, decent neighborhood kids, and from the sport itself, I learned to abhor the street fight where a bigger kid was beating up on a smaller one. It was especially disgusting when the bigger kid was known to be a bully, and the smaller kid was that nice kid who just didn't like to fight. When most of us see something like that happening, we reach a point where we just can't continue standing there without throwing a punch for the little guy—in this case—the American schoolteacher.

Our need to do something was the genesis for the writing of this book, *The Problem Isn't Teachers*. I'm sure as you read, the big kids won't be hard to pick out. The writing is pretty straight-forward stuff, so it's unlikely you will miss them. They are a formidable lot: The U.S. Supreme Court, members of legislative bodies, lobbyists, a significant part of the American and international business communities, and the influential members of America's wealthiest one percent.

So, which of these took the first shot? That would be the U.S. Supreme Court, which dealt a series of blows called *Tinker v. Des Moines School District, Goss v. Lopez,* Wood *v. Strickland,* and then finally *Honig v. Doe.* These shots were brutal enough to permanently crush nearly all of the efforts of teachers, in every part of our country. Maintaining civil and orderly classrooms became virtually impossible. It was as if, in a short period of years, all reasonable school authority and control had been stripped from the hallowed halls. But, as you will read, our champion managed, after several crashes to the canvas, to get back to his feet.

No sooner had he gotten to his feet, however, when classrooms were overrun by thousands upon thousands of new American poor. This new and broader condition of American poverty was brought about by the actions of his next adversaries the U.S. Congress, corporate lobbyists, the America business community, and the "one percent." Together, these groups created, over a short 30 years, the greatest disparity in American wealth ever seen. Their actions have resulted in the largest underclass of poor and poor children that the nation has ever known. Further, their actions virtually decimated our country's middle class. We now have millions of children coming through the school doors hungry, not just for knowledge, but for food to first sustain their young bodies.

Not many young boxers could come back after such pummeling, but you will observe that ours does. In addition to his daily teaching, he now helps in the feeding, clothing, and establishment of in-school clinics. He assists in providing tutorial assistance. He comes to his classroom much earlier and stays later. He attempts to nurture the added millions of poor children that fill the nation's classrooms in numbers not seen since the Great Depression.

As he assists daily the needs of the poor and fights off the continual consequences of the Supreme Court decisions, our fighter tires more easily. This is what his most recent opponents, the business/industrial community and many elected state politicians have been waiting for—this moment when it might be possible to finally crush forever the spirit of this champion.

When he enters the ring again, they attack. They attempt to wrestle from him his final dignities. First, they attempt to take from him his unions—his solidarity of comradeships formed over 100 years with other teachers like himself. And then they attempt to strip from his hands his grail of purpose entrusted to him by our country's forefathers.

Our young boxer is filled with anger as his adversaries cast aside the grail of his forefathers and replace it with their own work-preparation purpose of education. Their purpose declares a new direction for the lives of American children—lives to be spent as production components of the business/industrial complex as it reaches for economic world domination.

These, our champion's most recent adversaries, have convinced much of the nation that a narrow band of academic assessment of all children is essential. It is a narrow band that excludes music, the arts, history, languages, literature, and the thousands of years of man's philosophical thought—all of the magnificent disciplines that round out an enlightened education. Swept away is the dream of the Founders. These adversaries have cleared the road. And the process of measuring, judging, and then assigning a value to each child, as determined by some standardized measurement of their own creation, is already under way. Soon all that will remain will be to direct the children of the American nation into this new sterile destiny.

I hope, after you read this book, that you'll consider entering the ring with our champion. He's tired, but he's not beaten. He fights now to recapture his grail of purpose passed to him in sacred trust by the nation's Founders. Their vision had been that he continues the education of a nation's youth in order to sustain an informed and enlightened citizenry essential to the growth of a viable economy and an emerging democracy. They asked that he then send forth each new American generation into the forums of liberty so that the "apprenticeship of liberty," which was begun over 200 years ago, should never end.[1]

RJG June, 2012

Note:

1 Benjamin R. Barber, "Public Schooling—Education for Democracy," in *The Public Purpose of Education*, John J. Goodlad and Timothy J. McMannon, editors (San Francisco: Jossey-Bass 1997), 27.

Introduction:

Upside Down and Simply Wrong

Let us first begin by emphasizing the fact that this book is not intended to defend those teachers who never should have been permitted entry into this noble profession. We make no excuses for persons who are abusive, felonious, or unwilling to look for ways to improve their professional capacities.

Further, this book is not an appeal to return to the good old days where everything was perfect, for though we lost much as we moved away from those days, we all know that the past was hardly perfect. It is definitely not a call to dismiss children who have special needs or to demean children who come from cultures that are different from that of the majority. We support efforts to include these students along with efforts that ensure that they and all students behave in ways that are not disruptive to the learning environments of their classrooms or of their schools. We do not seek to push a particular set of values or squash creativity. And certainly this book is not an attempt to say that there is one simple answer to the extremely complex issues that surround American education. There are many. Finally, this book is not just for teachers. This is an in-depth discussion of often uninformed opinions that have led to the unjust charge that teachers are mainly responsible for the failure of our education system. This book is written for all of us, for we all have a stake in the education of our nation's children.

Using the lenses of history, morality, purpose, experience, and common sense, we seek to determine how our society has come to a point where people expect teachers to do their jobs, regardless of the profoundly complicated and overwhelming issues they must deal with, even though their power to do so has been dramatically diminished. As we try to clarify this deeply troubling situation, we examine the grave conditions that exist outside the school house such as poverty, racism, drug abuse, child abuse, and violence. We look at the critical necessity of engaged, effective parenting while examining what appears to be the diminishing control and guidance many parents are exercising over their children. We look at all of this, because it is our firm conviction that schools are a highly-polished mirror where the truth and reality of what we are as a nation enter schoolhouse doors every day. We believe that until we candidly and honestly look at these realities, the problems that are the nation's problems, not the problems of our teachers, will continue to cause the chaos and injustice that ignorance, greed, insensitivity, and unrealistic expectations have created and fostered for far too long.

We have been involved in education in a variety of capacities that have included classroom teaching, administration, consulting, speaking, and writing. During these years, we have had the privilege of coming to know thousands of educators. Further, we have come to know that the vast majority of teachers are well-prepared, intelligent, hard-working, and caring. Thus, it hurts us deeply to see attacks on teachers and on their unions. These attacks are becoming more aggressive and vicious as individual state legislatures, departments of education, professional experts, and special interest groups attempt to dictate how, when, where, and what they teach. We fear that if these attacks continue, no teacher will be able to secure either reasonable working conditions or fair compensation: they will not be able to continue to have for themselves those things necessary to carry out their mission with honor and dignity. We hope with this book we can echo their concerns and add our voices to theirs in an effort to create a playing field where their contributions are fairly evaluated and acknowledged.

People often point out the critical importance of good parents as do we in this book. It is often said that parents are the child's first teachers. What we so often fail to point out is that the teaching we do as parents, or as teachers, is being learned by the child in a pure form. Their early learning sees no shades of gray. They see no partial answers. They see no "once in a while" as the proper time to provide justice. As young learners they see only the pure forms. Therefore, as we pass through life with our children, they occasionally express what they have learned from us. They express this learning in its pure forms. And in so doing, they challenge us. They make us reflect on our own teachings. Could we, at our older ages, still say and mean it so purely? We are blessed to have had six children. Consequently, there are many stories we have that could illustrate this point. Let us share just two.

Some years ago, our family was sitting with friends and neighbors at our son Michael's high school football game. During a break in the action, a close friend, Dave Kralik, teasingly said to our then 5-year-old son Dan, "Boy, my yard is just covered with leaves. You know what, Dan? I'll let you rake them up, and I'll only charge you $10."

Dan continued eating his popcorn while he thought this proposition over. A minute or so later, Dan tapped Dave on the shoulder and said in a straightforward but polite manner, "Mr. Kralik, that's upside down." For a moment we were all taken aback, but then we burst into laughter as we realized that Mr. Kralik had just innocently, albeit politely, been slam-dunked by a 5-year-old. Dave told us later that whenever he thought of that moment, he would shake his head and laugh all over again.

We too have recalled that night over the years, but not just because we all shared a good laugh. We remember that moment because we were glad, of course, that Dan "got it right." But we were also really impressed that he was able to stand up for himself—not always an easy thing for any of us to do. You could see him thinking this through: "Hmm…$10. Wait. Something's not right here. Mr. Kralik's a nice man, but…I got it. I know what's wrong." Then came the tap on the shoulder, and with his 5-year-old language, Dan spoke truth to power. Simple, direct, quick, and pure. No dancing around the point. No "Let's negotiate." No hemming and hawing. Just a thanks-but-no-thanks answer to what was simply and "purely" unfair.

On another occasion, we were coming home from a football game with our 12-year-old son Tom. We had to stop to use a pay phone (no cell phones back then). When we opened the car door, a stray kitten from the nearby woods jumped into the back seat with Marion. He was tiny, skinny, and he seemed to have a cold. We thought at the time he was probably full of bugs too. But we couldn't leave him as there weren't any houses nearby, and we were afraid he might not make it through a really cold night. With the kitten on Marion's lap, we headed for home again. Not very much later, mom and dad were having some real second thoughts. "What if he was really ill?" "What if he scratched one of us and got us sick?" "What were we going to do with a cat anyway?" "How much would he cost to keep?" Rational and fearful thinking led to a decision to put the kitten back on the side of the road. We stopped the car, placed him a safe distance from the main highway, and pulled away. Rational thinking had overcome the initial desire to simply provide care to an animal in need.

Tom was very quiet as we slowly drove away. Ray looked over and asked, "What are you thinking, Tom?" With no hesitation, Tom said very plainly, "That was simply the wrong thing to do." The two "grown-ups" didn't need to hear anything else. We immediately U-turned our way back to pick up the kitten in an effort to redeem this lapse in moral behavior. Brought up short, we had to acknowledge our son's "purer" sense of knowing the right thing to do. You don't leave a helpless creature on the side of the highway.

At a very early age Dan had been given a glimpse of a tricky, unfair world, courtesy of a very kind neighbor who never would have taken advantage—who was, in fact, delighted that he had been "called-out." He chose to challenge something that felt wrong. Tom, a little older, but still very young, had seen his own parents do something he didn't think was right. He didn't argue. He didn't complain. He just knew that to abandon that kitten was "simply wrong," and he said so. Both had seen something unfair in the world and both had said so in no uncertain terms.

These little acts of courage may not seem very significant to some people, but they have left a lasting impression on us. They continue to remind us in a unique, moving way that there is a time to stand up to what is simply wrong—what is upside down. So, today when we look at what teachers are enduring, what they have been asked to do, how they have been abandoned, we sense again a lapse in moral behavior—this time on a large scale—and we feel a need to say like our young children, "That's upside down. That's simply wrong."

It's been many years since we sat at that football game, not as many since we brought home a little kitten that has grown into a lovely cat appropriately named "Lucky." They have been turbulent years for this nation and its institutions, and we think no group has borne the impact of that turbulence more directly than teachers. During this time, child abuse, drug abuse, poverty, and ignorance—social ills that have always haunted our classrooms—have worsened profoundly. Despite the desperately needed and long-overdue advances in civil rights for all kinds of minorities and despite the growing awareness of our many cultural differences, society's racist attitudes and prejudices have not gone away. In some ways they seem worse. Attempts to accommodate vast numbers of children with special needs without adequate funding have required extraordinary efforts and have caused an additional financial and emotional strain on the whole educational system. All of these factors have burdened teachers with such unreasonable demands that they have become increasingly unable to cope with what has become, for many, a hostile work environment.

Starting in the late Sixties and continuing through the late Eighties, the United States Supreme Court rendered a series of decisions that broadly enhanced the civil rights of students. One of these decisions declared that education was no longer to be considered a privilege. Rather, the Court declared education to be a property right, thus requiring schools and classroom teachers to provide proper legal due process procedures for even the most routine of disciplinary matters. They further broadened a student's right to free speech within the schools and classrooms, leading to disruption and controversy that still exist as teachers and school administrators daily try desperately to handle the extra burdens these decisions engendered. All of these decisions have come with obligatory record-keeping and legal processes that have also swamped an already overburdened and exhausted system.

Tragically, in more recent years, the most frightening kind of event has become all too common. Acts of violence such as we never would have imagined possible have made teachers and students the victims of physical and psychological assaults. We are bombarded with stories about teachers and students who have been seriously injured and even murdered. We have heard with alarming frequency about students who have committed suicide as a direct result of being bullied. These tragic events have taken place in our schools—places we had understood to be safe harbors. Even now, as this is being written, the nation is reeling once again from the terror another disturbed young man has wrought. This time the people of Chardon, Ohio, must heal from the shattering loss of some of their children.

For a very long time now, this country has witnessed the gradual transformation of what we once felt was a safe place, a stable place—indeed a sacred place—a place called school. During this time, we have often felt the need to write about what was happening in schools—about the overwhelming problems that were becoming part of the fabric of every work day. Over the years, we have read the writings of many professional experts inside and outside of education. Over the years, we have had hundreds of discussions with administrators, school board members, parents, students, and teachers in an attempt to find out why our educational system has become so complex—so overwhelmed, so vulnerable to vicious attacks. What issues, events, or attitudes have caused the education of our children to become such a struggle for so many who have only the best intentions?

We now feel we can no longer wait to write about these profoundly complex issues and events that have resulted in schools where teachers struggle to sustain order while passing on knowledge and values such as perseverance, honesty, civility, and love of country. We do so in the hope that more people will begin to understand how misguided court decisions, complicated regulations, unfair criticisms, irrational expectations, inappropriate testing, and shifting attitudes regarding behavior have all but drowned out our teachers' best efforts to give our children the unique gift of education this nation has intended for them to have.

We anticipate that some people will disagree with our conclusions. We suspect that even some teachers will not be able to relate to what we have said, for they may never have had the misfortune to teach in classrooms where students are ill-prepared, crude, apathetic, or defiant. They may never have wanted for appropriate and sufficient supplies. They may never have been verbally or physically attacked. These teachers might ask, "What are these authors talking about?" Our response to this question is, "If you don't know, you have been spared and blessed." But there will also be others who will criticize us because, in their opinion, we did not go far enough to describe the horrors and frustrations that some teachers live with daily. We say to them, "You are right. Our discussions could have been much more graphic, much more brutal." Thus, we say to any reader who finds what we have written as unimaginable, "Be advised that there are even deeper and more depressing levels of misery and stress that are endured by teachers who continue, under the most dreadful circumstances, to give all that they can."

Lest we be misunderstood, we want to make it clear that the problems we illustrate and examine are not confined to a particular school setting. *Please do not assume that only large schools with large minority populations are struggling with these issues.* Regardless of size or location, teachers everywhere are confronting actions and attitudes which challenge, sometimes profoundly, their capacity to teach. As a consequence, whether a school is located in an inner city, suburb, a small town, a Native American reservation, or a rural setting, societal attitudes and legal decisions are having an impact. The stories you will read in this book reflect this reality.

For all those teachers who feel discouraged, exhausted, or abandoned, we think you will find in these pages voices of colleagues and others that expose the extreme challenges to your ability to do what you have always wanted to do—what you were meant to do: *Teach*.

We hope this book will contribute to this end by arming teachers and citizens with a better awareness of what has gone wrong in this nation and what needs to be done to restore, revitalize, and recapture the purpose of one of this nation's most valued gifts—a proper education for all of its children. Above all, we hope that though there will be strong debate about the issues we raise, it will be clear that teachers are not to blame for the failures of our educational system.

Finally, we urge you: Tell your own stories. Respond to the ugly letters to the editor which appear in the newspaper. Challenge the lies and rumors that so often are levied with broad strokes against all teachers. Join with your colleagues, with parents, with students, and with the broader community to demand that all teachers have the safe and orderly environment necessary to ensure the education of the next American generation.

Start by looking around, seeing what is unfair, and saying, "That's upside down and simply wrong."

MJG June, 2012

SECTION ONE

HERE, THERE, AND BACK AGAIN

The essential strengths of any successful school are order, civility, and supported teacher authority. In chapter 1 of this section of the book, we have selected stories that reveal what has happened to schools of today when such strengths have been stripped from schools or permitted to erode. Chapter 2 takes you back to a calmer time. You will find yourself relaxing in school settings where order, control, and civility are commonplace. Hopefully, you will also feel the gentler nature of these times as you witness not just the condition of civility, but the product of such civility. We reveal here that as a consequence of this kind of environment schools can be places where profound teaching and learning can take place. Also, we think these stories reflect the kind of environment where teachers can more easily direct their efforts to offering the kind of broad education that is necessary to produce the enlightened citizenry essential to the preservation of this democracy.

In chapter 3 we return to today's schools where many of our American teachers and students must attempt to eke out some semblance of an education in a much more savage environment. It was our intent that these contrasting chapters provide a clarity that sometimes only extremes can reveal.

Chapter 1

"America, We Have a Problem"

In 1970, the nation watched as Apollo 13 was launched into space. Families everywhere gathered around television sets. They watched and listened to the media coverage which detailed not only the technological wonders, but the lives of the astronauts themselves who had "the right stuff." Suddenly, the excitement turned to fear as it was revealed that Apollo 13 was in deep peril. Something had gone really wrong. Now Americans watched this epic event with great fear. The simple, calm statement by Captain James Lovell, Commander of the mission, "Houston, we have a problem," caused a nation to completely refocus in a different way until the astronauts of Apollo 13 returned safely to Earth.

Their safe return was by no means an easy accomplishment. It took all the resources of scientists and personnel at NASA. Technological knowledge combined with experience and the ability to come up with innovative solutions brought our courageous astronauts home.

The investment and sacrifice this nation had made in the space program was truly significant. The dream of exploring space had taken on a very special meaning for most Americans. It was a telling moment in our history and represented the best of what America could be.

We are at another time in our history when we need to call on our ability to be the best we can be, for we face a crisis of much more importance than the development of a space program. This crisis may not have brought any dramatic television coverage. There are no vast numbers of people holding their breath. But it is critical that we address the problems discussed in this book, for their solutions are essential to the survival of not only our educational system, but to the survival of our democracy and our way of life. Both are in great peril. We need the same kind of focus, dedication, knowledge, skill, and innovation that we have always demonstrated when we have been faced with a crisis, but the first step we must take is to recognize that something is wrong. "America, we have a problem."

Your immersion into this chapter is fairly brief. There are only five stories. Each is surrounded by tension and pressure. Only one of these five stories is taken from an inner city of one of our nation's major metropolitan areas. The remaining four come from smaller cities, suburbs, or rural settings. We mention this because the prevailing belief in our country is that stories such as these represent the experiences of only inner cities. They do not. Sadly, what you are about to read is a sample of a pervasive condition that exists throughout the entire country. Pockets of civility and order continue to exist everywhere in America, but there are fewer of them. Today, no classroom, school, or community in our country is immune.

Please, join us now for the first of these five stories titled, "Off the Record?"

"Off the Record?"

Our central office administration center had originally been an insurance company that was built around 1910. It had been built using fine hardwood throughout the interior. In the entrance was a rotunda where marble interior staircases took you to the second floor. The outside of the three-story structure was brick and stone. Some of the corner offices on the main level had wood-burning fireplaces and stained glass windows. The building was kept clean, but more recently was showing wear and was in need of repair. Nonetheless, it had charm, and I enjoyed working there. My office was one of the smaller ones on the main floor and had no view except that of the alleyway behind the building, but again the total charm of the architecture plus the extensive interior hardwood made up for the lack of beautiful scenery.

It was a Friday in late October, a little past 4:30 p.m., and I was wiping down the glass on my desk—the last task I normally did at the end of a workday. I would soon be in my car and on my way home. At that moment, Lynn, the receptionist for the building and switchboard operator, came to my door.

"I have Mr. Matcina from Washington High School on the line, but the switchboard is closed, and I can't transfer it back to you. Can you call him at his school?"

I responded, "Sure, Lynn, I'll call him right away. Have a good weekend."

As I picked up the phone, I said to myself, "Never fails—Friday afternoon, 4:30—never fails." I had no idea at that time about the events that would soon unfold.

"Hello, Phil."

"Yeah, Ray, thanks for callin' back."

Then, in a voice slower than he normally spoke, sentences somewhat choppy and to a degree disconnected, he began, "Ray, enrolled a transfer kid this late afternoon. Came in by himself. Nice lookin' kid, kind of preppy, sharp dresser, nice smile and good social skills—made my secretary Helen laugh. Ray, you know Helen."

"Sure, sure, Phil."

Then he continued, "Ray, been workin', as you know, with kids this age for twenty plus years. Have taught, coached, you know. Twenty years of workin' with kids is just screamin' out at me that somethin's wrong with this kid, Ray. Somethin's wrong, really wrong, and it's really got me undone, and, worst of all, I have nothing concrete to base it on—just a hunch, you know?"

"Where's he from, Phil?"

"Papers he brought with him say some institution in Southern California—Hillcrest Institute. Papers say he's placed with his aunt in town. I've called several times, but can't get anyone at this place to talk to me, and his aunt is at work. What do you think, Ray? What do you think?"

Over the years I had learned a few things about the school business, and one of them was to trust the intuition of guys like Phil—guys who, as we would say, were out there "in the trenches."

"Phil, what do you want me to do?"

"Well, let me give you the phone number of this institute. See if you can get anything."

"Okay, Phil, but if you couldn't get anything, I don't know why they would talk to me."

"Well, tell them you're the superintendent or something."

We both laughed. Then he gave me the number, and I told him I'd try and then would call him back.

My first two calls resulted in dead ends. Persons who had some responsibility for this kid's care while at the institute had left for the weekend. On my third call, I tried a different approach and asked for anyone at all in their psychology or psychiatry departments. I hit the jackpot.

"This is Dr. Wilson. How can I help you?"

I explained who I was, the incompleteness of the young man's records, our inability to contact his local caregiver, and Phil's apprehensiveness as well as my confidence in Phil's judgment. There was then a long moment of silence while neither of us spoke. And then he said, "I'm sorry. There's nothing I can do for you."

It seemed to me quite a strange answer, so I persisted and persisted, and politely, yet pleadingly, persisted. Then again a long moment of silence, and finally he said, "Off the record?"

And I responded, "I'll take it any way I can get it."

Then again that long silence and finally he said, "Off the record.

About a month ago he raped a woman employee in one of our housing units and five days ago he was caught in the act of attempting to rape a night nurse. The next day we were near a staff walkout. He's been cleared to leave this institute. His aunt is the only one we could find to take him. So, he's yours."

I sat there stunned and momentarily speechless. I heard him say again, "This is off the record." He then hung up. I sat motionless with the phone still to my ear while it did its customary multiple clicks until finally the long, uninterrupted tone signaled a disconnected line. I set it down and just stared at the top of my desk. My eyes slowly moved to and then focused on a six-inch long cutout made of round poster board circles glued together to form a child's pretend worm, a smiley face drawn on the first circle. It was a gift from my oldest daughter, Tanya, made when she was in kindergarten. I kept it taped on the side of a black metal accordion file near the phone.

It was now nearly 5:30 p.m.—best call Phil. He answered immediately, and I brought him up to speed. I told him everything.

"Any thoughts, Ray?"

I simply replied, "Stay in your office. I'll call you back."

I sat there alone, staring but not really seeing a cutout worm and its smiley face. I knew the law. Hell, I ran workshops on it. I had been the school district's first hearing examiner and understood the Supreme Court decisions well: *Goss v. Lopez, Tinker v. Des Moines, Baker v. Owens, Wood v. Strickland*. The kid had a property right to an education. In addition, there was the state code pursuant to federal law. And regardless what I had been told about him, on the record or off, he was to be admitted. Furthermore, he had a right to remain in our schools until he did something in our schools that warranted an expulsion hearing or until he was arrested and under the jurisdiction of some police authority or court. I knew it all. The kid was probably special education too—records too incomplete to know, but it was reasonable to assume. That, of course, made it even more complex.

But what if he rapes a girl in our school? How do we explain something like that to a father or mother? How do Phil or I sit across a table and explain what we knew or thought we knew? How do we…? I looked back at the smiley-faced worm and pictured the smiling face of a little girl who made it for her daddy—my little girl. I took a deep breath. It had been a good run. Really didn't want it to be over yet, but what the hell. Had driven a truck in my younger days, even drove a beer truck. Not bad work. Marion would back me. She had told me that many times. She even teased about how we could live in a tent if we had to. I took one more deep breath and then picked up the phone and dialed.

"Yeah, Ray."

"Phil, I'm gonna tell you something that I'm also going to put in writing for you and bring to your house this weekend. On my authority, I am telling you not to allow that young man in any classes in your building on Monday. If he comes to your building on Monday, he is to immediately leave and then come to my office with his aunt at his earliest convenience. He is being denied his right to a public education at this time. I don't know where the hell this is going to go, but that's my decision."

Phil said nothing, but after a long while, "You don't have to bring the letter over, Ray. I wasn't going to let him in anyway."

We both laughed. Then we laughed and laughed some more. We then talked as friends sometimes do at the end of a long workday. I told Phil to give me a call over the weekend and we would strategize, but I asked him not to call me on Sunday during the Bears-Packers game. We both laughed again, then hung up. It was closing in on 7 p.m., so I called Marion, and then went home.

Sunday came and at half-time of the Bears game, it was Bears 13 Green Bay 0 at Lambeau Field. The phone rang. Marion got it and called from the kitchen. It was Phil.

"Did you hear?"

"Hear what, Phil?"

"It's been on the radio all morning."

"Phil, I haven't had the radio on. What are you talking about?"

"Last night, about 1:30 a.m. our kid from California attempted to sell heroin and marijuana to a female undercover agent assigned to our schools in the high school parking lot. Hammond narcotics guys Jimmy and Ted witnessed the sale. The kid's under arrest right now, and they took him to Crown Point. No court date set yet. I got a call about an hour ago from Jimmy. Said he was going to give you a call. I told him that I'd be calling you at half-time, so he told me to bring you up to speed."

"Thanks, Phil. Thanks a lot."

I hung up, left the kitchen, and stepped onto the screened-in back porch. My older daughter Tanya, creator of the smiley-faced worm, was in the backyard out near the little house I had built for the kids out of an old picket fence several years earlier. She was teaching her little sister Jocelyn how to hold a baton and then spin it. They were having great fun together as sisters should. The last of the leaves were falling from the big oaks and surrounding their play. I stood there for a long while without their seeing me. I knew that if anyone ever hurt one of them I'd.... I pushed the dark thought out of my mind.

I then went back into the house and the living room. My two older sons, Mike and Scott, were sitting on the floor in front of the T.V. The second half was about to begin.

Slowly over the next years, I would be told about or hear of stories that would reveal to me that Phil and I were not the only two who nearly went back to driving a truck. There were countless administrators and teachers throughout the nation who, though circumstances for them may have been different, were faced with the same moral decisions, and they chose to risk on the side of the common good and reasonableness. They still do make these same moral decisions. They still do risk their careers.

The Trees Didn't Look Quite So Lovely Anymore

I had been invited to keynote a conference in Phoenix. As I often do, I came a day early in order to avoid the possibility of unanticipated travel problems which might cause me to miss my scheduled obligation. The day before my keynote address, a friend invited me to visit a couple of elementary schools. I always enjoyed such visits. So off we went.

As we were walking through an elementary school hallway, we both noticed a young teacher farther down that hall on one knee with what appeared to be two first or second grade boys. We could see that she was attempting to explain to them why they shouldn't fight. Tears streamed down the face of one boy. The other still had his fists clenched and a scowl on his face. As we neared, she looked up and said, "I'm so sorry, as soon as I settle them down, I'll take them back into class." I responded, "No need to apologize. We'll move along here and get out of your way." We continued our tour, but said little of the incident.

The next morning I gave my keynote address. Immediately afterwards, four or five participants approached the stage wanting to get my attention. As I briefly talked to each, I could see at the back of the line the teacher who had been working the day before in the hallway with the little boys. When she finally approached, she appeared quite distressed. Then, with her voice quivering, she said, "Dr. Golarz, can I please talk to you?"

We left the stage area and found a quiet spot outside near a fountain and some very lovely trees. She began, "Dr. Golarz, today in your presentation you said that we must also remember to take care of ourselves, the caregivers. I knew then that I had to try to talk to you. Yesterday in the hallway at my school, I was so ashamed. I knew I should have been in my classroom teaching math, but they were fighting and I had to …I had to…" She began to get choked up and was momentarily unable to continue.

I said to her, "Don't be ashamed. Don't ever be ashamed. Your job is not simply to teach math and science. Your job is also to assist each student to understand the meaning of good conduct and civility. Don't ever be ashamed. You were doing the right thing."

Then she blurted out, "But Dr. Golarz, you still don't understand. It happens all the time...all the time. I have five students in that room that I cannot control. I've had lots of administrative help. I've tried all the new instructional strategies they've given to me. I've done everything that I've been told to do. Several veteran teachers have confided in me that no one has ever been able to handle these kids. They've told me to just try to hang in there and make it through the school year. But I don't know if I can. It's only October, just October. I can't sleep. I'm losing weight, and I'm jittery all the time. Last Friday, the principal and I had a parent conference with the mother of the worst one of this group. She yelled and screamed at me the whole time. She told me I was picking on her child and that there were other children just as bad. She said that I didn't know what I was doing. She said that I was boring and even suggested that I might be racist.

"Dr. Golarz, I'm from Iowa. It was my idea to go into teaching. My dad only agreed to it if I kept my other major in business. Therefore, I graduated with a double major and a 3.7 GPA. At night when I call my parents, I can hear my dad hollering in the background. He says that if things don't change soon, he's coming out on a plane, gonna punch some people out, and take me home. Dr. Golarz, I so wanted to teach. It was my dream since childhood." She took a deep breath, dropped her head, then turned and slowly walked away from me. She didn't go far, just nearer the fountain in the center of the courtyard garden. I didn't follow. She needed a moment alone.

As I looked up and away from her, the trees didn't look quite so lovely any more.

Raymond J. Golarz and Marion J. Golarz

"I Don't Know How Much Longer I Can Do This."

I recall a day when Marion came home from work quite late, looking very depressed. She wanted to go out to dinner. She said she really needed to talk. I got my coat, and we were on our way to one of our favorite restaurants.

At the time, Marion was a teacher at the secondary level. After we were seated and had ordered our dinner, she began, "Ray, I need to talk to you about my fourth period class."

Beginning with the first student, she described all of the things that she knew about his childhood—the abuse, neglect, and the movement from foster home to foster home. Then she explained what she was attempting to do for this student on a daily basis, despite his continual class disruptions. Next, she told me about a second student who was as needy and rebellious, if not more so, than the first. And again she explained what she was attempting to do during class to help him. Then I heard story number three, number four, and so on, until I heard a total of twelve stories. When finally she finished, she looked up, her uneaten dinner now cold, and said, "What do you think?"

I remember being quite overwhelmed and not really having anything helpful to say, so I just sat there looking at her and nodding my head. She then continued, "Ray, my additional frustration is that I don't just have those 12 in my class, I have 30, but the immense needs of those 12 daily absorb all of my time and energy, and I can't get to the others sitting there and waiting to learn. If I do attempt to direct my attention to them, a disruption breaks out immediately, and I have to refocus on one, two, or several of those twelve. She then concluded with what has become an all-too-familiar lament heard now in education, "I don't know how much longer I can do this."

The Problem Isn't Teachers

The Rookie

I had just completed keynoting a Canadian school superintendents' convention in Vancouver. The weather was questionable, so rather than head home, I rerouted and flew to another part of Canada. I would be early, but I wouldn't need to worry about the predicted snow and the possibility of not making it at all.

By 10 a.m. the next morning, I sat smiling in my hotel room with a hot cup of coffee while I watched the blizzard unfold. I had made a good call. My work in this part of Canada would be a keynote address to over 4,000 teachers and then smaller group work with administrators. I was soon to be reminded that teachers are not the only ones feeling profoundly stressed.

It was about 10:30 a.m., and I was working with a group of about 80 administrators. We were only ten minutes into the session dealing with work-related stress when a young, rather attractive woman administrator began to sob. She was seated at one of the round tables nearer the front of our group, thus clearly visible to virtually everyone in the room. There was really no ignoring her, so I stopped. In that now very silent room her sobs began to become more frequent and louder. Finally, she just lost it and broke down completely. No one, including myself, knew quite what to do, so our silence continued. Finally, she looked up, her face now a complete mess with running mascara and she shouted out, "I've only been an assistant principal for two months, and I hate it. I hate it. I get spit on, attacked in my office, cursed out daily by parents and kids, and never get out of there 'til seven or eight at night." Then she continued, "I used to be a nice person, a really nice person, but no more, no more. I hate people! I hate everybody!" She continued to sob, only now a bit more subdued. Finally, she looked up again and pleaded rather quietly, "Dr. Golarz, what am I going to do? What am I going to do?"

Some of us began to move toward her while she just sat, shaking her bowed head back and forth. At that point, an older veteran woman administrator pulled her chair up behind the distraught rookie. She then grabbed her by both shoulders and turned the young woman to face her. With a clean white handkerchief she gently wiped her face and, as she did, she said in a deep, confident, gravelly voice, "Sweetheart, what kind of pill you want—we got 'em all." The offer to medicate was made in jest, but it did the job.

The place went up for grabs. The tension in the room broke into intense and sustained laughter. Every person in that room had been there. They had all had their moment of unparalleled agony and terror in some earlier time and some other place, but they had all had the experience. The continuing and sustained laughter was simply affirming their deep understanding and empathy for this new colleague and her pain.

They would not let her flounder. In this immediate moment, several hustled her off to a bathroom to clean her up and help restore at least a part of her damaged soul while the rest of us took a break. A new administrator was experiencing her baptism by fire, but she would sleep better tonight, for in this very moment a network was forming—a network of seasoned veterans who would not let her fail. She would not fail on their watch. Not on their watch. Or so they prayed.

"They Will Here!"

The text that follows is accurate. The incidents described occurred in an inner city high school that had had a long history of being out of control. The story focuses upon the experiences of a brand new teacher just out of college. What follows was written by that teacher. For purposes of anonymity, he is referred to in the text as Mr. John (Jack) Harris. The writing is often in the form of dialogue. It is authentic and often graphic. The only changes that we have made to the original text have to do with the idiomatic peculiarities used in the dialogue portions of the text. We have removed these and replaced them with standard English, making the dialogue text more easily read and understood. Where vulgarities were used, we chose not to completely alter them. Our editing was done with the approval of the author who wishes to remain anonymous.

As you read you will probably experience almost immediate discomfort not only for the plight of this young teacher, but also for the pupils who chose to disrupt and those who suffered from the disruptions—students of all kinds who had never experienced school as a sacred, civil, and safe place. Put your eye near the keyhole and view our opening scene titled "The Interview."

The Interview

The principal is inquiring of this future teacher about how well he can relate to difficult students. Note the principal's unapologetic acknowledgment of a lack of civility on the part of students in her school.

"But are you prepared to teach young people who aren't ready to listen?"

She paused briefly and then continued, "How are you prepared to deal with defiant students, students who have psychological problems, come from abusive homes and the like? How well are you prepared to approach these kinds of kids?"

"Well, Kendra, I'm glad you've asked me this question because

I've never kidded myself about the nature of our work. That's why I did my student teaching on the Bilmaka Indian Reservation which, as you may or may not know, is one of the most economically depressed places of the country. I could've student-taught at a mainstream school but I felt that, had I done that, I would have denied myself a real interesting experience. Thanks to my being on the reservation, I feel that I've had an opportunity not afforded to a lot of other student teachers. I feel I've had to deal with problems, and I feel that this will prepare me for anything Central can throw at me."

"How were the kids on the reservation? What's the worse thing that happened to you?"

"Well, for the most part, I mean the majority of them didn't cause many problems. But a significant number of my students out there were quite disrespectful. I've been told to "f--- off," "get outta my face." Y'know, stuff like that. As a matter of fact, I had a girl in my algebra class whose behavior necessitated a parent-teacher conference. I didn't deal with a lot that was very severe. I mean nobody ever got two inches from my face and told me they were gonna kick the shit out of me or anything else…"

"They will here."

I stopped. I couldn't respond. What did she mean: They will here? Wouldn't she stop them? It wasn't so much what she said, it was how she said it. She leaned back in her chair, folded her arms. She smiled a little. And she repeated, "They will here."

I kept looking at the floor. She kept looking at me. After about ten more seconds of silence, I braved more words.

"I think it's important to remember that I am very much a student of teaching, and I hope, I trust, that should I work here, that is, if you should hire me, I trust that you're the type of people who will assist me and coach me along with these issues."

Administrative Authority?

We pick up the story again on day one of the new school year. Assistant Principal Baker attempts to get a student who is attending a school assembly to comply to a school rule.

As Baker stood there, a young man walked past him. He had his pants sagging down to his knees, a direct violation of the school dress

The Problem Isn't Teachers

code. He walked past Baker and sat by himself on a bleacher and looked at the ground. Baker approached him.

"Excuse me. You're going to have to pull your pants up to waist level."

"Man, get outta my face!"

"Michael, listen to me. This is a school rule. Now pull your pants up to waist level. This is not..."

"Motherf---er!"

The young man got up, walked about twenty feet away from Baker, and sat down again by himself. Baker stayed where he was, folded his hands behind his back, and looked down at the floor. About ten seconds later, he started walking toward him very slowly and cautiously.

"Page 14 of the student ethics code obliges you to pull your pants up to waist level. Please conform to school policy."

The kid looked up at Baker and gave him a dirty look. He then looked down at the floor. He finally stood up and said, 'Goddammit, man. Motherf---er!"

He then pulled his pants up. Baker looked at him and said, "Thank you," and walked away.

Attempting to Gain Classroom Control

Later in this same first day of school Jack is attempting to establish classroom order.

As I was trying to get everybody back in their seats and quiet, the announcements came on. It was Kendra Leonard, the principal, giving school announcements. I was standing three feet away from the overhead speaker that the sound was coming out of, and I could hardly hear her. I just couldn't get anybody to shut up.

Two minutes after the announcements were over, I had succeeded in getting most of the students in their seats. As I was standing next to the door, I saw a large boy get out of his seat and walk up to my computer on the other side of the room.

"Excuse me. I need you to get back in your seat." He ignored me. "Excuse me. Did you not hear me? I said, Get back in your seat!"

He looked at me from across the room, elevated his arms over his head and yelled, "You gonna kick me out?"

As I was looking at him, I heard, "F--- you, bitch," from another boy standing two feet away from me. "Excuse me, you're not to use that language in here."

"Man, get outta my f---in' face!"

As he said that to me, he got out of his seat and walked out of the classroom door.

"Hey, get back in here. Did you hear me?" I said, "Get back in here!"

Then the dismissal bell rang. When it rang, he laughed at me and walked off.

As the students walked out, I leaned up against the wall next to the phone. I put my head in my hands for about five seconds. When I uncovered my face and opened my eyes, I saw a girl pick up the telephone.

"Excuse me...excuse me. You're not allowed to use the telephone in the classroom. You're going to have to use the phone in the main office. Hey, did you hear me?"

After figuring out that there was no way she was going to put the phone down, I looked out into the hallway for Baker, Leonard, or any administrator. When I saw that an administrator was not to be found, I looked around the general area and saw the phone wire plugged into a phone jack on the wall. Not seeing any other options, I reached over and pulled it out of the jack. She was pissed.

"Goddamn, n----! You a bitch!"

She walked out and slammed the door. I walked slowly toward a seat and sat down. I didn't say or do anything. I just sat there and stared at the wall.

A Warning from "Hustle" the Security Guard

There are two full time plainclothes security guards in the school that are additional to uniformed officers. Their names are "Hustle" and "Tank." Hustle becomes alarmed at what he sees.

I could tell right away that this was a hostile group. I tried for three minutes to get them to be quiet so that I could start the activity period. As I was trying to get them quiet, I could see out of the corner of my eye Hustle standing outside my door. When we made eye contact he signaled me to step outside. I did.

"What's up, Hustle."
"Hey, Baby. We've got to talk."
"What's up?"

He wasn't looking at me. He was looking inside, through the door window at my class, toward the back of the room. But he continued to talk to me without looking at me.

"Hey, Baby, you...uh, you gotta be careful, man. You, uh, you got some real assholes in your class...some real assholes!"

He continued to look inside at the class and after a few moments of silence he continued.

"Be careful, man. Any of 'em give you problems yet?"
"No, not yet."
"Yeah...uh...yeah. Look, uh, just watch your back...you just watch your back. Don't worry. I'm gonna look out for ya...uh...yeah, you're gonna be all right, Jack. Just...uh, yeah, you'll be all right. I've got your back, I'm lookin' out for ya. Just uh, be careful, man. These guys are some real assholes."

Upon hearing this, I returned to the classroom and continued to try to get my students to be quiet—all 48 of them.

A Classroom Incident

The following has to do with a" request" to use the bathroom that created an ugly incident for our teacher Mr. Harris.

As this was going on, I saw Antonio looking at the ground somewhat harmlessly. And then it happened. Antonio sprang up out of his seat and marched to the front of the class and literally screamed, "I gotta take a f---in' piss, Harris. I gotta take a f---in' piss! I gotta go to the bathroom, Harris! Hurry up, Harris, let me go."

"You're just going to have to wait. You had the whole lunch period to use the restroom. Now go sit down."

"I gotta go! I gotta go! Right now! Right f---in' now! You let me go. You let me go. I'm gonna piss in my pants!"

He paced back and forth across the front of the classroom several times. Then he suddenly picked up a trash can and started to unzip his pants.

"You let me go now, Harris! I shit you not, Mr. Harris! I'm gonna piss in my f---in' pants! You let me go now!"

"Get this through your head. You're not using the bathroom. Now, sit down!"

"You better f---in' let me use..."

Then, a kid named Jesus shouted from the back of the room, "Harris, you ain't gonna last a f---in' week in this school!" He then stood up and pointed his finger at me and shouted at me again, "You hear me, Harris? I said you ain't gonna last a f---in' week here...not one week...not one f---in' week! You might as well get the f--- outta here right now."

I didn't hear the rest of what he said as I was trying to stop Antonio from walking out the door.

MELTDOWN

Day six—the last straw:

11:54 A.M.

"Now I want everyone to listen to me. You all owe me two minutes of silence. As soon as the bell rings we're all going to sit quietly for two..."

"Soon as that bell rings I'm walkin' out of the f---in' door!"

"Two minutes! Y'all owe me two minutes!"

11:55 A.M.

The dismissal bell rang. Then there was a sudden dead silence. It was really weird. It was the quietest they'd all been in the whole hour. A group of students in front, including the football player, suddenly turned toward each other. It was like a huddle, but nobody was standing. They were all whispering to each other. The football player got up and walked toward the back of the room. Whatever was about to happen, he didn't want anything to do with it. As he was walking to the back of the room, he turned to look at me with a desperate look on his face. He said something to me, but it was a faint whisper. I couldn't make it out. I gathered he was trying to warn me about something, but I just couldn't make it out.

11:56 A.M.

They were still whispering. I could only make out bits and pieces of what they were saying:
"What you wanna do with him?"
"Girl, I don't wanna get expelled!"
"You ain't gonna get expelled."
"Look, if we're gonna do this thing, let's do it."
"I'm in."
"I'm in too!"
"F--- it. Let's do it!"
One of the girls stood up, "Let's do it!"
Lara Torres stood up, "F---in' A!"

Girl, after girl, after girl stood up until they were all standing, I counted nearly fifteen of them. Then Lara Torres looked me in the eye and said, "I'm gonna punch you in the f---in' mouth!"

Then they charged me in unison. It was a mob! I secured the door handle with my left hand. They were not going anywhere! At least ten of them charged ahead to within inches of my face then came to a halt. We stood there nose to nose. We could all hear each other breathing heavily.........I felt something on my left hand. I looked down. One of them was trying to pry my hand off the door handle.

Lara was leading the mob. Her face was six inches away from mine. Then she suddenly lunged at me. She struck me in the chest with her shoulder then quickly backed up. Then she crept closer. I was holding a cup of coffee. She pushed on it with her fingers. A few drops of coffee dripped down my hand. Then she smiled at me. Then she whispered,
"What the f--- are you gonna do about it?!"

Lunch with a Veteran Teacher

Several days after the incident, Jack had lunch with a veteran teacher who tells our rookie that his lack of action puts all teachers at risk.

"Well, Jack, how are your classes going?"
"Pretty rough. I'm not gonna lie to you, but I seem to have things under control today."

"That's good. I hope when you say 'rough' that it's not anything too drastic."

She started to lift a cup of coffee up to her mouth.

"Well, I was mobbed by my class on Wednesday." She stopped her cup in midair.

"Excuse me?" she whispered.

"Yeah. It was pretty ugly. Basically it went down like this. To make a long story short, I tried to keep my class after school for a couple of minutes. The last class of the day, y' know."

"Yeah, OK. So then what happened?"

"Well, basically, I was mobbed by about ten girls at the door. This one Hispanic girl, the one who was sort of leading the group, threatened me."

"What did she say?"

She said, 'I'm gonna punch you in the f---in' mouth' Then before I knew it, I was nose-to-nose with about ten of these girls. One of them, not this Hispanic one, tried to pry my hand off the door handle. She was never identified. Then this girl, the Hispanic one, lunged at me with her shoulder. She also jabbed at this cup of coffee I had in my hand. Then they all just kind of backed off, and I waited a minute. Then I dismissed them. Yeah. Yeah. It was pretty crazy."

"Jesus, Jack!"

We both paused, she took a sip of her coffee, then leaned forward. "So, Jack."

"Yeah?"

"When is the expulsion hearing?"

"The what?"

"The expulsion hearing, you know, to expel this girl...when is it... and where is it. Here? Downtown? Where and when?"

I looked at the ground.

"Dhana, there isn't going to be an expulsion hearing. We handled it."

"Who handled it? What's this supposed to mean? Who handled it?"

"We did, Mrs. Leonard, Mr. Baker, Tank, the cop who responded, uhmm...ya' know...we handled it. So, what are you doing this weekend? I heard there's going to be a..."

"No! No! No! No! No! Jack, explain this to me like I was a 5-year-old. What do you mean...you handled it?"

"Well, we, uh, well, it's like this. When it first happened, I was all hell-bent on pressing charges and all that. Then, well, Leonard and everybody else, well, we had a talk."

Her eyes got big. I continued.

"And basically everybody involved, especially Leonard and Tank, pretty much indicated to me that pressing charges against this girl would not be the best course of action. They made it clear to me that it was my decision, but they also made it quite clear that things would, well, not necessarily work out to my favor if I did proceed with expulsion."

Now she was breathing heavy. I could see her body inflating and deflating as she breathed into her lungs. I continued.

"So...well, hey, I'm a first year teacher. There's no question here who has more know-how and experience, so I went along with them. And well, I guess in retrospect I made the right decision. I was advised by people, namely administrators who've been in this business for at least ten years. I feel that I was advised correctly about how to handle this thing. So now, she's not gonna be expelled, but she is gonna be suspended. I feel as though, I mean, we all felt as though that would be the wisest thing to do. Baker made it very clear to me that he would support me in any decision I made, but he also stressed that assaults similar to the one I was involved in Wednesday don't usually result in expulsions. But he did say he would take my side. We probably would've had a tough time with expulsion anyway because Tank pointed out to me that, in accordance with the student ethics code, students can't be expelled for assaults such as these. Tank seems pretty astute when it comes to these things. I think this school is pretty lucky to have somebody with his knowledge of the law. He seems pretty cognizant of school law."

She interrupted, "Tank wouldn't know the law if it bit him in the ass!!! He's the head of security! He has absolutely no business whatsoever talking to you about this assault! This responsibility rests with the principal and vice principal, and he doesn't have a f---in' thing to do with it! What did Leonard say? Who is this cop? Not only do you have the right to press charges, it's your goddamn responsibility!"

She paused. Some of the people sitting at the other tables were starting to look at us. "Jack, you have got to stick up for yourself! What... what...you just let Leonard and Tank and that cop walk all over you!"

"I wouldn't say I let..."

"I mean...I mean, shit, I mean I guess I'm glad Baker was sticking up for you!"

She leaned forward and whispered.

"Jack, you can't do this. When a student assaults you, you have to stick up for yourself. You have to draw a line in the sand. I'm not pissed at you, but you know what? Your lack of action is probably going to endanger the physical welfare of other teachers. If the students at the school know that this girl got away with this, the rest of us are going to be punching bags!!"

Jesus was wrong. Mr. Harris made it through the first week, but not the first month. He had been advised that the girls might be part of a bigger gang and known to retaliate. Shortly thereafter, tragically, the school lost a fine teacher.

Note: Over fifty percent of all teachers who initiate their teaching careers in the United States do not complete their fifth year.[1]

No Longer Uncommon

Teachers and administrators are increasingly finding that the violence and lack of civility in today's schools are making the decision to stay in the profession fraught with great difficulty. They often find that even though they truly desire to continue to educate young people, the rising incidents of violence and abuse are causing them to reconsider this choice of careers. The excerpts taken from a document by Kristina Goetz demonstrate why they are concerned about the risks they are exposed to and why they are conflicted about continuing to fulfill this mission:

"The fatal stabbing of a private-school principal last week shined an intense light on the potential danger in Memphis area classrooms once regarded as safe havens."

Noting that such violence is being seen across the country, Goetz also reports, "In Philadelphia, more than 4,000 assaults on teachers were reported in a five-year period. In Kentucky, a teacher suffered a traumatic brain injury earlier this year after he was knocked unconscious while trying to break up a cafeteria fight."

Goetz quotes those knowledgeable about school safety to point out that the violence is not just being seen in the upper grades:

"The part that concerns me a great deal is that this

violence has migrated to the lower grades," said Ronald Stephens, Executive Director of the California-based National School Safety Center, who has been involved with school crime prevention for more than 25 years. There appears to be a greater number of assaults on teachers in the elementary grades.

Finally, Goetz comments on the disturbing fact that teachers are often afraid to report incidents of violence and that there is a growing lack of discipline even among younger children:

> Memphis Education Association president Keith Williams said that while the MCS administration may encourage reporting, city teachers are still fearful of doing so because of concerns about retaliation. Profanity has gotten to be a common-day language in some schools. The principals are saying, "Don't even write them up for that." It's getting to be whereby it is acceptable.[2]

Looking at statistics on a broader scale, Michael D. Simpson reports on a truly alarming number of acts and threats of violence which occurred in just one year:

> According to the U.S. Department of Education, 127,120 (4 percent) public school teachers (K-12) were physically attacked at school—hit, kicked, bitten, slapped, stabbed or shot—during the 2007-08 school year. Another 222,460 teachers (7 percent) were threatened by students with acts of violence.[3]

Notes:

1. Lisa Lambert, "Half of Teachers Quit in five Years," *Washington Post* com. http://www.washingtonpost.com/wpdyn/content/article/2006/05/08/AR2006050801344.html
2. This and the following quotations are taken from Kristina Goetz, "Assaults on Memphis-Area Teachers not Uncommon, Records Show," *The Commercial Appeal*, Memphis, August 14 2011, http://www.commercialappeal.com/news/2011/aug/14/assaults-on-teachers-not-uncommon.
3. Michael D. Simpson, "When Educators Are Assaulted. What NEA Affiliates Are Doing to Protect Their Members from Violent and Disruptive Students," *National Education Association*, http://www.nea.org/home/42238.htm.

Chapter 2

The Way It Was

Following is a set of stories reflecting an earlier time. These stories are a contradiction to the stories that you just read. The stories are about teaching and learning as it was experienced by most students and teachers in earlier days but tragically being experienced today in fewer and fewer American classrooms. [The stories are titled "Miss Virden," "Opening the Treasure Box," and "A New Teacher in Old Cloth."] Together the stories are intended to paint a picture of the commonalities that are the hallmark of effective teaching and learning essential to classrooms. In each of the stories, the reader will see and, hopefully, feel the positive learning environment that can only result in ordered schools and classrooms where there exists meaningful teacher authority and control. This kind of environment was so very common to classrooms of earlier times. As the stories are read, we hope that you will come to see that the intended instructional outcomes of teachers these earlier days extended far beyond the typical expected outcomes of today's standardized tests, a deep concern noted and repeatedly expressed about today's schools in *The Death and Life of the Great American School System* by Diane Ravitch.[1] Further, we hope that the stories reveal a simpler time of long walks to school and rushing to one's seat before the class bell rang. Finally, and overarching all of these commonalities, we hope you, the reader, can sense and feel the learning atmosphere that resulted—an atmosphere most conducive to good teaching and relaxed learning. This is the teaching and learning that can and will result if classrooms are safe, orderly, and under the control of teachers. We hope you enjoy reading about a slower and more civil time, a time we have titled "The Way It Was."

Miss Virden

It was the winter, and I was beginning the second semester of my senior year in high school. Early January was bitterly cold that year. There hadn't been a great deal of snow thus far, but morning temperatures were often in the mid-teens, sometimes below. The one-mile walk to school on those mornings required a heavy coat, gloves, scarf, and an insulated cap. Chic was often sacrificed for warmth.

On the first day of class immediately after lunch, I left the cafeteria and went to my locker. I grabbed the appropriate books and then climbed the staircase that was filled with fellow students and went to the second floor, north side of the building. I was looking for the English Literature class with a teacher I'd never had—Miss May Virden.

As I approached, I could see her in the doorway of her classroom greeting students as they entered. She appeared to be about age 60 or so, no more than four feet, ten inches tall and couldn't have weighed 100 pounds. She was wearing a light gray dress with a high collar and sleeves to her elbows. The dress had dark buttons down the front and a fabric bow at the neck. Her hair was cut several inches above her shoulders, off the face, and was very neat. She held an open book in her hands at waist level, and on her face she had a smile that was warm and compelling.

She received her bachelor's degree in English from Cornell College in Iowa. Later she did advanced work at both Iowa and Northwestern Universities. She had been teaching high school English and literature for nearly 40 years. She had never married and was, for me and many of my classmates, the epitome of grace and dignity. She brought to us and to each of her classrooms the essence of civility.

From her first class, she established the mood of the learning environment consistent with classrooms of that day. From the moment the bell rang it was clear that she was in charge. We had entered "her" classroom. Even on that first day, if you were unfortunate enough to come late to class, she advised you in a quiet but firm voice to go to the main office for a tardy slip. If you were foolish enough to begin an excuse, she simply waived her index finger slowly, then pointed to the door, and said again in that same voice, "As you leave, close it quietly." You could tell that she meant what she said and that she was confident that she could, if necessary, back it up.

The first use of her chalk board was to write her name. Then once written, she would pronounce it several times and then select, at random, someone to pronounce it aloud for the class. Once done to her satisfaction, she would smile and say, "Correct." She would then add, as she often did, the reminder, "Always remember that with language, precision is essential if one expects to communicate in a manner that will be understood."

In class she seldom referred to us by our given names, but rather as Mr. Golarz, Miss Simpson, or Miss Luchene. As she learned our names she would ask us for the pronunciation used. She many times also asked us for the origin of our names—ethnic background. After advising her, she might then inform us as to how our name might be pronounced in that native tongue. She never criticized or commented on our anglicized version. Her effort seemed to be more of an attempt to expand our understanding. I can recall in my own case bringing home to my father her pronunciation of our last name and his response. "She's absolutely correct, Raymond. Is she Polish?" "No, Dad." He smiled and added, "Then she's just a very good teacher. I had teachers like that when I was in school at Hammond High."

What I remember most while sitting in her classroom and the classrooms of other teachers in those days was the feeling of relaxation that I experienced. It seemed to permeate the entire room. That was, of course, assuming I had done my homework. There was no fear that some fellow student might create a disruption and thus break the tranquil and safe learning environment, or that several students would begin talking during her teaching moments and thus distract the class. All knew that they were sitting in a special place, a place that I have come to refer to as a sacred place. We were being permitted to participate in a gift that she daily was creating for us. We were being given a privilege that she and many others like her had taken a lifetime to prepare. Disruption was unthinkable and, furthermore, would not have been tolerated by her, nor by any other responsible educator. It would have been inconsistent with the nature of schools of that day.

One day in mid-January, she announced to us that she had prepared a special treat for us, a treat that had been given to her by one of her professors many years earlier. So, she had us close our books and asked us to listen attentively. She then began to recite for

The Problem Isn't Teachers

us line by line the poem, "The Bells," by Edgar Allan Poe. Throughout her presentation, we were totally captivated. But our capture was not the result of the words of the poem, rich though they are, but rather by her immersion into the poem: her eyes, the movements of her body, the gestures of her hands, the inflections of her voice, her pitch, her tone, at times almost moaning, the pace of her words, both rapid and slow. The bells became real, and we could feel as well as hear their many variations as Poe had intended. She seemed so totally alive in that long moment of presentation and then, as quickly as she had started, it was over, and the room was silent. She had taken us on a journey to a place most of us had never been, and in that journey she had introduced us to poetry as we had never known it.

I recall a movie from years ago titled *Blackboard Jungle*, in which a young teacher in an attempt to give a similar gift to his students brings to class his cherished personal record albums. Without his even having the opportunity to play the records, his students break and shatter them. The gift was thus never received—not because of a young less effective teacher, but rather because of the loss of an atmosphere for learning, a loss of civility that was no longer a part of that school.[2]

I and my friends who attended high school with me were the sons and daughters of steel workers and iron workers. Soot spewing from open-hearth furnaces miles away from our homes during the night covered our cars each morning. Most of our grandparents and some of our parents were born in foreign lands. In our homes many of us heard a foreign tongue spoken more frequently than English. We were rough and crass, and we butchered the English language. We butchered it with our Chicago area dialect mixed in with Eastern European idioms and peculiarities as well as with our own street vulgarities. We were as hard an audience as you would ever like to have. Yet, when Miss Virden finished her eloquent delivery, we continued to sit there stunned. Then, spontaneously, we began to applaud. We applauded and applauded, and then began to rise and applaud. We applauded as she stood there before us, and then she smiled.

It would be years later, only after I had myself become a teacher, that I understood what teachers experience in such rare moments. It's the moment that makes a teacher's journey worthwhile. It is the magical instant of real communication that sustains teachers as nothing else does. It is why they stay.

Shortly after her presentation of "The Bells," it was our turn. Our assignment was to select some piece of poetry or prose, or write a piece of poetry or prose, and present it to the class. I had not presented to a group of any kind since my presentation of a Polish prayer at Trinity Hall in East Hammond while in the second grade. I was, therefore, quite nervous. After some deliberation, I chose a verse from "A Psalm of Life," by Longfellow. It was a favorite of my dad's from his high school years. I remember working diligently. I even presented alone in front of a mirror. Finally, the day arrived. It was my turn to present. I was confident. I got up, made my delivery with appropriate hand gestures, then when finished sat down. As I did, Miss Virden said, "Mr. Golarz, may I see you after class?" I looked up, smiled and replied, "Why, certainly." I was by now quite confident that she wanted to compliment me, but not embarrass any of my classmates. After class, I came up and stood to the side as the last of my classmates exited. Then she turned to me and asked, "Do you realize you have a speech impediment?"

Not recognizing that word and fully expecting a compliment, I said, "Why, thank you." Then very gently, but clearly, she let me know what that meant. I remember being so embarrassed that I wanted to slide under the door into the hallway. She immediately recognized my distress and said, "Come to my class after school." I did.

For the next several months twice a week after school she guided me past a speech impediment and past the set of inaccuracies of usage that came both from my ethnic heritage and from that South Chicago dialect. In finishing one of our final language sessions she turned to me and said, "Mr. Golarz, you are not finished. You will need practice, practice, and more practice. However, what I believe you now know is when you are wrong. Therefore, if you choose to say it incorrectly it will now, I believe, no longer be said out of ignorance. The capacity to choose makes us free. Choose wisely."

As I have keynoted conferences across the country and Canada in my adult professional years, I have often started an address with a story of a young man with a speech impediment, a limited vocabulary, and a caring teacher whose gift to all of her classes over so many years was, "Always remember that with language, precision is essential if one expects to communicate and be understood." She and others like her gave such gifts and so, so much more in a sacred place called school.

Opening the Treasure Box

Life occasionally affords you an encounter that you never forget. Such was knowing Mr. Nelson who taught us literature. I remember the first time I saw him. I was a high school freshman looking for my locker. He was dancing down a half-filled hallway greeting, waving, and laughing as he came my way. When he got to me he stopped, looked me over, smiled, and asked, "Freshman?"

I responded, "Yes, sir."

Then he replied, "Ah, good breeding. Good breeding. And, its number, young man?"

"Sir?"

"Your locker number?"

"186, sir."

"All the way to the far end of the hall, turn right. You can't miss it...has 186 written on it."

He winked and then continued his waving, smiling, greeting mode down the hallway. Life occasionally affords you an encounter that you never forget.

It wasn't until my sophomore year that I had him for class. Each day, just before our class, he would appear, as if by magic, outside in the hallway. As the bell rang, he would leap into our classroom from the hallway, land in a half-squatting position, throw his books on his desk, and exclaim in a voice filled with joy, "Am I excited today!" Next, he would look at us and pose the question he had taught us to respond to, "And what, my young friends, have we gathered together to be excited about today?"

We would respond in unison with gusto and with heavy emphasis on the first syllable, "LITerature."

"Yes, my young friends, the nectar of life, literature."

One particular fall day in mid-October, he entered our classroom in his normal ritualistic manner and exclaimed, "Ah, my young friends. I have for you today a rare gift, a gift so rare, a treasure—a treasure that is a poem. A poem called "Thanatopsis."

As he spoke, he was already passing it out to us. Soon we each had a copy. With continued excitement he said, "I want you to read it. Several days from now, I want to do something special with it in class."

Unable to wait for our reading, he began to read the poem to us. Then he read it again and, finally, a third time. With each reading he seemed to go deeper and deeper into something he was feeling inside of himself. Somehow, it was as though the poem were talking back. He wasn't just reading. He was in a conversation. When he finished, many of us looked around at one another in order to see if others had felt as we had, and then the magic was over. Almost as quickly as it had come, it was over. He had taken us far that day. He had shepherded us into the beating heart of a poem and he seemed to know. He knew that he had opened a treasure box and that some of us had peered in. So, he smiled on his way out of class that day, knowing we now needed to come back. Our souls had seen but a glimpse. We would need to peer in again.

The following week on Monday we again addressed "Thanatopsis." William Cullen Bryant would most likely have grinned, shaken his head, and rolled his eyes. We dissected, carefully pondered, discussed, analyzed, and did some pretty deep thinking for 15-year-olds. Carefully, Mr. Nelson guided us into an open discussion of mortality where we continued our cognitive analysis. Finally, I can clearly remember that we felt as though we had exhausted the topic and had captured a clear understanding of death.

At that point Mr. Nelson looked at us and said, "My young friends, I have but one final question for you." We eagerly awaited, confident and cognitively ready. And then he said, "What would you do if your mother died?" I recall that it seemed a strange question and that for a moment it had caught us off guard. But we regrouped quickly, and our hands began going up. As he acknowledged us with his pointed index finger, the responses from various corners of the room came quickly.

"I'd call other members of our family. They would need to know."

"Have no idea where she keeps her insurance papers. Would need immediately to be searching her records."

"Would call the funeral home."

"Be writing an obituary—that takes time and needs to get into the newspaper as soon as possible."

As we were giving our answers, Mr. Nelson had been slowly

walking to the far right front seat in our classroom, a seat occupied by Tony. Tony sat in the front seat nearest the chalk board. Tony never said much, often doodled, though during discussions he seemed to be listening. We all knew he was kind of slow, though no one ever laughed at him. He was just a big, nice kid.

When Mr. Nelson finally got to Tony's seat, we had completed our responding. Then Mr. Nelson, with the fingers of his open right hand placed under Tony's chin, gently raised Tony's head so that Tony was looking directly into his face. In a quiet, gentle voice he asked, "Tony, what would you do if your mother died?"

Tony quietly responded, "I'd cry."

Mr. Nelson looked up at all of us as the room fell silent. The lid of the treasure box had been opened wide by a big, nice kid named Tony, and an artist named Mr. Nelson watched us in the silence of that classroom as we all peered in.

He stood there and said not a word to us. He didn't need to. We now understood. The writing of "Thanatopsis," the open discussion of mortality and of death, was not to conclude in a cognitive response. The reading of the poem—the journey to its heart—was not to be cognitively understood, but rather to be felt. Therein was its conversation with humanity—a conversation not of minds, but of hearts.

We left class that day richer than when we entered. We left a bit less convinced of our own greatness and intrigued by the wisdom that could be found in the "Tonys" of the world. Somehow, in that brief moment in that classroom, an artist named Mr. Nelson showed us where to find our real humanity, and he did it through the magic of "Thanatopsis," the magic of poetry. I don't really remember what else he taught us that year.

I suppose those were the things on the standardized tests.

New Teacher in Old Cloth

It was the fall and my first year of teaching. I had secured a job in Schererville, Indiana, where I would be teaching comprehensive seventh grade and have the extra duty assignments of head football coach and track coach. I had picked up my books and class lists several weeks before school started, and from mid-August I had had access to the school and to my classroom. So, after football practice, I would come to the building and go to my room for an hour or two to prepare. By Labor Day, I felt as though I was as prepared as a young new teacher could be. Was I nervous? Of course. My feelings of anticipation ran from very scared to terrified and back again. I clung to a piece of advice given to me by a beloved college professor in the hallway outside of his philosophy class:

"Golarz, hear you're gonna be a teacher. Want to be a good one? Then just remember to do two things. Love what you teach and love those you teach. The rest will follow." Then he turned on his heel and with a spritely gait walked down the hall, half-humming and half-singing some Guy Lombardo or Al Jolson tune, as was his manner.

I sat at my classroom desk that late Saturday afternoon before Labor Day and revisited again my class list of 34 students as I had been doing the past several weeks. I had a good handle on the pronunciation of their names by now. I even had faces for eight of them as they were players on the football team and knew me as coach.

A fourth of my students, many of them football players, would be coming daily to school by bus from Hoosier Boys Town, a facility for court-placed neglected, abused, and delinquent youth. I had several weeks earlier met with Fr. Campagna, the director of the home, who had advised me that the boys in my charge, either as football players or students, would know that when I spoke, I spoke for him. In other words, what I said in his stead was law. I gathered my papers together, placed them in my new briefcase, then walked to the window nearest my desk for a last look before the students came. Nice view from the third floor—could see all the way down the rather quiet, tree-lined street.

But now it was getting late. Long shadows stretched along the ground below. I crossed the creaky hardwood floor to the light switch at the back of the room adjacent the hallway. I then turned off the light, went down the staircase and past the principal's office where she was still working at her desk.

"Mr. Golarz."

"Yes."

"Could you come in for a moment, please?"

"Certainly."

"Sit down, please. We have not really had a chance to talk. Things have moved so quickly the last week and with you coaching football, well, there has not been much time."

I sat down and listened as she continued.

"We have a philosophy of schooling here that is fairly consistent with all American schools. You will hear me speak of it time and again in our faculty meetings. And I'm sure that by the end of the school year you will be able to recite my words verbatim. Nonetheless, I just wanted to take a moment to share this school's mission with you before school starts next Tuesday. May I continue?"

"Please do."

"Well, Mr. Golarz, this is how we judge our worth. First, we do not want you to ignore the value of the yearly progress test scores of the students, but be mindful that we look to many other things to judge our true progress. Some of the elements we consider most important are as follows: Are students gaining a fondness for personal reading? That is, do they read for pleasure? Secondly, are their studies in music, art, history and literature broadening them as human beings? Further, can you notice that they are becoming more sensitive to the needs of their fellow man? And finally, as the school year progresses, can you notice enrichment in their relationships with classmates, their families, their country, and their God?"

I was, to say the least, stunned and replied, "I'm overwhelmed."

She smiled, looked at me and said, "You didn't think that we just taught numbers and letters did you?"

We both laughed, and then she said. "Don't worry, we won't look for you to get everything done this year. Enjoy what's left of your weekend and Labor Day."

"I will, thank you."

"Oh, and Mr. Golarz, if I've not told you before, and I'm sure I have, remember on the first day, first item on your teaching agenda is to make sure you let them know who's in charge. It will make your year and my year much easier."

"Yes, Ma'am. Thank you. See you Tuesday."

I got into my cherished white Chevy. The feeling of apprehension on my internal nervous-meter was now reading "terrified." Maybe the weekend would bring it down.

Thankfully, my first days of teaching were generally uneventful. On day one I introduced myself, writing my name on the chalkboard and pronouncing it several times. Then as instructed by my principal, I set the tone. I neglected to understand, however, that for most of my students I was their first male teacher, and my six-foot, two hundred pound build and deep-voiced threats of potential medieval torture for the least transgression may have been a bit over the top. The football players took it in stride, but almost no one else did. I remember spending the remainder of that day smiling and speaking in much softer tones so that those most timid would stop shaking before they went home.

During the first week, the only challenges to my total authority were from little Bobby, who just loved people but couldn't figure out how to be quiet, and from Linda on the other side of the room who loved to write and pass notes. Neither condition presented much need for deep thinking. Bobby found himself in row four, front seat right next to my desk. A parent conference with Linda's lovely mother and father, followed by a new front seat, row five next to Bobby, seemed to resolve all immediate issues. In the ensuing days and weeks, even when I might permit some desk study or reading time while I was at my desk, if whispering got to be a bit loud, all I would need to do was raise my head, look around, and all would be quiet.

As we moved along with our studies, I began to notice that some of the strategies, time-tested as they might have been, seemed boring and somewhat non-productive. As an example, they read from the American history text aloud, one student after another, seat by seat, and row by row. Retention of what was read or heard seemed, upon testing, to be negligible.

"How would you like to study history a different way?"

They responded enthusiastically, "How, Mr. Golarz, how?"

"Well, we have two chalk board walls adjacent to one another. What if I get some butcher board paper, 36 inches wide, and then we roll it out and tape it to the chalk boards. Then we will draw several lines on the full length of the paper. On the top line each inch of paper will represent one year of American history, beginning with 1492 and Columbus to the other end of the paper and the present time. A line just below the date line would be for important events such as the signing of the Constitution. The line below that would be for famous people, and the line below that might be for significant inventions or such."

"Mr. Golarz, a next line could be for when new territories became states."

"Exactly. Good idea. And you can work in groups of three or four. Then when you're ready with something to put on one of the lines, your group presents the idea orally to the class and then tapes the information on the butcher board paper in the appropriate year."

Their enthusiasm could hardly be contained.

"Now understand, this is to be done in an orderly and quiet manner, or we'll have to stop the project and go back to reading one by one from our desks. Clear?"

"Yes, sir. It's clear."

"And who's to make sure this project is done properly?"

"We are."

"Correct. Not me, but you."

"Don't worry, Mr. Golarz. We'll make sure everyone does it the right way."

This and other projects in English, mathematics, and additional content areas were initiated and carried out successfully. As we became more successful, they would come up with additional ideas such as the book they created for American history. They asked me to run off pages of the outline of the continental United States. I ran off more than the project would require. They then labeled each page with its own date, beginning with 1492 and then every five years thereafter, 1497, 1502, 1507, and so on. Each page represented a five-year movement forward of American History. On each page, consistent with the proper year, they would identify the location and addition of each state, the beginnings and growth of cities, the development of railroads and railroad lines, and a host of other items. When they completed the project, one could flip through the book slowly and observe the visual growth of the nation in five year spans. The project, when completed, was almost always on someone's desk. They were so proud of it.

The classroom next to mine was vacant, so I secured permission to use it. Occasionally, I would take the handful of students that most teachers often find are far ahead of their peers in any content area. In math, for example, I had seven students who were able to perform at extraordinary levels on any seventh-grade math achievement assessments. They were very bored with their grade-level materials. So, we went to the vacant room with the high school freshman algebra book. Sometimes I would work with them. Sometimes one of their fathers, an electrical engineer, would have time to come in, and sometimes they would work alone. The remaining students, those not engaged at that time in such projects, would have some other assignment. Seldom did I find it necessary to come in and give my look of "little too loud in here."

As a first-year teacher, I was quickly beginning to understand the critical importance of classroom order. If there were order and students behaved in a way that respected the rights of their classmates to learn, then we could accomplish anything. I am reminded of this need for quiet each time my wife and I go out to a movie. Just before the movie begins, this recording is played: the sound of a baby crying, the sound of loud conversation, and the sounds of cell phones. These sounds conclude with the following message: "Please don't interrupt the movie by adding your own sound track." The obvious intent of this message is to request that all in the theater respect the silence that each needs in order to follow, understand, and enjoy the movie. A movie theater is hardly a sacred place, but if such distractions continued, even for a little while, many of us, in frustration, would leave and ask for a refund of our money. None of us can watch and enjoy a movie or learn in a classroom environment filled with significant distractions.

Paula was the teacher in the classroom across the hall. Like me, it was her first year. She taught comprehensive fourth grade. Her class had thirty-two students, but as Paula would often lament, "I have thirty-one and Mary. That makes forty-one." Mary's behavior was like one of the Westside Gang in the Little Lulu comic series, and she was nonstop, always after someone. I'll never forget one early afternoon in September. I was in my class teaching, when through the rectangular glass window in my classroom door, I could see Paula in the hallway. She was pacing back and forth, so I went out to see if anything was wrong.

"Paula, everything all right?"

"Just waiting for Mary's mother—called her, you know."

At that moment, coming up the stairs behind us was a rather large, stocky woman wearing a buttoned down the front red sweater, that was obviously several sizes too small. She was breathing heavily and had quite a scowl on her face. As she reached the top stair, she grabbed the banister hard, spun on her left foot, then moved quickly toward Paula while saying, "Okay. What the hell's going on? What are you doing to my daughter? Where is she?" Paula turned her head toward her closed classroom door, then pointed at her rectangular glass window with her extended index finger and said, "She's right in there. She's the one standing on her desk throwing books at her classmates."

I could hardly contain the laughter that came out almost reflexively, so I just looked at Paula, shook my head, and went back into my classroom. The behavior of Mary, her nemesis, did not improve much despite continued parent conferences, principal interventions, behavioral contracts, and a host of additional strategies. Most times, Mary's continued presence and disruptions were a catalyst to the negative behaviors of several others. Consequently, Paula, despite administrative support, never had the calmer classroom atmosphere that I experienced nor did she have the student learning benefits that resulted. During most of her school year, she spent much of her free time and class time addressing the impact of disruptive behavior. It was as though there were always a smoldering mass in the middle of her room looking for the slightest breeze to spark the flame and ruin another day.

Over the years, I've often thought of Paula. She was a fine young woman and I believe learning daily how to be a good teacher. Our conversations over the months were infrequent and sadly often focused on her need to leave. I'm not sure that the Marys in her classroom were the only reasons she left. But I am sure that they were the primary reason, for we've talked often since she left. She didn't return for a second year.

Jesse

Early on in the school year, I found that the playground was a great place to get to know so much more about my students. Their informal interactions or lack thereof, revealed a great deal. My observation time was either when I had playground supervision, or when I observed out of one of my third-floor classroom windows. One of the students I very clearly remember observing was Jesse Domingo, who came from Hoosier Boys Town. He was one of my seventh-grade students. Jesse was also the best player on our football team. He was a running back that opponents could neither catch nor stop. He was fast and powerful and was probably the real reason we went undefeated that year.

On the playground, Jesse never engaged in play with his classmates. He often walked the perimeter of the schoolyard by himself. Then, if time permitted, he'd walk the perimeter again.

So, on one early fall day, I caught up with him. "Jesse, mind if I walk with you?"

"No, not at all, coach."

We walked for a while, talking of nothing more than football. After some 15 or 20 minutes into our walk, I said, "Well, need to get back to the building and give you a few minutes to play with your friends." He looked at me and just said, "Uh…don't really want to play with the kids, coach."

I let it go, but was struck by the use of his choice of the words "the kids." This prompted a meeting at Hoosier Boys Town with Fr. Campagna. So, on a Sunday afternoon about a week later, I met with Fr. Campagna and Mr. Gabriel, a staff person, in Fr. Campagna's quarters. For almost an hour they filled me in on Jesse's childhood. It was information that I wished I hadn't needed to hear. When I left that afternoon, my heart was heavy for this young man. Beginning at age four, Jesse's life and the life of his younger brother had been tragic. The details of that early tragedy were so horrific and personal that it seemed insensitive to include it here. From that early age the boys had been separated and placed in foster homes. They each had, over the years, been moved to additional placements. Finally, Jesse was remanded to the care of Hoosier Boys Town. Once there, Jesse pleaded with Fr. Campagna to find his little brother. Fr. Campagna's staff was successful and six months later Jesse and his brother were reunited. In the years before Hoosier Boys Town, the two boys had resided in 15 foster placements. The transient history had resulted in Jesse, who was now age 15, being placed in the seventh grade—two full years behind his age-appropriate peers. Then it all made sense, "Uh…don't really want to play with the kids."

Several weeks later I was handling the chains at a high school game as a favor to a coaching friend. It was a great game, close and hard fought. The only element missing for my friend's team was a hard-running half-back. As we walked to the locker room after the game, Jack said to me, "Your kid Jesse still sure he's gonna come our way?"

"He says he wants to. Year after next you'll probably have him on your team."

Jack looked startled, then responded, "Year after next? Damn, Ray, I need him next year."

"Sorry, Jack. He's only in seventh grade."

"Seventh grade? Oh no, Ray! Damn!"

All the way home I couldn't get the conversation out of my mind. I kept thinking, "What a shame. What a shame." The following Tuesday night I was at St. Joseph's College in East Chicago. I needed some teaching advice from my old philosophy professor Mr. Brinley. After we finished and he was walking me down the hall to the college entrance, he said, "What's got you down, Ray?"

I responded, "Does it show?"

Then I told him the story about Jesse. He looked at me, smiled and said, "Can he pass the entrance exam for the high school?" I responded, assuming he had not understood my issue. "But that exam's for eighth- graders, right?" His smile filled more of his face and he said again, "Can he pass the entrance exam?"

You know, there are times when you really feel slow, like when you're the only one who didn't get the punch line of a joke, or when you can't think out of the box like the smiling professor standing in front of you. I started to laugh.

Then I said, "Really think so?"

"Won't know unless you try, will you?"

I left the campus and drove toward home. The following days were filled with evening meetings with Fr. Campagna, the principal of my school, and the principal of the high school, to name a few. Finally, the path was cleared and approved, but he would have to pass the entrance exam. My last talk would now be with Jesse.

The principal took my class while Jesse and I went for a walk. Out on the grassy edge of the playground, I told him everything and cautioned him as I did. Then I asked the question, "Do you want to go for it?"

To this day, I can still picture him standing there in front of me, his body swelling up with emotion until it reached all of the parts of his face. He breathed in deeply as if attempting to hold it all back. Then the tears rolled down both cheeks as he brushed his eyes with his open hands. He then turned from me, bowed his head, and wept. I held him in my arms for a long, long moment while he tried to regain some composure.

Finally, brushing back his tears again, he said, "I'll make it, coach. I'll pass that test. Will you help me?"

"You know I will."

Then after another deep breath, he said, "Can I stay here for a minute by myself?"

"Sure. Come back in when you're ready."

I returned to the building holding back my own tears. As I walked, I looked up and said a "Thank You," for until that moment I had not really understood the depth of that young man's pain. Jesse seemed to change that day. I know he stayed up late in his bed with a flashlight studying for that exam. Fr. Campagna told me so.

The following year Jesse made a great high school halfback, and for me it was always a pleasure to go and watch him play for I knew that his contentment was coming from much more than football. He knew that he had earned being there and that was a feeling he had never had before.

Danny

Danny was a tall, lanky kid. As we used to say, "He was all arms and legs." He was also a very timid, quiet soul who seemed to always be trying to get out of someone's way. It was as if deep down, he felt like he had no right to be there. On the playground, he appeared to be quite content to play with the first- and second- graders. The second day of the school year, I had asked my students to write a little story and tell me about themselves. I asked them to take their time, but to make the story no more than a couple of paragraphs. That night after school and football practice, I sat at home at the kitchen table reviewing the stories. I came to one paper that thoroughly confused me. There was scribbling at the top where the name should be. Then in paragraph form there was scribbling, a space, scribbling, a space, a shorter amount of scribbling, a space and so on. There were no discernible words on the entire page, but from a distance of, say, four feet, it looked like a written piece of work. I checked against my class list of stories received. The only odd-man-out was Danny. I was off to the college for a consult.

"Is this a boy or girl, Ray?"

"Boy."

"Well, Ray, I've seen this before. If I'm right, this young man can't read or write and probably doesn't know his alphabet either. However, he is demonstrating fairly good cognition, because he's giving you the closest thing that he can as he attempts to mimic what his peers are doing."

Several days later, I had a meeting after football practice with Danny's parents. In the meeting I found that they were, in fact, his aunt and uncle and that they had recently secured custody of him. His mother had passed away. His father's whereabouts were unknown, and his young childhood to that point had been a series of tragedies. The aunt and uncle seemed to care a great deal for Danny, and they were willing to do anything they could to help him. They said he enjoyed basketball. Alone most evenings, he would shoot baskets at a rim that his uncle had fashioned on a homemade backboard that was attached to the front of their garage.

During the next late afternoon that we met, we fashioned a partnership and a plan. His uncle, though not a carpenter, was good at woodworking, so he would cut out an alphabet out of blocks of wood. Then he would color code them so that each of the twenty-six block letters would be a different color: dark red, light red, yellow, dark green, etc. Danny would study these at home with his aunt and uncle. I, on the other hand, would spend time in school with the alphabet doing some one-on-one tutoring with him when I could.

The second part of the plan would need to be handled more delicately. Danny had some skill at basketball. Could I find a seventh-grader who would be a good match for Danny—someone who was very interested in learning a sport, someone gentle and quiet like Danny—someone to whom I could give, with Danny, time for such a sporting activity? That is, could I facilitate a friendship? One candidate who came to mind was Charlie. On the playground, during recess and after school, most of the other young men in my class were engaged in some sport, including a basketball game at the far end of the playground where there existed a rim secured to an old pole. Only one young man stood out as having no place to go—Charlie. As I later came to find, Charlie was one of my most capable students, regardless of the content area. But, in the area of sports he had virtually no developed skills. Besides being one of the shortest boys in my class, his girth was impressive. He had told me early on that if he could be anything other than what he was, he would like to be a professional athlete. Once he confided in me that it didn't even really matter what sport it was—just something. Over the next month, I periodically gave Danny and Charlie a basketball during class time and would have them go out alone. Sometimes I'd give them 15 minutes, occasionally a half an hour.

In late October, after school on a very crisp and sunny fall day, as I was preparing to go out to football practice, Charlie and Danny came to my desk. They stood next to each other. I remember looking into two smiling faces, one directly across from me at eye level and one about a foot and a half higher.

Charlie spoke. "Coach, can we use a basketball?"

"Well, sure, boys, but what for?"

"Well, we both talked to our parents, and they said it would be okay if we stayed after school to play some ball and then walked home."

I gave them a ball and they walked off. "Thanks, coach. Thanks, coach." After practice, I came back to my classroom. I had some papers I needed to take home that evening. As I sat at my desk shuffling papers and deciding what I needed to take, through the closed windows I could hear dribbling and the occasional shudder of the iron rim being hit by the ball. I opened the window and watched them as they finished.

As they passed my window far below, they saw me and yelled up, "Good night, coach. See you tomorrow." I waved and then continued to watch them as they walked the sidewalk lined with autumn-leaved trees and long shadows. They walked with their arms over each other's shoulders, a difficult reach for Charlie. I watched till they faded down the hill that the sidewalk took as it passed the old church. I watched till I could see them no more, though the vision still today remains in my heart along with the words of a very wise principal, "Finally, as the school year progresses, can you notice enrichment in their relationships with classmates, their families, their country, and their God?"

Danny stopped playing with first-and second-graders that late fall. By the end of the school year he could write and read, though not yet at grade level. Charlie, by spring, could play a fair game of basketball.

Danny had begun to unravel the mysteries of language. Charlie had begun to use his body in a way he didn't know was possible. Jesse had his hope restored. And I? I had begun to understand the wisdom of those words of advice given me by my philosophy professor as I ventured into teaching: "Love what you teach and love those you teach. The rest will follow."

By most people's standards, my first year of teaching would probably have been judged a good year. In all content areas my students gained as a group substantially more than a year's progress. Most did better. Few did worse. Danny's four-to-five year growth was due to the fact that he had been so far behind. We had done lots of personal reading, and the students seemed to enjoy it. In addition, we studied music, art, literature, and history.

As to their growth in terms of their humanity and civility, I think they taught me more than I taught them. Yes, I was an enthusiastic young teacher who wanted to do a good job. But I was also given many of the gifts and tools that all teachers need in order to be successful. In addition to the gifts given to me by helpful college professors, I was supported by the following:

1. My class list was available in a timely fashion.
2. My room was available for my use several weeks before school started.
3. I had no want for paper or supplies.
4. My books for all content areas had been ordered long before I came and were available before school started.
5. Each of my students received books for each content area on the first day of school.
6. My students were permitted to take their books home and use them both at home and in school.
7. I was given a current and accurate phone list for the parents or caregivers of all of my students two weeks prior to the start of school.
8. The school secretaries made calls and arranged the logistics for my requested parent conferences.
9. With few exceptions, I had parents or appointed caregivers who were supportive and available.

10. My room was clean, neat, and orderly.
11. I had the desks I needed for the number of students expected plus four extra desks.
12. All student desks were neat, clean, and in working order.
13. I had total support from the administration in the event of my needs regarding student discipline.
14. My classroom authority was never second-guessed by any secretary, support staff member, or administrator.
15. I did not have in my class any of the kinds of students whose behavior can be so disruptive that they can make each day a living hell and destroy the opportunity for a successful year of learning.
16. The school administration and parents of my students supported the quiet and orderly learning environment necessary for good teaching.
17. Finally, though I had not yet graduated from my college teacher education program, I was afforded any and all of the college's resources, including counsel and advice whenever I experienced that need.

As a consequence of all of these things and so much more, when I came to this assignment, those who had preceded me and those who continued with their arms around me, had stocked the cupboards, set the table, and handed me the keys.

It's all that teachers really want and need. Stock the cupboards, set the table and give them the keys. With gracious and kind guidance they'll do the rest.

Notes:

1. Diane Ravitch, *The Death and Life of the Great American School System* (New York: Basic Books, 2010), 16-30.
2. *Blackboard Jungle*, Metro-Goldwyn-Mayer, Dir. Richard Brooks, March 1995.

Chapter 3

"Watch CNN. Our School Is on Lockdown!"

With chapter 1, "America, We Have a Problem," we explored via a set of stories the present American educational scene filled with its anxiety and stress. In chapter 2, titled "The Way It Was," we provided a contradiction. Again with a set of stories, we journeyed with you to a gentler, more civil time, a time very different from today. It was a time filled with the conditions that supported and allowed for relaxed and safe teaching and learning. An atmosphere of trust was pervasive. Learning at very many levels could and did occur. We hope that you felt its safety and security.

Now with chapter 3, we bring you back to the present where we will continue your roller-coaster ride of this section of the book, "Here, There, and Back Again." And now that you're back, we will slowly take you to the top and then abruptly drop you into "Watch CNN. Our School Is on Lockdown." Hold on tight. Keep your arms in. Don't stand up. We are going to make sure with this chapter that you know you are back in the present. You'll find soon that being back can be terrifying.

Detroit

I got a call from the newly appointed Superintendent of the Detroit Public Schools, Dr. Eddie L Green. He had read our book, *The Power of Participation*, and he asked to meet in order to discuss his desire to implement the design proposed in that book in all of the Detroit schools. We arranged to meet a month later in Traverse City where

I was keynoting a convention. During meetings with Green and his cabinet in Traverse City, we agreed that I would work directly with all of the administrators in the Detroit Schools, but would prepare video presentations for each school staff because of the size of the district. One of my earliest video presentations was taped at a districtwide video tech center located in the southwest corner of a large inner city high school. Space for the video tech center was available in this complex due to years of declining enrollments. About half-way through the taping session, I needed to use a bathroom. I advised the taping crew. After some hesitation, their response was, "Do you really need to go?"

"Yes, I do."

They left and soon returned with the media director who said to me, "Dr. Golarz, do you really need to go?"

"Is there some kind of problem?" I asked.

"Well, the bathroom we use in this part of the complex is closed for repair, so we will need to get you a security guard and find you a bathroom to use somewhere in the high school itself."

Some ten minutes later, I was being led down a locker-lined hall by an armed security guard. When we came to the midpoint of this long hall, we encountered a floor-to-ceiling metal security screen that needed to be opened by a second security guard on the other side of the screen. The first security guard then turned me over to the second guard while the first relocked the screen and waited for my return. The second guard now walked me down the hall and advised me that I was now in that part of the facility where classrooms were in session behind locked doors. I noticed as we walked that the wall graffiti was becoming more pronounced. Also, since quite a number of overhead lights had been vandalized and were not working, it was fairly dark. I could see too that a significant number of lockers had been vandalized in this part of the building. Clearly they were not usable. We traveled a second, similarly vandalized hall to a midpoint where we met a third guard. This guard took me into a rather dark men's bathroom while the second guard waited outside.

I relieved myself in one of the least-clogged urinals. While in the bathroom, an immense sadness overwhelmed me. On the way out I said to the third guard, "Do the kids use this bathroom?"

He replied, "Not many. Most kids learn not to drink fluids till after school is over, because if they go in to one of these, it could be dangerous, and we can't protect 'em."

"Can't protect 'em?"

"From the gangs of students who wait for 'em in here, you know. Hey, man, there's only three of us for this whole damn building."

Lockdown

I was sitting in a restaurant with Marion and a dear colleague, Dr. Tony Broadwell, and his wife Dorothy. We had just ordered lunch. We had been reminiscing about Richmond, Indiana, where I had been superintendent of schools and Tony had been my associate. My cell phone rang. I answered. A teacher colleague from Southern California who had traveled with me on various speaking engagements was on the phone.

"Ray?"

"Yeah, Mickey."

"You watching CNN?"

"No, I'm out having lunch."

"Watch CNN. Our school is on lockdown. I'm lookin' out my classroom window. I can see two—no—three helicopters. At the entrance way of my school building are platoons of police in helmets and shields separating hundreds of black and Hispanic students—multiple fights all over the campus. God, hope they can get this under control. Damn, shot just fired through the window of my classroom. "Everybody on the floor. On the floor now. Now! Now! Damn good thing we're on the second floor. Ray, call you later. Can't talk now."

As I put my phone down, a rush of memories filled my mind, and as I caught Tony's eyes across the table, I was transported back in time to my office in the administration center of the Hammond Public Schools. The phone was ringing and my secretary Phyllis was shouting to me to pick it up.

"It's Chief Wise of the Hammond Police."

"Hello, George?"

"Ray, we have a full-blown situation here at Central High. We're working with your building administrators. But this thing between our black kids and southern whites may overrun our resources, and we may need help from East Chicago and the Chicago police. Wanted you to know. Please advise your superintendent. Get back to you as soon as I can."

I made the short walk over to the superintendent's office. The condition around the high school was now being picked up by all of the T.V. and radio stations. Outside of our building I could hear the sirens of squad cars coming from all parts of the city and moving toward the high school. A second high school, only a short three blocks from the Central High School epicenter, was catching the spill-over effect and hundreds of its students were now vacating that building and moving down the street to join the fray.

I drove to the scene. Calumet Avenue was blocked by squad cars. Behind and beyond the City Hall, a block from the high school, black citizens and high school students were gathering in groups in Maywood Park and the adjacent black neighborhood. I could see young people whom I knew and had worked with standing on corners holding hand guns and carrying rifles.

I got out of my car near the football field. It was at that moment that I was most terrified, for coming out of a neighborhood of mostly southern whites were seven or eight young men. They were carrying weapons of all kinds, notably shot guns and hand guns as they moved toward the high school. My terror was that if they walked far enough in that direction, the corner of the building would no longer block their sight-line, and they would then see the armed group of blacks on the corner of Calumet Avenue.

I began walking quickly toward them not really knowing what I could or would do. I recognized only two of them. Most of them were adults from that community, not students. At that moment a Hammond squad car, siren and lights on, came careening around the corner from Sohl Street moving directly toward them. They scattered quickly into the neighborhood. It took the next three hours for the police to steadily regain control of the neighborhoods and streets. By 6:30 p.m. there was a tense control being maintained by an overextended and very tired group of law enforcement officers.

Somewhere near 7:30 p.m. faculty and staff were beginning to gather in the high school cafeteria. Many were still in a state of shock. Some had vomited or would soon do so. Others were sitting and shaking, while still others just stared blindly into space. Pat O'Rourke, President of the Hammond Teachers' Federation, and other union leaders as well as the principal, Dr. Elizabeth Ennis, were moving from

The Problem Isn't Teachers

teacher to teacher, trying to calm frayed nerves, or just holding those who could not stop shaking. They would continue tending to their colleagues until all were safely out of the building that night.

The pockets of students who had earlier clustered together in classroom corners were now safely out of the building. The hallways were strewn with litter of all kinds. Those who had earlier walked these halls, some armed and prepared for violence, were now gone. The potential for in-school deaths had come close—very close.

For at least a month, the school would be run more like an airport under siege. Some parents would refuse to allow their children to return. Many students who did return would be dropped off and picked up by parents. Security officers, inside and outside the building, would be visible virtually everywhere. Preparations for and the conducting of expulsion hearings for those found most responsible would be running nearly around the clock. Teachers, classroom after classroom, would be attempting to reestablish order and restore some feeling of safety despite the shattered pieces of a calmer past that still lay strewn across their halls and classroom floors.

Our initiation into the fraternity of violent schools had taken place. We now held with them a place of honor. Those who had known us before would not again look at us in the same way. Our only consolation was that we were by no means alone. The fraternity was expanding. Members were being accepted from across the country. New membership was being given to schools with documented incidents of rape, physical attacks or fights with weapons, robbery, and violent deaths, including murder.

Statistics

In February of 1998, an extensive and definitive report on violence and discipline problems in U.S. public schools was published by the National Center for Education Statistics using the 1996-97 school year. Following are some of the findings reported:

> 4,170 incidents of rape or other types of sexual battery;
> 10,950 incidents of physical attacks or fights in which weapons were used;
> and 187,890 fights or physical attacks not involving weapons.[1]

In April of 2012, Terence P. Jeffrey of *CNS News* reported that the United States Department of Education and the U.S. Department of Justice were jointly reporting that during the 2009-2010 school year their structured studies were suggesting approximately 1,183,700 violent crimes committed at public schools while only a part of these were being reported to police. Segments of his article specifically state:

> Many of the violent crimes that occurred at public schools were classified as physical attacks or fights without a weapon (there were 725,300 of these of which 194,200 were reported to the police).
>
> About 14,300 physical attacks or fights with a weapon occurred, but only about 4,400 were reported to police.[2]

If the National Center for Education Statistics had correct figures for the school year 1996-97, and we compare those with the actual figures for the 2009-10 school year, then we are confronted with something frightening. In the category of incidents of physical attacks or fights in which weapons were used, we increased from 10,950 incidents in 1996-97 to 14,200 incidents in 2009-10. For fights or physical attacks not involving weapons, the increase was from 187,890 to 725,300.

Statistics Never Tell the Whole Story.

As if these figures and comparisons were not frightening enough, consider the fact that most children who are victimized do not fight back. Consequently, for them, there is no statistic to report. They did what the perpetrator told them to do. They passed on the lunch money. They submitted to the sexual advance. They just got beat up and said nothing.

I can remember in my own case being the victimized child. The school and its playground were the safe haven. The streets and neighborhood were not. The nuns made transgressions on their grounds something you didn't want to do twice, but they couldn't walk you home. And the cultural norms of the streets of the old Polish neighborhood forbade your bringing home what happened to you on the streets. So, I was a silent victim. I said nothing for several years. I turned over the money. I took the beatings. Finally by the age of ten I had had enough and fought back. I got tired of walking or running the twelve long extra blocks out of my way to get home to my grandmother's house. I kept getting beat up, but I had decided to no longer make it an easy thing to do. Within a couple of years the beatings diminished. They never stopped. But diminished seemed okay. Once in a while as a result of intense provocation, I would fight at school and make the statistics list. But that was rare, for the consequences of such transgressions were never worth giving in to your momentary anger.

If there was anything positive about victimization, I found it in only one place. It was in one's capacity to notice other victims and if touched by their agony, to try to help. In my own case it was timid and shy Catherine. A short story of Catherine follows, taken from one of our recently published books, *Sweet Land of Liberty*:

> Then there was timid, shy Catherine. She was in my class. She seemed to have only one dress and her shoes were extremely worn. She did very poorly in class and tended to shake when she was tense. I sat a seat behind her and one row over, so to me it was obvious. On the

playground, she stood alone in the corner of the school building, usually for the entire recess unless another girl or group of girls decided that they needed to tease her by poking her or spitting on her.

One day as school was dismissed and I began my walk to Busia's (grandmother's) house, I found her on the edge of the playground, surrounded by four or five girls who had already thrown her things to the ground and were circling her, yelling at her, poking, and calling her "filth." I came up, frightened them all away, and they went running off, screaming warnings to her that it wasn't over. She was down on both knees crying. I leaned over, put my fist under her chin and raised her face. She looked up at me and big tears streamed through her dirty face onto her dress. I picked up her things and began to walk her home. She actually lived close to Busia's on Tapper, directly across from Koch's Bar. She lived alone with her mother, who was seldom there, in one of the five one-room apartments on that side of the street. We didn't talk at all until we got to her door.

Then she said to me, "They'll get me tomorrow for your breakin' that up and walkin' me home."

I began to say in anger "No, I'll get 'em....."

But she stopped me and just said, "No, it's okay. You can't stop 'em, and I want to thank you for walking me home. Nobody ever did that before and I'll remember it."

Then she opened her door to go inside. As she did, I got a glimpse of a room with no furnishings, a crate for a chair, and an old mattress on the floor. She went in, and I walked down the alley to Busia's. The picture of that empty, dark room with no furniture still haunts me as does the tear-streaked, dirty little face of the girl who lived there, Catherine.[3]

While the statistics of national school violence cannot really be absorbed by us, the image of a vulnerable child with a tear-streaked, dirty little face can bring us all to tears and rage. That rage would certainly intensify if the tear-streaked face belonged to our own child who had endured such indignities alone.

Civility and order do not simply make better schools and classrooms. They do not just make great teaching and effective learning. Civility and order are the right of every vulnerable child.

Notes:

1. Sheila Heaviside et al. "Violence and Discipline Problems in U.S. Public Schools: 1996-97," (U.S. Government Printing Office, Washington D.C., March 1998).
2. Terence P. Jeffery, "1,183,700 Violent Crimes Committed at Public Schools; Only 303,900 Reported to Police," *CSN News..* April 23, 2012. http://cnsnews.com/news/article/1183700-violent-crimes-committed-public-schools-only-3.... 5/20/2012.
3. Raymond J. Golarz and Marion J. Golarz, *Sweet Land of Liberty*, (Bloomington, Ind. AuthorHouse, 2011), 174-75.

SECTION TWO

PAIN COMES TO SCHOOL

Section 2 of this book is focused upon the kind of pain that children bring into their classrooms, sometimes every day. They are the pain of poverty, the pain of abuse, and the pain that comes from living with adults who are hooked on drugs. As we reflected on these three chapters, we remembered a story we heard recently of a little girl who pleaded with law enforcement officers to please arrest her daddy who was at that moment in the throes of the effects of multiple toxic drugs. As she stood helpless on the side of their rural trailer, she did the only thing she could think of to help her daddy: beg for help.

The following three chapters are not easy to read, though the manner in which the "Parent Center" got established may amuse you. Please join us now for a hard look at how pain comes to school—pain which is often seen only by teachers.

Chapter 4

Child Abuse

Recurrent Image

It had been a great conference. I had been able to convince my father to come along with me, which was a special treat. The conference planners had prepared a packet for him, including his own name badge. I don't think he ever took it off. He just kept greeting strangers, attending sessions, taking notes, and having a ball.

Saturday morning the conference concluded at 11 a.m. Our flight back to Chicago was not scheduled to leave until 2 p.m. We got up early, packed, checked out, had breakfast, and went to the closing ceremony in the grand ballroom. By 9:20 a.m. we were finished. There was a handful of breakout sessions left starting at 9:30 and running until 10:45 a.m. We debated: "Should we head for the airport or squeeze in a final session." The only session that looked like it might fit my criminal justice focus was a child abuse session to be conducted by a medical doctor from the Coroner's Office of the City of New York. We decided to stay, went in, and found two seats. The session was quite well-attended, and we didn't have a lot of time to settle in. She was beginning.

"Ladies, gentlemen, and colleagues. As you can see in the brochure identifying this session, there is a caution. Unless you are law enforcement officers assigned to crime-against-person units or are department of public welfare personnel who deal with severely abused children, the content of this session may be too much for your personal sensitivities. So, if anyone feels a need to leave, don't be ashamed. Just leave now. The session will include untouched pictures of abused children that I will show enlarged on the screen above me as I explain each. I will now wait five minutes before I begin just in case anyone still wishes to leave."

The room got absolutely silent. After two minutes or so, several people left, and then a few more followed. Finally, near the five-minute mark another large group, about twenty in number, got up and left. Then she started.

The next twenty minutes or so were a visual blur interrupted only by occasional images of a tortured child or infant showing injuries that I did not believe human beings capable of causing. Several participants around us vomited. A number left in tears. I finally looked at my dad and saw tears streaming down his face. I motioned to the door. He nodded and simply said, "Yeah, let's go, kid—seen enough." We didn't say much on the way to the airport, nor on the plane ride home. Some months later we talked about it, but only that once. We told each other of the images that still wouldn't go away, especially at night when we closed our eyes and listened to our own voices as we said our prayers.

A year later, I joined the county child abuse task force and several years after that I was privileged to be elected chairman of the Indiana Chapter for the Prevention of Child Abuse. The saddest thing I learned during those years was that the condition of child abuse and neglect has no social class boundaries. These conditions exist in upper class homes, middle class homes, and the homes of the poor. Teachers everywhere in our country see and must respond to their fair share every day.

I've gotten to where at night only one image keeps recurring. Maybe it always will. But I've also learned as a result of my work that teachers tragically often have to deal with the same night-terrors.

A Fragile Decanter

I had gone to Lafayette Elementary School situated in a working-to middle-class neighborhood to visit a kindergarten teacher. It was an overdue visit. I had often wanted to stop in and watch her teach. Irma had a reputation throughout the school district for her fine teaching. I hadn't been there more than an hour when the bell rang announcing that morning kindergarten was over. As she and I walked toward the door, a little girl, one of her pupils, came to her side, and they then held hands as we continued to walk through the door and to the outside. I could soon tell that Irma was somehow now totally preoccupied and was hearing nothing that I was saying, so I stopped talking. Busses and cars arrived to pick up children who were not walking home. A black Ford with a single male driver came for the little girl whose hand she held. The child got into the car, closed the door, and they drove away.

Irma then turned to me and said, "Each time I walk her out, Ray, I pray that the black Ford will not come. When it does, she squeezes my hand so tight I at times believe that she might snap one or two of my fingers. I can feel the terror and fear building in her. She will be sexually abused this afternoon, and it will be violent. I've called and called the Department of Public Welfare, but they've not responded. She'll return tomorrow physically hurting. I can tell just by how she walks. That pain I know will pass. The psychological pain will never go away, and it will stay at a high pitch for three or four days after the rape. During these days, I just pet her head often and allow her to draw and color. Her ability to refocus and again be ready to learn sometimes takes that full four days." She then grabbed my hand and squeezed it a bit, turned, and went back into her classroom.

All the way back to my office I reexamined what I knew about abuse. Anxiety, fear, and terror crush our capacity to learn. The harsher the abuse, the more powerful is its impact. An innocent child is such a fragile decanter that can be so quickly shattered.

That afternoon a young Hammond police officer, Linda Lawson, who had a deep concern for the plight of such abused children, along with the Director of Child Protective Services out of Gary, and two case workers from the Department of Public Welfare in Hammond, removed the little girl from her home in the Lafayette School District and placed her in the protective custody of the state. She never had to go back there.

A Sick Nation—Just a Few Statistics

According to a UNICEF report, the following facts provide a grim picture of life for some in this country:

> The United States ranked as one of the two top nations in the world in child deaths due to maltreatment. Among developed nations we have nearly the youngest mothers of first-born children. We are one of five developed nations with new born lowest birth weights. We have nearly the highest number of newborns in the world born to mothers who are on drugs. [1]

It should come as no surprise, therefore, to find that as one writer reports the following:

> Annually nearly 90,000 infants are abused or neglected within the first month of life. Further, in the United States poverty is significantly related to incidence rates in nearly every category of maltreatment. Current statistics from virtually any reliable source will reveal that children of poverty today are: fifty times more likely to die from maltreatment and twenty times more likely to be seriously injured. [2]

Since I walked to my car with the police and that little girl removed from her home in the Lafayette school district, child abuse and neglect in America have continued to rapidly rise. Knowing that and remembering Irma's last words on that day bring me no peace:

> I can feel the terror and fear building up in her. She will be sexually abused this afternoon and it will be violent. Ray, her psychological pain will stay at a high pitch for three or four days after the rape. During these days I just pet her head often and allow her to draw and color. *Her ability to refocus and again be ready to learn sometimes takes that full four days.*

On the evening news in November of 2011, multiple television stations reported a story which really got our attention. It was also reported in an article by Deborah Williams. The media reported that the children of Shanghai, as a group, perform at the top of international competition on standardized tests. Reporters who went to find out why concluded and reported back to the United States that the major reason for such success was that these children of Shanghai began each day ***ready to learn***.[3]

Notes:

1. Retrieved from UNICEF, "Child Maltreatment Deaths by Country 2011," http://www.nationmaster.com/graph/hea_chi_dea-health-child-maltreatment-
2. Anastasia Mott Austin, "90,000 Babies Abused or Neglected in the First Year of Life," 4/42008, http://www.buzzle.com/articles/90000-babies-abused-or-neglected-in-the-first-year-of-life.
3. Deborah Williams, "Why Shanghai Students Outscored All Others in the World," 2012, http://www.tutorfi.com/wordpress/index.php/why-shanghai-students-outscored-all-others-in...

Chapter 5

The Crush of Poverty

The United States has never been a country that has managed to get its national condition of poverty under control. During the Great Depression of the Thirties, the condition became catastrophic for millions of Americans. We still hear talk today of the bread and soup lines, countless meatless meals, cardboard in shoes, homes without heat, and "tabs" at the corner grocery store. Only because of WWII, labor unions, the GI Bill, and federal programs like the WPA and CCC camps that gave work to the poor did we emerge into the Fifties and Sixties with a viable middle class, relief to the poor, and some financial equity for all of our country's people.

In the middle of the 1970s this move to economic justice began to dissolve. As a nation, we began to drift back into increasing poverty and inequality. The Great Recession of 2008-09 did not alone cause our current condition, for we were already well on our way. What the recession did was to catapult us the rest of the way into a hole so deep that in actual numbers there are more Americans in poverty and serious need than we experienced in the very depths of the Great Depression of the 1930s.

Joseph E. Stiglitz addresses this current issue clearly in his recently published book, *The Price of Inequality*:

> By 2007, the year before the crises, the top 0.1 percent of American households had an income that was 220 times larger than the average of the bottom 90 percent. Wealth was even more unequally distributed than income, with the wealthiest 1 percent owning more than a third of the nation's wealth. The last time inequality approached the alarming level we see today

was in the years before the Great Depression. The economic instability we saw then and the instability we have seen more recently are closely related to this growing inequality.[1]

Finally, Stiglitz summarizes for the reader what he calls a "snapshot of America's inequality":

The simple story of America is this: the rich are getting richer, the richest of the rich are getting still richer, the poor are becoming poorer and more numerous, and the middle class is being hollowed out.[2]

No other modern, developed nation must shamefully admit to such dramatic inequality—only the wealthiest of nations, the United States. For despite our wealth, we have the greatest concentration of poor that we have ever had. Further, on the issue of who these poor are, the media and the strength of our long standing racial prejudices have given us the wrong image. The image of poverty that most of us continue to picture is that of a black adult. Further, it's an image of a black adult who we've been conditioned to believe is culpable for his or her own condition. What we don't visualize is the truth of poverty. And the truth is that the person most often in poverty in America is actually *a child*. He or she might be white or black, Native American, Asian, or Hispanic. What we need to be aware of is that their numbers are growing. A full fourth of all American children are now in poverty. The image of these children that our teachers see daily is of a hungry, scared, often ashamed, poorly-dressed, sad child—a child who most often attends a school where there are lots of other poor children—a child who finds few, if any, resources at home that will help ensure success in school. This is the child who pushes the grocery cart for a mother at a cheap discount store, the child who knows of paying with food stamps and vouchers, the child whose dress or jeans is a hand-me-down or comes from the racks of Goodwill. At night this child may eventually try to go to sleep while listening to a frightened mother fight off the advances of a drunken boyfriend. Yet this child may dream of having a nice bed to sleep in, of living in a safe neighborhood, of getting good grades, or of not being hungry. If a girl, she may dream of being older, and unlike her mother, still having pretty teeth. If a boy, he may dream of having a father who has a regular job from which he comes home every night. We find these children everywhere. They might live in an inner city, a small town, on a Native American reservation, or in a remote, rural area. Increasingly, they might be found living in an old car, an alleyway, an abandoned church attic, or in a homeless center. They might not live that far from our own neighborhoods, yet they are often unseen.

Following is a set of stories that open the front door of the "homes" of the children of poverty—children who daily enter the schools of our American nation. These stories, we believe, are their stories. They are the stories of all of our children of poverty. Please look around as you step inside. Despite the best efforts we make with our current limited resources in schools, despite the sandwiches teachers often bring to them from their homes, despite the coats, shoes, dresses, free lunches, Christmas gifts and squeezed-in moments of tutoring, we are able year after year to save only some. We are not able to give them the gift they need most—the gift of an education. Many will drop out and live lives less fulfilling than they should have been. Poverty is a brutal reaper. Few will have their dreams fulfilled. Unless our nation changes its practices with respect to the poor, most will live the harsh and hopeless lives of their parents.

The Real World

I spent my early childhood years in East Hammond, Indiana, a Polish working-class ghetto. There was a small number of African American and Russian families, but, for the most part, the community was Polish, Roman Catholic, and poor. Oh, it was not the poverty of my parents, though they told stories about having to drop out of school at the age of 15 for want of a second housedress, or of leaving home and wandering the nation via the tops of trains and bum camps so that a mother would not have to set one more supper plate that she could not fill. They told of being denied hospital admission for lack of insurance and later losing, after days of labor, a baby too big. They told of the shame and anguish of the poor. But those brutal days of poverty for my family were gone, and now we were just poor. So, out of my Busia's (grandmother's) rear side door, then through her back yard and down the alley, I made many childhood trips for her to the corner butcher shop. Three slices of bologna and a loaf of rye bread made up the usual short list.

As often as I made that trip, I also made the trip to Koch's Polish bar next door to get my Dziadzia (grandfather). These bar trips were more fun than the trips to the butcher, for upon entering Koch's bar, I would be hoisted into the air by one of the several men in the bar closest to the door, danced with, then set on a stool at the end of the bar with my own coke, complete with straw. It was a festive place filled with hard-working Poles focused on a Friday night moment of camaraderie in the form of a series of shots, beers, and salutes of "Nazdrovia" (to your health). Eventually, the grandmothers would come. There would be loud shouting, words of consternation, waving of fists in the air directed at Koch, the bar owner, downing of the last shots, and finally walks back down the alley bordered by its cyclone or wood-slat fences and occasional back walls of unpainted dirt-floored garages. In the immediate years that followed, I gave little thought to that alley way. But then why would I? It was just an alleyway in an old Polish neighborhood, an alleyway with broken fences and unpainted wood-slatted garages with dirt floors, or so I believed.

Degree in Hand

Years later with a master's degree in hand from Indiana University, I got a job with the Hammond Public Schools. I had already taught middle and high school for several years, so I was a perfect fit for their new federally-funded delinquency prevention effort. They wanted staff that had some teaching experience.

My first day on the job, at 7:45 a.m., I met my mentor at a house in a heavily industrialized part of town off of Sibley Boulevard. The house was one of the few remaining in an area of old condemned houses being razed as a part of a redevelopment effort. I pulled up, and Andy Hiduke was already there waiting for me.

"Have a hard time finding it, kid?"

"No, not really. Just didn't realize there were still homes in this area."

"Won't be for long, kid. Won't be for long."

I followed him up the broken concrete sidewalk to the house. Andy was an old salt—reminded me of some Navy petty officers I had served under, the kind of guys you could work with for thirty years and still not tap all that they knew or could teach you. He had been doing police and court work for years during which time he had been Chief Probation Officer for the Lake County Juvenile Court.

As we cautiously continued down the dangerously cracked and broken sidewalk to the house, Andy turned to me and said, "These are poor but proud people, Ray. She will have cleaned for our coming, but it smells so bad in there that you won't notice. She may also have gotten a little coffee from somewhere and made some for us. If she offers, accept. She has nothing else to offer. Their last name is White. They have 14 children. Nine still live in the house. The two oldest sons are doing time at the Michigan City State Penitentiary for armed robbery. The whereabouts of the two older girls and an older son, all dropouts, are unknown." As we approached the front door it was opened to us by a barefoot and scantily dressed boy who appeared to be about 4 years old.

"Hello, Mr. Andy."

Andy replied, "Joshua."

Then we heard from within the house, "Mr. Andy, you just come in here and bring your friend too."

We walked through the living room and into the kitchen. There we found Mrs. White. She was an extremely large woman. I knew from earlier conversations with Andy that she was in her mid-forties, but she appeared much older. Life had been hard. "Would you want some coffee?" We accepted and sat. One of the several young girls near the kitchen served us. Andy then advised Mrs. White that I would be working with her and her family. At this she seemed quite distressed.

She turned to me and asked, "Will you remember to bring us a food order if we need one?"

I smiled and replied, "Yes, ma'am. I'll remember, I promise."

She smiled back and seemed to relax. As Andy took over the conversation, out of the corner of my eye I watched a large roach working its way along the kitchen door frame toward a fairly sizable hole in the ceiling. While I continued to glance around from where I sat between the kitchen and living room, I could see in the living room stacks and stacks of disorganized clothing, blankets, bedding, and badly torn furniture and mattresses. In and amongst these stacks and piles were small half-naked children playing everywhere.

I turned back to the table at the very moment that a large roach dropped from the ceiling hole. It landed no more than an inch from Andy's hand which was gripping his coffee mug. He did not move. He did not in any way act startled. He did nothing to shame or humiliate this poor woman who was attempting to give us her best. He was the noblest of gracious guests. As we left the White's house that day and went to our cars, I looked up and said a little "thank you." I had come to this job with my new university degree, but I had been taught more on my first day, in an old run-down house, by a seasoned mentor than I ever could have imagined. Andy looked back as he entered his car and with just a trace of a smile on his face, he slowly nodded and with a knowing look said, "Welcome to the real world, kid. Welcome to the real world."

Snakes on Her Legs

Occasionally, on these work days I would stop at my grandmother's house for lunch. I'd sit at her kitchen table as I did when my feet wouldn't touch the floor and enjoy her company, a bologna sandwich and, if I were lucky, some Polish homemade *kapusta* (sauerkraut).

It was a cold, Lake County winter day in early February. There had been snow several days running, and now the temperature was dropping into the low 20s. I had just been assigned a new family to work with in the 900 block of Conkey Street just across the alley from my grandmother's house in the 900 block of Ames, so it made sense to stop at her house for lunch, and then make my stop at the newly assigned family on Conkey. The ten inches of fresh snow made the drive over to Conkey Street ill-advised. So, instead, it would be a familiar walk. Boots on, out the rear side door, through the alley, past the butcher shop, Koch's bar to Conkey Street. Once there, however, I couldn't find the house. I knew this neighborhood well, but possibly I had been given the wrong address? I decided to take a stab at asking for directions at a couple of neighboring houses. At the second house, a pleasant, middle-aged woman told me to go back to my original address. She added, "Go to the back. In the back. She lives in the back." On faith alone, I went back and trekked through a foot of melted and refrozen snow and ice between two houses. I found nothing, just an old unpainted wood-slatted garage, the back of which was visible from my grandmother's backyard. It was a garage I had walked past many times as a kid.

I knocked. The door moved, so not wanting to open the door without permission, I held it and knocked again. I held it again and knocked a third time. Finally, it opened, and standing before me was a very slight African American woman wrapped in a blanket. Her face seemed ageless—neither young nor old. Yet it was clear that she was very tired and defeated.

I had never before looked into the face of hopelessness, but I believe in that moment that I did. As I looked down at her, the dim light of the February afternoon shown on her exposed legs, and from her knees down to her feet, her legs appeared to be wrapped with black snakes. As she stood there motionless, they seemed to move. A chill cut through me. Behind her in the shadows of the far corner of the dirt-floored garage appeared to be a cot covered with blankets. Under the blankets, there also appeared to be movement. A single light hung from the garage rafters. Past the cot in the farthest corner of the garage, I could see light where the back wall of the garage met the earth. Towels, blankets and such had been jammed into the opening of broken slats in an unsuccessful attempt to block the weather. Snow and very cold air continued to come in. Eventually the moving cot revealed its secret as the head of one, then two, then three little children appeared.

Once in a while, life impresses an image on both our conscious and unconscious minds. Time moves on, but the images remain. For me, one of these images will always be the lady with snakes on her legs, complete with all of the background pieces of garage rafters, little children's heads, and cold snow.

Time and familiarity eventually completed this picture, and I came to realize that the snakes were really extreme varicose veins. The little heads became eight children. The ageless woman, then twenty-six, younger than I when we first met on this cold February day, had had her first child at age thirteen.

For years we worked with her and her family. We provided tutorial interventions for the children, medical assistance, most of which focused on attempts to keep her alive, and primary care such as food, clothing, rent, and heat. She and her children became the focus, along with many other families, of an inter-agency task force involving the General Relief Agency, Lions Club, Trustees Office, Department of Public Welfare, police, and police support groups. We gave her and these other families as much of the limited resources that we could provide. In the end, she never learned to read or write, had two more children, and died prematurely of a venereal disease her body was unable to fight. Within four years of our initial contact with her, three of her children also died of what we shamelessly call natural causes.

Our successes with such families or their children in those days were few. One of the few successes that I vividly recall took place around this same time. A family of five had been referred to us by the police department. The family lived in a rat-infested two-room basement apartment on Marble Street across from Junior Toy Steel Corporation, a non-union industrial sweat shop that I had worked in while in my late teens. The family was made up of a mother, a 13-year-old daughter, a younger daughter, age 8, and two boys, ages 6 and 7. The mother earned her money by providing sexual favors to men who would come to the apartment at various times of the night. They were usually intoxicated when they came and often, before or after sex, would vomit or urinate in various places in the apartment. Most early morning hours, the apartment, therefore, smelled heavily of alcohol, vomit, and urine. The children would get to school on their own, if they got there at all. Worst of all, the 13-year-old girl, most vulnerable in this situation, was beginning to appear desirable to some of the drunken men who frequented at night.

My first visit to the apartment was with Fred Monberg, a giant, barrel-chested high school counselor from one of our inner city high schools. As I recall, Fred sized up the situation immediately. His eyes swelled with tears, and then he looked at me and said in a voice of total authority, "There's no way in hell she's staying here. No way!" By that late afternoon, the young girl had been removed by the Department of Public Welfare and, as a consequence of Fred's persistence, a system that normally moves very slowly went into high gear. She was temporarily placed that very night in the Mayflower Home for Girls adjacent to Fred's high school.

Over the next several months, a multitude of social agencies as well as the Lake County Courts took over. The temporary placement became permanent. A charming and caring Mrs. Kucer, who was part of the high school's non certified staff, voluntarily became the young lady's surrogate mother. The girl was provided with clean and appropriate clothing and was tutored regularly by volunteer teachers. Eventually she graduated from high school and went on to Purdue University. She never had to go back. But we were never able to help her siblings or so many, many others in the same way.

The Drop out List

In later years, I became the Director of Child Services for the school district. One of my tasks was to forward annually the school district drop out list to the appropriate state agencies. Each year I would sit in my office and slowly review that list. There were years when the list would exceed 500. Yet, for these many years, no matter how long that list was, no child or their surroundings were unknown. I could picture their houses, the dark and dirty interiors, their kitchens where plaster had fallen off the walls and floor tiles lay loose and cracked. Their siblings and extended family members were all a vivid memory. And I, and all others like me who did such work, even remembered to which stores we wrote their food orders and remembered the teachers who drove them to those stores and helped them shop. All of us spent our days, countless evenings and many weekends working with these families. We were interacting with and breathing in the soft underbelly of an otherwise wealthy and prosperous American society. Tragically, our successes were few—our losses many. The only commonality that remains from those times and continues into today's America is the relentless power of poverty. Its wrath continues to overwhelm our best efforts.

For years, often as I would drive home from work, I would first drive past my grandmother's house, then past her alley. I'd stop for a moment and remember a little boy hurrying along to purchase bologna at the butcher shop, then an older young man trekking through the snow to meet a sad young lady with snakes on her legs. I'd continue to drive all the way to Sibley Boulevard. Turning left where there were no longer any houses, I would remember Andy. As I looked out at a set of industrial plants, I could still hear him, *"Welcome to the real world, kid. Welcome to the real world."*

Raymond J. Golarz and Marion J. Golarz

Shades of Gray

The money that Congress approved to fund the Safe Streets Act was also approved to provide college tuition money for active duty police officers. Because much of the work I did was adjunct to law enforcement, I was asked to teach Psychology for Law Enforcement Officers. I must admit that when I taught, I always received more than I gave. One of the side benefits I gained came from becoming friends with many of my students who were Chicago police officers. Illinois had more extensive child services than Northwest Indiana and occasionally, when needed, they permitted my tapping into such services.

It was a dark, wintry, late November day, and I was checking on a referral that came to me from the court system in Lake County. The referral took me to an apartment in an old home that we called "the maze." The house, built in 1890, was one of the old, original Hammond, Indiana mansions. The more recent owners had cut it up into no less than twenty small apartments. Rickety staircases lined the outside of the house and the entire structure had the look of braided hair from a distance. I found 22B in the back near the top of the building. The door was ajar. I knocked. It opened, and in the gray, dark, empty room near the back wall was a child about a year old. He was just sitting there, whimpering, and he had a deep cough. He was shivering almost uncontrollably, wearing nothing more than a very wet and soiled cloth diaper. I yelled for an adult but no one responded. I searched the other partial room but found no one. I knocked on apartment doors in the adjacent apartments, but no one responded (I hated late Friday afternoons). I cleaned the baby and then left a note, "Have your baby. Come to the police department at the City Hall."

The drive to the City Hall was a short one. All the way there I couldn't get the picture of the interior of the apartment out of my mind. There were no toys, no furniture, no pictures on the wall, just endless shades of gray. The floors, walls, doors—all shades of gray. I thought of my own children's bedroom, the array of colors, music, chalkboards, toys of all kinds, books, big rocker, mobiles, and records. I thought of their smiles and the warmth they must feel when being held, rocked, played with, and read to. I put my hand on the child lying next to me, a child wrapped in my warm coat, trying to sleep between his deep coughs. I arrived at the station, turned off my car, and took the baby inside. Sgt. Wlekinski met me.

"Ray, what do you want us to do?"

"Well, first send a squad car to the apartment. See if a parent or an adult shows up."

"Okay. No problem. Got a squad car out in that area anyway. Will have 'em check every hour or so."

Then I said, "Can you do anything with the kid?"

"That's gonna be a little more difficult. We've already contacted the Department of Public Welfare, and they don't have a placement. Want to know if we can keep him here till tomorrow."

"Damn. That's not good. Kid seems sick, Sarge."

"Yeah. We know, bad cough."

I thought for a moment and then said, "Can you get the Chicago 79th Street Police Substation on the phone? Doesn't matter who's handling the desk. I'll talk to whoever is there."

I made my call and then came back out into the squad room. "Can one of you guys take me and the kid to the Chicago Skyway in Roby, just beyond Five-Points in Whiting? Need to go under the Skyway at the Indiana-Illinois State Line."

Wlekinski looked up, smiled, and then said, "You got it all worked out, didn't you?"

I nodded, smiled, and responded, "They have space and can on their own authority take the child directly to the protective child-care unit at South Chicago Hospital and make a temporary placement."

Wlekinski then said, "Well, let's get this little guy into the right hands."

All the way over to the Skyway through the rapid flashing red and blue lights of the squad car, all I could see were shades of gray. Some images just won't go away. Poverty and its tragic vestiges create painful and indelible memories.

Next morning about 7 a.m. Wlekinski called me at home. With a trembling voice, he told me that the hospital had just called. Despite their best efforts, the little guy didn't make it. He was dehydrated too long. There was too much pneumonia, too much fever, just too much of everything for the little guy. I thanked him and hung up. I walked to the open doorway of my own children's bedroom. They were all still asleep. As I stood there watching them with my head leaning against the door frame, a tear ran down my cheek and then several more. I didn't want to cry, but it wasn't going to be something I would decide. There are times when it happens that way. And inside of you, it just hurts.

No one to our knowledge ever came back to that apartment, nor did anyone ever inquire about the little guy.

The Parent Center

It was a spectacular spring day. Over the last two weeks we had gotten more than our fair share of mid-America rain, so the grass that had been waiting all winter was growing, touched everywhere by spring flowers. As I looked out of my office door that morning, I could see Johnny, the Director of Buildings and Grounds, walking briskly through the sun-filled hallway.

"Johnny, found that portable classroom yet?"

I was having a little fun with him. We had a dozen portable one-room classrooms that we moved around to different locations in the district as enrollments shifted and we found a need for additional space. Last year we were using ten of the portables. Two were sitting idle—well, one was sitting idle. The whereabouts of the second was unknown. In the school business you get used to having some things occasionally disappear: library books, a computer, cables needed for electronic equipment, a basketball, baseball equipment, even once a fairly sizable, portable soccer backstop. But a portable classroom? Never lost a portable classroom.

I knew it was a sensitive spot for Johnny, so I let up, laughed and said, "Johnny, don't worry. We'll find it. I mean, really. How far can you get with a hot portable? Where would you fence it?" I laughed again. Johnny just looked up and shook his head.

A week or so later, Johnny and I were visiting some of our elementary schools in the central city. We were trying to get into as many classrooms as we could. Teachers never get enough visitors. When they do, they seem never to tire of having their pupils show off regarding something that they had just learned. I always found it to be an uplifting experience. We left the last school on our list of morning visits, got into our car, and as we drove around the school grounds, we marveled at the manicured lawn and beautiful flower beds. The flowers surrounding the new parent center behind the school were particularly well-tended. The new parent center—what an attractive, wonderful welcome to the poor parents of this community.

We stopped on the street for a moment of admiration. As we sat there, not looking at one another, Johnny asked, "Ray, what would you estimate the size of that freshly painted, one-room parent center, surrounded by beautiful flowers to be?"

"You mean is it possible that the parent center with the flower boxes under the windows and new white gutters and down spouts is about the same size as a missing classroom portable?"

We parked the car and went into the building to find Nancy the principal. On the way to her office we ran into her. "Oh, I'm so glad you've not left. I just came from some of the classrooms you visited. They're so pleased. Have you time to stop at the parent center?"

"Nancy, that's what we need to talk to you about. Can we go to your office?"

"Sure. Or we can talk at the parent center. It's not as full now as in the morning. Can't even find elbow room in there in the mornings."

"Full? What are you talking about, Nancy?"

"Well, we opened the center about six weeks ago. Within a week, by 6:30 a.m. it was full of young mothers. They found out that a number of our teachers were coming in early to teach a few mothers how to read. Well, they all wanted to learn to read. Run four morning classes now, an hour each, starting at 5 a.m., about thirty in a class. Teachers rotate the teaching of the classes."

"They come at 5 a.m.?"

"Some would come earlier if we were open. If they stay at home, their drunken exes or boyfriends coming in from the bars look to beat them up, then rape 'em unless they consent. It's a bad situation in this neighborhood for these young women and their kids. Bad, Ray—really bad. Poor is not a good thing to be in America. But, I'm sorry. Here I am running off at the mouth, and you wanted to talk to me about something."

I looked at Johnny, then turned to her and said, "It can wait, Nancy. It can wait."

We had our visit at the new parent center, even enjoyed doughnuts made by a few of the teachers. As we passed by the center in our car, we stopped for a final look.

"What do you think, Johnny?"

"Think the portable we're lookin' for is smaller. Matter of fact, I'm sure it's smaller." I looked at Johnny, smiled, nodded my head slowly, and responded, "Think you're right, Johnny. Think you're right!"

Old Neighborhoods and Such

It was a very hot Bloomington, Indiana summer. Our son Daniel who resides in L.A. and teaches calculus in the inner city was home for a short break. He had some personal business to tend to at the Social Security office on the far side of town, not a part of town that we frequented, so we got lost. We noticed as we drove that the properties, block after block, were taking on a more dilapidated, cluttered, and unrepaired look. I commented on it to Dan who responded, "This is the poorest part of town, Dad. Lots of needs out here."

As he was speaking, we both noted two young men ahead of us standing in the middle of the road. They were waving at us to stop. We slowed to a crawl and could hear them yelling to us, "Can't continue this way. Up ahead there's a guy in the street with a gun to his wife's head. Police asked us to stop cars. Not enough police here to block all the streets." We didn't argue, simply turned around and headed back into the mid-afternoon heat as we watched them stop the next car through our rear view mirror. We got to a boulevard, and then turned right.

"Dan, about a quarter mile ahead I think there's a street we can turn on, avoid that neighborhood and get to the Social Security office. Want to try it?"

"Go for it, Dad."

We took the turn. We drove about a mile. Things were going well. Then up ahead, "Dad, squad car." Without knowing it, we had gotten back into the neighborhood.

"Need to turn around, gentlemen. We have a dangerous situation up ahead."

"Okay, officer."

As we turned around, I noted again the tattered, unpainted, and dilapidated condition of the properties. We had lived in Bloomington nearly 15 years, yet there were parts of the community I was unfamiliar with—these parts, these poorer parts. As we drove, making an extensive circle around this part of town, my mind raced back to my office years earlier. It was much the same kind of day, quite hot, though later in the year, early October. I was alone in my office.

My secretary Ruthie came in and announced that Jay Henderson, a very prominent business man from the community, was in the outer offices and wanted to see me. She concluded her message with, "Dr. Golarz, he seems quite shaken, almost trembling."

"Please invite him in, Ruthie."

"Ray, really sorry to bother you, didn't know who else to bring this to."

"Sit down, Jay, relax, I've got plenty of time. Just sit down and take a deep breath."

He did. As a matter of fact, he took several deep breaths. Then he began, "Ray, I'm born and bred in this town, and life's been good to me here. Went to school here, married my high school sweetheart, started my business here. Things have gone well and as I'm sure you know, I'm quite well-off. Well, Margaret, my wife, is presently running for city council, so in my spare time I've been going house-to-house, campaigning for her. You know, handing out literature and such. Well...."

Then he stopped and got kind of choked-up.

"Take your time, Jay. Take your time."

"Well, you know how you, the school board, Dr. Stolle, and Marshall are always talking about the hidden poor?"

I nodded.

"And a bunch of us guys in the Chamber of Commerce are always giving you a hard time about that?"

I nodded again.

"Well, I found them today. Was passing out literature door-to-door in my own neighborhood—neighborhood I grew up in. Haven't been down those streets in 25 years, Ray. Never have a need to. Ray, the poverty. My God. House after house. Rats, roaches, garbage, the smell of filth, run-down houses. Ray, I saw two kids digging through garbage—I swear. Minister down there told me last week they found two kids sleepin' in the church tower. No home. No parents. No food. Ray, my own neighborhood. I played there. I grew up there."

He stopped, then lowered and just kept shaking his head. We sat there in the quiet of the late afternoon. We left the lights off as it got dark and just talked of growing up in old neighborhoods and such.

In Bloomington, as twilight came and Dan and I were once again home, a police sniper took out the man in the street with one round.

A Couple of "Right-On" Articles

The following article, titled, "Class Matters. Why Don't We Admit it?" was written by Helen Ladd and Edward B. Fiske. It is taken from the opinion pages of the New York Times:

> No one seriously disputes the fact that students from disadvantaged households perform less well in school, on average, than their peers from more advantaged backgrounds. But rather than confront this fact of life head-on, our policy makers mistakenly continue to reason that, since they cannot change the background of students, they should focus on things they can control. No Child Left Behind, President George W. Bush's signature education law, did this by setting unrealistically high—and ultimately self-defeating expectations for all schools. President Obama's policies have concentrated on trying to make schools "efficient" through means like judging teachers by their students' test scores or encouraging competition by promoting the creation of charter schools. The proverbial story of the drunk looking for his keys under the lamppost comes to mind.
>
> The correlation has been abundantly documented notably by the famous Coleman Report in 1966. New research by Sean F. Readron of Stanford University traces the achievement gap between children from high- and low-income families over the last 50 years and finds that it now far exceeds the gap between white and black students. Data from the National Assessment of Educational Progress shows that more than 40 percent of the variation in average reading scores and 46 percent of the variation in average math scores across states is associated with variation in child poverty rates.[3]

In addition, the following article *"Schools Can't Manage Poverty,"* written by Patrick Welch, takes aim at one of the more thorny aspects of the requirements of No Child Left Behind. It appeared in the "Forum Section" of *USA Today* in September of 2010:

> Last week Secretary of Education Arne Duncan gave the keynote address at the Back-to-School convocation for the 1,200 teachers in the Alexandria Virginia Public School System. The meeting was held at T.C. Williams, the high school that Duncan's Department of Education labeled as "persistently low-achieving." Why? Our failure to meet Adequate Yearly Progress (AYP), the No Child Left Behind requirement that each of six sub-groups of students—black, white, Hispanic, economically disadvantaged, special education, and English Language learners—must attain higher scores in tests each year until in 2014 all children in all schools across the country reach the 100 percent pass rate.
>
> We teachers were told that Duncan would take questions after his speech. Being an English teacher, I prepared a little analogy to ask him about the rationale for labeling schools on the basis of Adequately Yearly Progress. Duncan's biographies often mention that he was co-captain of the Harvard basketball team during the 1986-87 season, his senior year. I reminded him that his team won only 7 games and lost 17. Such a record, I told Duncan, was the mark of a "persistently low-achieving" team, which made no "annual yearly progress." I meant the analogy to be humorous, but teachers sitting near Duncan said he didn't seem to take it that way.
>
> I went on to say that I assumed Duncan and his teammates did the best they could with the talent they had, and that no matter what improvements they tried to make, it would be foolish to think their team could ever reach the highest benchmark in college basketball—the final four. Like his basketball team, many schools are doing the best they can with the students they have and it is unfair to label such schools as failing.
>
> Duncan answered that all schools are not doing

the best they can and ended our little go-around with the cliché that "poverty is not destiny." Anyone who has taught at public schools as long as I have—I've been at T.C. since 1970 would agree. We have seen former students raised in the most impoverished circumstances go on to the best colleges in the county and then shine in various professions, but those wonderful success stories are the exceptions that prove the rule that the effects of poverty—especially the multi-generational poverty that we see in so many of Alexandria's schools—cannot be overcome by schools alone.

As J. Glenn Hopkins, President of Alexandria's Hopkins House, which runs a nationally recognized pre-school and provides other services to low income families, notes, "The real problem is that education officials don't realize—or won't admit—that the education gap is symptomatic of a social gap." He says student achievement is deeply affected by issues of family, income and class, things schools have little control over. Education bureaucrats naively assume that if they throw in a little tutoring and mentoring and come up with some program they can claim as their own, the gap will close." [4]

In this chapter so far we have tried to accomplish three things. First, with a set of stories we have attempted to give you, the reader, an up-close-and-personal view of the harsh daily life of American poverty. Then with two articulate and pertinent articles, we have further supported our position regarding the fact that low school achievement is highly correlated with the depth of poverty in America. Finally, we think these same articles restate that low achievement is the result of American poverty and not the fault of schools or teachers.

Now, in the final section of this chapter, we would like to crack the really tough nut of poverty—the tough nut of poverty that begins with this question: How can a nation as extraordinarily wealthy as the United States have such deep pockets of poverty and also such a rapidly diminishing economic middle class?

Raymond J. Golarz and Marion J. Golarz

Poverty Is No Accident

There are several groups that have been directly responsible for supporting and passing such self-defeating educational legislation as No Child Left Behind. These are the same groups currently attempting to crush teacher unions and eliminate long established teacher benefits. They have pressed for standardized tests, supported with money and legislation charter schools, and screamed that poor teaching is the cause of low national test scores. These groups include the vast majority of America's wealthiest, many of those we have elected to represent us in state and federal legislative bodies, and their huge number of paid lobbyists.

They have with their policies, their legislation, and their lobbying tactics effectively trampled much of the American population into the depths of poverty and crippled the American economic middle class. <u>In so doing, they have caused millions of American children to live in conditions that preclude their capacity to succeed in school.</u>

Their exploits in manipulating governmental procedures are well-documented. For over 30 years they have been ruthless in their own pursuits. Jacob Hacker and Paul Pierson write persuasively in their recent book, *Winner Take All Politics*, describing first how the current state of politics has created an emboldened privileged class with the power to manipulate and control our entire economy:

> The story of America's winner-take-all economy isn't just about political leaders actively passing laws to abet the rich, but also about political leaders studiously turning the other way (with a lot of encouragement from the rich) when fast moving economic changes make existing rules and regulations designed to rein excess at the top obsolete.[5]

A second passage from that text reaffirms the same point—that government has been a partner in this assistance to the rich in securing market advantages:

> When, that is, we look at what's happened at the very top, take political efforts to block the adaptation of government policy seriously, and look at how markets

have been politically reconstructed to aid the privileged—a conclusion that can't be mistaken comes into view: government had a huge hand in nurturing America's winner-take-all economy.[6]

Finally, the authors warn that if there is no effective governance, then there is a risk of returning to a medieval stranglehold of power from an ever-more powerful class made up of the rich:

> Effective governance could help provide citizens with basic economic security, a healthier environment, legal protections from predation in pursuit of profit, and the needed social investments—from decent roads to good schools—that would lay the foundation for further opportunity. All of this could improve citizens' lives while simultaneously diminishing the threat that a new economic aristocracy would replace the hereditary aristocracy that the Founders had risked their lives to defeat.[7]

As early as 1992, in *The Culture of Contentment*, John Kenneth Galbraith added an additional dimension to this caste type American social system as he described and explored the intent of the American rich to perpetuate for their own needs what he refers to as the "underclass:"

> The underclass are concentrated in the centers of the great cities or, less visibly, on deprived farms, as rural, migrant labor or in mining communities...the greater part of the underclass consists of members of minority groups, blacks or people of Hispanic origin...what is not accepted, and indeed is little mentioned, is that the underclass is integrally a part of a larger economic process and, more, importantly, that it serves the living standard and the comfort of the more favored community.[8]

Once again in *Winner-Take-All Politics*, the authors remind us of an observation made by David Hume that seems especially relevant to this discussion:

> David Hume observed that "[W]here the riches are in a few hands, these must enjoy all the power and will readily conspire to lay the whole burden on the poor,

and oppress them still farther, to the discouragement of all industry."[9]

When I attended college and took my first course in economics, I was taught that the foundation principle underlying the study of all aspects of economics was that man has unlimited wants and a limited amount of resources to fulfill those wants. I presume that those in our society who have immense wealth, hold positions of influence, sit on the boards of multinational companies, or hold high-paying jobs as lobbyists all took the same course. What must they then think happens to the least fortunate in a society when the top one percent secure and then control approximately half of the nation's wealth with the support and blessings of the majority of those who hold offices in our state and federal political structures? What do they think happens, or do they simply not care?

Where do they get the unmitigated gall to do what they've done while they attempt to publicly hold schools and teachers responsible for not succeeding at a task which they themselves have significantly contributed to making impossible to complete?

As we have said before in this book and will continue to say, the problem isn't teachers. It never has been.

If you, the reader, find this section particularly intriguing, consider reading *The Culture of Contentment* by John Kenneth Galbraith, *U.S. Politics and the Global Economy* by Ronald Cox, and, finally, *The Future of Capitalism* by Lester Thurow.

We the authors hold that:

The poor of America, if given equal economic opportunities, coupled with the assistance of schools, are only a generation away from beginning to contribute their splendid and lasting gifts to our democracy as well as our national economy. This has always been the American experience. To provide the poor with these opportunities, we must compel those now standing in the way of their potential to cease and desist. If necessary, we must force their heels off of the necks of these fellow Americans.

The present course being forged by many national and state politicians and the greed of the business/industrial complex are toxic to the future of the democracy and our economy. A nation can only be properly served when all of its people have been empowered with the capacity to make their unique contributions. Poverty and an uneducated citizenry serve no nation well and are the shame of any nation that claims to make liberty and equality available to all of its people.

Notes:

1. Joseph E. Stiglitz, *The Price of Inequality* (New York: W. W. Norton, 2012), 2-5.
2. Ibid., 7.
3. Helen F. Ladd and Edward B. Fiske, "Class Matters. Why Won't We Admit It?" *The New York Times*, December 11, 2011, http://www.nytimes.com/*2011/12/12/opinion/the-unaddressed-link-between*-poverty-and-education.
4. Patrick Welsh, "Schools Can't Manage Poverty," *USA Today*, September 15, 2010, 9A.
5. Jacob Hacker and Paul Pierson, *Winner-Take-All Politics* (New York: Simon and Schuster, 2010), 43.
6. Ibid., 45.
7. Ibid., 298.
8. John Kenneth Galbraith, *The Culture of Contentment* (Boston: Houghton Mifflin, 1992), 31.
9. Hacker and Pierson, 75.

Chapter 6

Drugs and Schools

I never would have guessed when I became a teacher that some day I would, as a part of my work, be sitting in an obscure bar in Calumet City, Illinois, meeting with three raggedly-dressed, bearded narcotics officers who were introducing me to a very attractive young woman whom we would soon be enrolling in one of our high schools as an undercover drug agent. But here I was.

"Take a guess at how old she is. C'mon, Ray, take a guess."

She just sat there across the table, coke in hand, with a trace of a smile on her face and looking directly at me.

"Nineteen. I'll say nineteen."

Jimmy Lawson, Teddy Hargrove, and Bill Vandembemden just smiled. Then Jimmy volunteered, "She's twenty-nine, but you're right. She looks a lot younger and that's why she works undercover. She fits in real well with the high school crowd."

I nodded and thought to myself, "It all seems like a bad dream—a really bad dream. How the hell did we get here?"

The illegal use of drugs in the United States had ratcheted up dramatically during Vietnam and the Sixties. The heavy hit impacted schools in the late Seventies and early Eighties. I had recently gotten reports from school building administrators whose older and most experienced teachers were noting a significant increase in the number of students exhibiting such conditions as lethargy, sleeping in class, memory loss, and bursts of hostility. These were students who had no past history of such behaviors. Superintendents and school boards were feeling the pressure from communities and the media to do something. Schools were now really being hammered to go to battle with another social problem and, of course, they would succumb to that pressure. In so doing, this new problem would soon be called theirs. They would own it, and more of the limited, precious school resources once dedicated to the teaching of mathematics, literature, science, and the arts would be directed to this new social need—drug abuse prevention and intervention. Within a short period of years, the government and private vendors would be pushing their programs and selling their wares, and schools would be obligated to try them out. To name only a few:

    Drug Abuse Resistance Education (DARE)
    Partnership for a Drug Free America (PDFA)
    Alcohol, Tobacco and Other Drugs Curriculum (ATOD)
    Prevention Curriculums
    Teacher Education Curriculums
    Drug Information Assessment and Decision Support (DIADS)
    Just Say No

Some schools chose to use the approach of surprise searches. Some chose, as we did, to partner with law enforcement and use undercover agents. So, we would be enrolling our young undercover agent at a local high school on Monday. It was not an inner city high school, but served a working-class population in a more suburban setting. Her identity would not be revealed to anyone at the school, and her presence would be known only to the assistant principal. Our narcotics team had assisted with such undercover operations in Detroit and Chicago and had learned through those experiences that the fewer who knew, the safer for all involved.

    Monday afternoon after having enrolled that morning, our undercover agent was suspended from school for writing with her index finger, "Harley f---in' Davidson," in the icing of a freshly-baked cake in foods class. Jimmy advised me that she usually had a quick, non violent way of becoming known to her fellow students as a trouble-maker and someone not averse to illegal activities. She was readmitted on Thursday and by that time had already arranged for her first drug buy on Friday at noon.

    At 11 a.m. on Friday, we were in a run-down white van, parked some forty yards from the southern boundary of school property adjacent to the bleachers of the football field. The van belonged to Chicago narcotics and had a large one-way glass window on one side. Through it, we had a center stage view of the out-of-doors lunch time activity. By 12:15 p.m., the amount of buying and selling was incredible and relatively easy to see as Jimmy and Teddy explained what we needed to look for. Our undercover plant was having no trouble fitting in and making buys.

The assistant principal in the van with us was making identifications while Teddy was writing them all down. About half way through the lunch period, a car that had been circling the area pulled up about 20 yards from our van. Two male occupants got out as eight or ten of the students in the general area slowly moved to their car.

Jimmy commented, "They're from East Chicago and selling some more sophisticated stuff than these kids here are used to. They have been coming here about once a week."

Billy added, "They've been makin' it to two other high schools in town. We've been watchin' 'em now for about two months. Have just about what we need to bust 'em and get 'em off the streets for a long time."

The time in the van was eye-opening and sad. The kids buying, selling, and ultimately using represented the full range of the student body: cheerleaders, athletes, honor students, and band members, along with those who had a history of suspensions and disciplinary actions. They represented all of our students and came from every grade level. Over the next week, as the activities of that day and the spin offs got sorted out by administrators, it would be found that the illegal drugs ultimately seized ran the gamut from cigarettes, alcohol, and marijuana to uppers and downers, crack cocaine, LSD, and heroin. Subsequent locker searches, with and without dogs, at these same schools resulted in findings of additional drugs of all kinds.

The American community had turned a new page in illegal activities and the fall-out from this new chapter would not see an end. The older days of cigarettes, alcohol, marijuana, and LSD were not going to go away, but rather new, and in some cases, more frightening alternatives such as crack, crystal meth, ecstasy, and inhalants of all kinds would be added to the arsenal. The abuse of illegal drugs by our children would make a heavier and heavier impact on the strained financial, time, and energy resources of our schools—resources of money, time, and energy that could have been spent on the teaching of science, mathematics, humanities, and the arts. [1] This urgent need to deal with illegal drug activity would come from the past and slam like a tsunami into the resources of the twenty-first century.[2] That wave to this day has not receded. If anything, it has swelled. So, as we now stand on higher ground and watch, we view a world of illicit drugs that has, in the United States, gone insane.

Raymond J. Golarz and Marion J. Golarz

Drugs from Hell: Meth Labs

None of us saw this devil from hell coming. Nor did we see what this demon would bring with him, particularly to the children of the American poor. There would be new levels of social, psychological, and physical pain introduced to these already desperate children. Learning and the joys that come from a normal childhood would be torn from their lives.

The manufacturing process, risky and extremely dangerous because of the highly volatile, hazardous chemicals used, is occurring in the homes and trailers of thousands and thousands of school children. Lifelong and immediate adverse consequences to children living in such conditions are brutal. Note the following excerpt that comes from the government bulletin titled, "The Dangers to Children Living in Meth Labs:"

> The inability of meth-dependent and meth-manufacturing parents to function as competent caregivers increases the likelihood that a child will be accidentally injured or ingest drugs and poisonous substances....Children developing within the chaos, neglect, and violence of a clandestine methamphetamine laboratory environment experience stress and trauma that significantly affect their overall safety and health, including their behavioral, emotional, and cognitive functioning. They often exhibit low self esteem, a sense of shame, and poor social skills. Consequences may include emotional and mental health problems, delinquency, teen pregnancy, school absenteeism and failure, isolation, and poor peer relations.[3]

The research quoted here represents only a very small portion of what is now being written about this current epidemic. In all cases, the children—primarily poor—are the losers. They are losers for want of a normal childhood. They are losers for want of a safe, nurturing home. They are losers for want of parents or care-givers who can focus love and attention on them. They are losers because they are the very children society is leaving behind without a look back.

Again, the problem isn't teachers. Yet through school house doors these children come. They come psychologically or physically abused and battered. They come socially impaired. They come simply needing to be hugged or patted on the head. They come academically behind. They have lost much of what cognitively could have been. A normal childhood will never be theirs. They have little understanding of normal sleep. Many have witnessed extreme violence. They come, most mornings, having experienced hunger, fear, and shame.

Through the schoolhouse doors they come. They come and are not turned away, for teachers will not leave them behind. Teachers never do, for it is not their nature to do so. It really never has been.

Wonder where this fits into standardized assessment?

Notes:

1. Hanley Center, "Warning Signs: How Can I Tell if a Student Is Using Alcohol or Drugs?" 2011, http://www.hanleycenter.org/prevention/resources/warning-signs-for -teachers.html.
2. National Drug Statistics Summary, 2007, http://www.adolescent-substance-abuse.com/national-drug-statistics.html.
3. "Dangers to Children Living in Meth Labs," http://www.ojp.usdoj.gov/ovc/publications/bulletins/children/pg5.html

SECTION THREE

"AND THE WALLS CAME TUMBLING DOWN"

Order and control in American schools began to erode about ten years before the U.S. Supreme Court rendered the decisions which dealt crushing blows to the ability of the educational system to cope with problematic student behaviors. This early erosion took place first in high schools of our larger metropolitan communities. However, by the mid-1960s one could find schools suffering this loss of control everywhere in the country.

Then, from the late Sixties through the 1990s the decisions of the Supreme Court almost brought American public schools to their knees. The new requirements imposed upon schools by these decisions made the maintenance of civility and order in many schools and classrooms virtually impossible.

Chapter 7

What Ever Happened to Safe and Orderly?

Assistant Principals' Meeting

It was a crisp, windy, autumn day. The afternoon sky was filling with clouds, and rain was sure to come unless it turned to snow, which appeared to be a strong possibility. It was nearing 4 p.m., and assistant principals from across the district were beginning to arrive at the administration center for our monthly meeting. We all seemed to enjoy these monthly moments of camaraderie. I walked into the large boardroom on the second floor and took a seat at the table with the early arrivals. The custodial staff had unfolded eight-foot tables and arranged them in a square for our meeting. The normal attendance was anywhere from eighteen to twenty.

I had spent the morning training two new administrative hearing officers for the school district. Eventually, when trained, they would be handling the brunt of requested expulsion cases. I would sit in on their first three or four cases in order to guide them. It was critical that their hearings not depart from law, making the district vulnerable to an appeal or legal challenge. They were always taped (recorded), and counsel for the student(s) and their parent(s) or caregiver(s) had a right to the tape. It would have been disheartening to the staff of a school if a school were to lose an expulsion case because of inadvertent transgressions from due process. These lapses could include such things as forgetting to swear in a witness or neglecting to give the name of an intended witness in the certified documents sent to the student and parents prior to the hearing.

I had been the district's first hearing examiner and had presided over several hundred cases, so training of new examiners fell to me. Those new to the role would come from the ranks of central office administrators and assistant principals, and I had recommended to the school board and superintendent that there be three of them who would rotate cases. The preparation, hearing itself, and post-hearing paperwork of simply one expulsion case could often consume upwards of hundreds of total hours for the teachers, administrators, and hearing officer involved, and for performing these legally required obligations no relief from normal duties was given.

It was now 4:30 p.m. and everyone who was supposed to come had arrived. Those desiring coffee had already filled their cups, and the 15 minutes of pre-meeting conversations were concluding and seats being taken. I passed out the agendas and, as I did, Jeff, the assistant principal from Spohn Middle School, interjected a question and a concern.

"Ray, before we get started, if you don't mind, got a question or concern that comes from a group of really great teachers in my building."

"Go ahead, Jeff."

"Early this morning we again had an incident that started in one classroom, spilled into the hallway, and ultimately disrupted a wing of the building."

"Go ahead."

"Started with a seventh-grade girl we've had a lot of trouble with before. She apparently wouldn't sit in her assigned seat and insisted on sitting in a seat that was vacant this morning next to one of her friends, a change that, if permitted, would have predictably resulted in her causing continuous disruption. The girl's teacher is Mrs. Wilson. You know her."

"Sure, I've worked with her on several committees. Very competent teacher."

"Well, she insisted that the girl stop talking and take her normal seat. The girl apparently just ignored her. So, Mrs. Wilson said it again and finally had to say it a third time. At that point the girl looked up at her and screamed, 'F--- you, bitch. Don't have to move if the seat's empty, and it's empty. So, quit botherin' me, bitch, and just teach.'

"Phil explained then how the teacher could not get the girl to quiet down and finally needed to call the office to get someone to come for her. This, of course, took time and during that tense waiting time, bedlam spread throughout the room, and other students whose behavior was often marginal joined in the fray. In the time it took to bring the whole classroom situation under control, the chaos had spilled into the hallway where two additional support persons were then needed. The loud screaming in the hall created a disruption to other classes, resulting in students from those classes also coming into the hallway. The entire incident resulted in immense stress for Mrs. Wilson and other teachers, as well as a loss of over four hours of teaching time for Mrs. Wilson and nearly an hour each for the other teachers. The child was removed from class and spent the rest of the day serving in-school suspension where she will remain for the next two days.

"We can't reach a parent or care-giver in her case...never can. So there likely will be no parent conference and the girl will be back in Mrs. Wilson's class this week on Friday. Before I came to this meeting, Mrs. Wilson was with me and the principal. Ray, she was completely distraught. How do we tell her to just write it up and keep a record, and then when there is a sufficient number of disruptions we can go for an expulsion hearing? Ray, somehow tomorrow I have to tell her that the girl will be back in her class on Friday. Tell her that the girl has a right to a public education. Ray, how the hell am I to do that? Have we all lost our minds?"

Jeff's remarks had struck a raw nerve with the administrators seated around the table and several spontaneous conversations had started. I looked around the table and understood. The freshly run-off agenda would be set aside and looked at another day. A hot potato had been pulled from a raging fire by a young assistant principal, and we needed to deal with it.

Each classroom always has its own uniqueness, but all should share certain characteristics. The essential characteristics that must prevail are civility and order. If an atmosphere for learning is to exist, then disruptions that crush civility and order, even for a moment, cannot be tolerated. To have a disruption, as described by Jeff, is catastrophic. Tragically, such a disruption very often results in the following instructions to a teacher: "Just write it up." Almost always the student is then returned to the teacher after a short suspension. Invariably, the cycle is then repeated, usually resolving nothing, even when mixed-in with interventions such as parent conferences, in-school suspensions, behavioral contracts, and a host of other strategies. The cycle continues until the administrator has a paper trail affirming sufficient disruptions to fulfill the legal standard of continuous disruption to the educational function. Only at this point can the school district initiate expulsion proceedings. It often takes several months for this cycle to reach that point, and during this time the classroom suffering such continuous disruption has long ago lost its viability as a learning environment. Students in that classroom may well have suffered the loss of no less than a semester of learning.

The law, as designed at present, creates the following cascading consequences: First, having a teacher who lacks clear and swift authority results in a loss of student confidence in that teacher's ability to maintain order. Second, this leads students to fear that this classroom is no longer the safe place they assumed it was. Third, students understand that those who cause disruptions of this kind and return after a short suspension are at least as powerful, if not more so, than the teacher. Finally, it is evident to both the students and the teacher that she has no real authority, leaving the teacher feeling impotent in the face of such on-going assaults.

Allowing such situations to go unresolved by a teacher who now cannot exercise swift and meaningful authority results in a violation tantamount to the rape of what we had always considered a sacred place. Up to this time, most citizens believed that our nation, understanding the critical importance of schools, would never allow for conditions that might lead to such mob rule, leaving vulnerable those who had come to learn as well as those who had come to teach. Apparently these citizens were wrong.

Order and Sacredness in American Courts of Law

Possibly had such classrooms been the places where judges discharged their duties, the Supreme Court would have had the empathy necessary to preserve the dignity and sacredness of schools. This insight struck me recently when I saw on television part of the Casey Anthony trial held in Florida. A young man (Matthew Bartlett, an employee of TGI Friday's in Orlando), seated in one of the rows of seats in the courtroom set aside for observers, raised his right hand to his eye level and then gestured his isolated middle finger at one of the attorneys in the trial. He flipped the DA the bird! An account of this act and its consequences was reported by David Lohr in the Huffington Post Social News:

> A visibly agitated Judge Melvin Perry called Bartlett to the front of the courtroom and showed him a photo of a man flipping the bird at the District Attorney Jeff Ashton earlier in the day. Bartlett admitted he was the man in the photo making the obscene gesture. Judge Perry then held up a sign that had been posted outside the courtroom door that read, "Any gesture, facial expression, or audible comment showing approval or disapproval during a court proceeding is absolutely prohibited."
> "Can you read and write?" Perry asked Bartlett.
> "Yes, sir," he replied.
> "Did you read this sign, sir?" Perry inquired.
> "I have read that," Bartlett said.
> Bartlett did not offer any explanation for his alleged action, other than to say it was "stupid…I'm not sure why I even did it," he said. "I do apologize."
> Judge Perry then sentenced him to six days in the Orange County jail and ordered him to pay a $400 fine plus $223 in court costs. He was told he had six months to pay and then was handcuffed and led out of the courtroom.

The account goes on further to explain:
> Bartlett is the second person to be held in contempt during the trial. The first, 29 year-old Elizabeth Rogers was sentenced to two days in the Pinellas County Jail for an outburst during jury selection. Rogers, who was watching the proceedings, blurted out, "She killed somebody anyway." Rogers claimed she is bipolar and mentally challenged. She also said she had not planned to say what she said. Perry found her in contempt and said that if she were not disabled, he would have sentenced her to 179 days in jail. [1]

Over the next week, I watched television carefully and read the news to see if there were any repercussions from Judge Perry's actions. I found none. Apparently there was a consensus of opinion that his actions needed to be swift and appropriate and, we would agree, necessary to preserve the order and dignity of a sacred place.

"Have We All Lost Our Minds?"

By 6:30 p.m. that evening our assistant principals' meeting was over. We had not come to any resolution, but it was good that we had taken the time to talk about it. As we parted company that evening, we promised one another that we would not let it drop. As I drove home that night, north on Hohman Avenue in the wet, falling snow, I could not get the picture of Mrs. Wilson's tear-streaked face out of my mind or the question of a young assistant principal that gave rise to our new agenda, "Have we all lost our minds?"

A monster had been released in our American public schools, and it was now rapidly eating its way through our cherished and sacred classrooms. Worst of all, on that cold fall night, it appeared as though we had no way to stop it.

Note:

1. David Lohr, "Casey Anthony Trial Spectator Jailed for Flipping DA the Bird," *The Huffington Post Social News*, August 30, 2011, http://www.huffingtonpost.com/2011/06casey -anthony-trial-spectator-jailed-n-888221...

Chapter 8

A Civil and Disciplined Environment

Unless someone has taught in a school classroom, it's difficult to understand the experience. There are so many variables that a teacher must constantly be aware of and manage. These are variables that somewhat naturally grow out of putting 35 children or adolescents in the same, rather small room, with one supervising adult. As a result, those who do teach, quickly come to understand that the conditions most needed to ensure successful teaching and learning are the undisputed authority of the classroom teacher and a school that has a high degree of order and discipline. If these conditions exist, then teachers and students will find that, despite the endless ever-present variables, the teaching/learning experience will have the greatest probability for success. Over forty years of continuous research screams out to us of the need for such safe and orderly school environments.

Schools that are safe and orderly are normally easily recognized. If you walk into such a school and hear the bell ring announcing the beginning of the next class, you should observe the following: hallways empty of students and students seated at their desks in classrooms and a general atmosphere of silence while teachers in each room begin class. If you observed this, you would be viewing, in part, what is meant by safe and orderly. Further, you would probably be in a school that has strong administrative leadership, coupled with strong teacher support and cooperation. Such conditions are the result of hard work, continual commitment, and vigilance. They do not occur accidentally. Furthermore, in such schools significant individual classroom disruptions are less frequent, for students understand the partnership that exists between their teachers and school administrators. Safety and order are seen as a shared commitment of all of the adults in that building.

There are essentially only two reasons why the development of such a shared-commitment could be crushed, despite the hard work and cooperation of classroom teachers with their building administrators. First, a safe environment cannot be managed effectively or smoothly if schools are serving a neighborhood in which a significant number of people repeatedly react to almost any school disturbance by blaming, challenging, and fighting with school personnel. Secondly, schools can be overwhelmed by the complexity and sheer number of provisions and procedural obligations that grew out of Supreme Court decisions and congressional actions that took place during the decades which began in the late Sixties and continued through the mid 1990s.

In addition to these two reasons, there is another important reason why this loss of school order and stability can take place. It can occur when a philosophical split occurs between the building administrators and the body of teachers regarding what constitutes appropriate behavior. In this case, administrators typically view the teachers as the problem, accusing them of insensitivity to the cultural, racial, or socioeconomic backgrounds of their pupils. Teachers thus find themselves accused of a lack of understanding and empathy. This administrative/teacher split does not occur often, but when it does, it can do immense damage to the esprit de corps of the total school. The following true story sadly illustrates this condition. It took place in an Ohio high school only a few years ago.

"Good Morning"

It was an early fall morning when Mr. Edison, high school track coach, was in one of the entrance ways to the building greeting students as they came in. The tardy bell had already rung, but he continued his greetings even to the late arrivals. Up the stairs to the building came J.B. Wilson. As J.B. got to the doorway, Mr. Edison said, "Good morning, J.B." The young man continued to walk into the building and responded, "Go f--- yourself." Mr. Edison stopped the young man, advised him as to his inappropriate response, and had him report to the office.

Dr. Shelly Wick, principal of the building, had been close enough to observe the entire incident. Edison turned to her and said, "Did you hear that? Been teaching 27 years. Never had that one. Sent him to your office."

"Yes, Mr. Edison, I did, but what you don't seem to understand is the young man's background. That was simply his way of saying good morning. I'll talk to him and then send him on his way to your room."

Edison just stood there speechless and watched her as she turned on her heel and walked down the hallway to her office.

The next morning around 7:15 a.m. Dr. Wick walked into the faculty lounge where approximately 15 faculty members, including Mr. Edison, were finishing morning coffee. She stepped in, looked around, smiled and announced, "Good morning." Edison looked up at her and replied in his normal, deep, booming voice, "Go f--- yourself." She looked at him. Then, without responding, she turned and walked out.

The most tragic aspect of this story is not simply that it is true. What is most tragic is the frequency with which similar kinds of incidents are occurring everywhere in our country. Some people seem unable to separate authentic cultural and racial behaviors from the acts of immature adolescents. They seem, further, to have lost an understanding of our broader society's demands for civility and appropriate behavior. If there is a group in America that seems to best understand the moral and appropriate expectations of our broader society, that group would be teachers. And if there is a group that has the most appropriate opportunity to shape civil behavior that would again be teachers. Therefore, if teachers judge that a student's behavior or attitude is really out of line, they are more than likely correct. If they judge that "go f--- yourself," wouldn't sit well with any prospective employer, they're probably right. The following is a caution: If we cause teachers in our schools to set aside their understanding of appropriate behavior and cease teaching civility to our children, as was the historical intent of our Founders , we will deny these young people some of the most important understandings they need to have in order to maintain healthy relationships and avoid unemployment, discrimination, poverty, and ignorance. Without this knowledge, it is likely that some of these children will never know why they were turned down by a potential employer, passed over by a person who could have offered an educational opportunity, or rejected by someone they wished to have in their lives—all because some adult did not have the necessary support to properly teach them.

A second story, the one that follows, is intended to once more demonstrate the confusion felt by teachers regarding their authority. This story again illustrates the consequence of a philosophical split between administrators and teachers, and it might also serve as an example of the confusion which was caused by the decisions of the Supreme Court.

I Don't Want to Get Married

Several years ago, in a crowded high school hallway between classes, a 16-year-old African American boy screamed out to an African American girl some thirty feet away, "Hey, I don't want to get married. I just wanna f---." Several adults, including teachers, heard him, but no one ever called the young man aside, or took him to an administrator or a counselor. When later asked why they did not do so, each responded similarly, "I'm not getting in the middle of that kind of situation only to be told that even though we might not like it, it is his right to talk that way, or be told that it was just a harmless way for him to joke around." As we said in the introduction of this story—a caution to a nation.

Earlier in this section we described the experience of walking into a school filled with order. What might we find in the environment that is less orderly? Come on in while we ring the bell again. Many students are still milling about in the hallways (often as many as several hundred in a school of 2,000). They are still talking in small and large groups at lockers, horsing around, shouting, or yelling to others down the hall. They are casually moving toward their assigned rooms or simply staying where they are. In this environment both classroom order and control of the school are jeopardized.

The lack of control in the building disrupts attempts by teachers to secure control of their own classrooms from the beginning of the period, as many of those students who do go to class, arrive late and enter in a manner disrespectful to the learning atmosphere others are attempting to create. They refuse to comply with the standards of traditional civility. Teachers attempting to control these near chaotic situations become extremely apprehensive. *Even from the beginning of class they are afraid to risk creating a more relaxed learning environment because they nervously sense that at any moment they could find themselves in a classroom out of control.*

On the other hand, where order and civility are maintained throughout the school, teachers can immediately engage in and facilitate more productive learning environments as soon as class starts. Under these circumstances, teachers feel comfortable creating a variety of learning configurations, such as small learning groups, independent study/learning experiences that do not restrict students to their seats, group and individual presentations, and the use of various technologies in the same room. There's almost no end to such variations if control and order exist. And virtually all American parents want their children to be in schools with these kinds of opportunities to learn. But they will be denied these opportunities unless the environment is safe, calm, civil, and orderly.

For too many years we have been listening to voices advising us that a student's use of vulgarities or obscenities or a student's disrespectful and disruptive behavior is rooted somehow in a unique cultural heritage and that it is supported by his family and community. Or we have been told that such behavior represents a more relaxed attitude toward what was traditionally considered proper but now is thought to be just old-fashioned. Isn't it time that we set such absurdities aside? Students who consistently disrupt the sacredness of classrooms and crush the learning environment have, as it were, a knife to the throat of the most viable avenue out of poverty, ignorance, and deprivation that is available to so many young Americans, whether they come from our inner cities, suburban districts, or rural communities.

Raymond J. Golarz and Marion J. Golarz

One Teacher's Nightmare

In 2005, Marion and I had been working with teachers in the school district of Cincinnati. After concluding a third session, a second-grade teacher in her first year of teaching was driving me back to my hotel. As we drove, our conversation began to shift to classroom atmosphere. Shortly into this conversation, she began to cry as she explained her situation. Very quickly she was sobbing, so I asked her to leave the expressway and find a place where she could safely stop. She pulled into a gas station and in her distraught state tried to explain.

"Dr. Golarz, I am terrified, afraid of each new day and unable to sleep at night. I have three students in my classroom of 26 that are daily out of control. I find myself spending virtually all of my classroom time just tending to them. If I try to teach the others, the behavior of these three gets worse. I have tried any number of strategies suggested to me, but nothing seems to work. I have finally resorted to sending them to the office, but that has simply resulted in conferences with the administrators advising me that good teachers learn how to handle their own affairs and use the office only as an absolute final resolution. I know my principal is losing faith in me. There have already been comments about how I may not be cut out for this profession."

As she sat there trying to regain her composure, I recalled an earlier time when I had sat with another young teacher, Paula, in the back of her classroom at the end of a tumultuous day. She had taught across the hall from me and was a fine young teacher. Her class was in a near continuous state of tension and disruption because of several out of control students. I had occasion to watch her teach without them. She was brilliant. She was like an artist who could totally captivate her audience. Paula also wept that day I sat with her in the back of her room after school. She too had wanted to be a teacher. We, of course, owed Paula more. Those who disrupted her learning environment daily should have been removed and not permitted to return. Their parents should have had to figure out how to get them an education.

The Problem Isn't Teachers

The young teacher from Cincinnati continued, "Dr. Golarz, my only help is Mrs. Shelly next door. She teaches a two-three split. When I'm totally at my wit's end, she will take one, two, or all three and give me a break. I think they are afraid of her. She laughs and tells me she is the drill sergeant in our hall and has been at it for 28 years. She tells me not to worry about how often I have to send them. But, Dr. Golarz, I do. Oh God, I do. I'm stuck. I have three of my own children I'm raising on my own. Before I started teaching, I went eight years to night school while working as a case worker at the Department of Public Welfare. I wanted so badly to be a teacher. God, what am I going to do? In my heart I know I'm a good teacher. The other children in class really like me and when I get chances to teach them, they learn. But I'm not getting those chances. What can I do?"

There's a movie I am very fond of. It's titled *The Edge*. It is set in Alaska. As the movie unfolds, it becomes clear to a billionaire named Charles, played by Anthony Hopkins, and to Bob, a character played by co-lead Alex Baldwin, that either they succeed in killing a giant grizzly that is hunting them, or the bear will succeed in killing them. Bob is frightened and skeptical. Charles shows him a picture of native children killing such a bear and then he says to Bob, "What one man can do another can do. Repeat it, Bob. What one man can do another can do." Then he continues to have Bob repeat the phrase until he's convinced that he has made Bob a believer in his new capacity to kill the bear. [1]

The only problem with the entire piece of cinema is that it's nonsense. It's pure Hollywood. It's the rare person who can kill the bear under any circumstances and then only with immense luck. We need to stop telling young teachers that if one can do it, all can do it, because they can't. Most simply can't. They can't, regardless of the strategies we attempt to arm them with, for the problem isn't a lack of appropriate strategies. The problem isn't a teacher who is not trying. The problem isn't a teacher who is not committed to the job, nor is it a young person who simply isn't cut out for this profession.

The problem is a classroom, or a school, or a handful of students in a classroom who are out of control. The problem is that American parents in growing numbers do not teach their young children how to be civil or how to behave. The problem is further aggravated because schools are obligated by our courts to protect this property right of children. They are obligated to protect a right that these children are often not able to comprehend. The consequence of this is that these pupils are able to test the limits of this protected right, time and again. And each time that they do, a part of an hour or day or week is lost to what could have been productive instruction for an entire class of students. What's the term for those who have thus been denied a part of their instructional day? Is it collateral damage? Is that the correct term? Most tragically, are we suggesting that such abuse of their right to an education is acceptable? Good Lord, how did we get to this point? Who can continue to blame teachers for this problem? Again we say: *the problem isn't teachers.*

We offer one more story to illustrate the unreasonable lengths teachers go to in order to attempt to engage students who are not able or willing to "engage." The story begins with a young new teacher, not unlike our Cincinnati teacher or Paula, who was struggling in the Indianapolis Public Schools.

The principal suggested that this teacher's students would be better engaged during an instructional period if each were given a dry erase board on which to quickly write their responses. Off the teacher went and distributed the dry erase boards. The students of this middle school were definitely engaged. One immediately wrote and held up for the entire class to see, "Will work for food," and another wrote "F--- you." A third student responded by hitting the student next to him over the head with his dry erase board. Chaos soon reigned in the classroom, and hall security was required. The teacher was later written up for his inability to successfully carry out the instructional strategy.

I'm reasonably confident that the day after my conversation with the teacher in Cincinnati, I could have gone into her second grade classroom and within minutes could have established myself as the other drill sergeant in the hall. I would not attempt this with middle and high school students who had a history of being hard to handle and did not know me, but I'm pretty sure I could have managed the second-grade classroom. I think this confidence comes from having raised six children with my wife and from having taught for many years, including kids who were hard to handle. The fact of my being a big man with a naturally deep voice wouldn't hurt either. Mostly, my success would just be the result of my physical presence, coupled with a lifetime of experiences.

Would this mean that my teaching methods were more effective? Would this mean I am a better teacher? Would I be better because the principal would seldom see one of mine in his office? Where did the obligation of schools to maintain order and safety get lost? When did it become the responsibility of gentle and caring teachers to demand, threaten, or cajole for their own respect?

Not long after Marion and I completed our work in Cincinnati, we accepted a dinner invitation from Paula and her husband at their club in Indianapolis to celebrate her promotion to full partner in her law firm. As we were leaving that evening, Paula looked at me and said sorrowfully, "I still often think I'd have made a great teacher."

As Marion and I walked in silence to our car that evening, she turned to me and asked, "What do you think?"

I said, "She'd have made a great teacher, a really great teacher."

Thousands Leave

Every year thousands of young, idealistic, and competent teachers leave teaching—not because they are bad teachers who have been fired, but because they have become disheartened, often bitter, and their dreams shattered. Many of them will use their education and training to enter other occupations where they will be successful. Most statistics suggest that fifty percent of teachers leave their profession by their fifth year. Can a nation which is intent on preserving its greatness afford to lose teachers at this rate?

Note:

1. *The Edge*, Anthony Hopkins and Alex Baldwin, stars: David Mamet, Writer DVD. Art Linson Productions. September, 1997.

Chapter 9

When Education Became a Right

I was in my office concluding a meeting with several building principals when my secretary came in and advised me that some professors from a local university were in the outer office and asked if I could meet briefly. I suggested to Ruthie to have them wait for I wouldn't be long.

Soon I was back in my office with the university staff. Johnny, one of the high school principals, at my request, had remained in the room with me.

"Dr. Golarz, we have been following the news reports on your school district and have noted that over the years your teaching staff seems unable to handle middle and high school discipline."

"By *unable* you mean?"

"Well, just the inordinate number of actions taken against students, including suspensions and expulsions is quite disturbing."

"Do you have a remedy?"

"We believe so. You see, we are experts at deviant behavior and corrective strategies. Two of us, in addition to teaching, also have our own private practices where we do work of a psychological nature. We would be willing to conduct some classes for your teaching staff to assist them with an understanding of more constructive alternative behavioral mechanisms."

"Have any of you recently taught?"

"Why, yes. We all teach."

"No, I don't mean at the university. Have you taught middle or high school low-functioning, disruptive students? You know, like where most of our suspensions and expulsions come from?"

The Problem Isn't Teachers

They looked questioningly at one another and then responded, "Well, no, but…"

I interrupted, "Have you been a disciplinary administrator in such a school?"

"Well, no."

"Have any of you personally ever attended such a school, say, during your high school years?"

They again looked around at one another and then responded, "No."

"Ladies, gentlemen, professors, I really appreciate your coming in. God knows we need the help."

I looked over at Johnny, and he was nodding affirmatively.

"Our teachers out there and their administrators can hardly make it through a day. Usually by 3 p.m. or earlier they are all exhausted, including even some seasoned veterans. They've tried virtually everything you can imagine, and they are experts at their profession. I like the idea of giving them some new ideas, but if we set something up with you, the first thing they'll want to know is whether or not you've taught or administered in such settings. If not, you'll have no credibility with them, and no matter what you propose it will result in a waste of your time and theirs.

"So, if you're willing, let's do this. I'll get a couple of principals to arrange to give to each of you one of these hard-to-handle classrooms for, let's say, three weeks or a month. The students will be told that you are substitute teachers. You'll be on your own to use your alternative behavioral mechanisms, and it will allow our principals to give some badly-battered veterans some time off to use as additional prep time or whatever they feel would be useful.

"The teachers will be told that you were the source of their brief respite, and your stock will go up. Then when you initiate your instruction cycle to the staff, you'll have some true and current stories to tell them about the effectiveness of what you'll be proposing. Furthermore, you'll be standing in front of a staff that will respect your commitment, though brief, to experiencing their condition."

I then enthusiastically leaned over and said, "What do you think?"

There was quite a long silence and then a somewhat icy response. "That's not what we had in mind."

"Well, will you consider it?"

Then a quick second response: "No, we don't think so."

They got up, said a hasty good-bye, and then they all left. They never came back.

I remember that after they left, Johnny looked at me and said, "Would have been nice, Ray. Would have been nice to have someone come in, actually experience some "firing-line" time and get a real sense of what we do day after day. They don't really understand, do they?"

"No, they don't, Johnny. They don't have a clue. They read a newspaper or a *Time* magazine article, go to a Christmas party and enjoy a half-hour conversation with an old friend, reminisce about their private or boarding school experience of thirty years ago, and think they understand. In the end, it's tragically sad, Johnny. Sad for them. Sad for us. Sad for all of American education."

Being uninformed is never a good thing, and if the lack of true knowledge is found in educated people of means and power, then it can be tragic and dangerous as well. Each time I read documents that relate to the several Supreme Court decisions that helped to crush order and civility in so many American schools and classrooms, I am reminded of the professors who came to my office. They were good, educated people of means and power, but sadly lacking in the experiences they needed in order to truly understand what we were up against.

I sometimes wish I could have, along with a group of teachers and school administrators of my vintage, had the U.S. Supreme Court Justices who delivered the majority opinions in *Wood v. Strickland* (1975), *Tinker v. Des Moines* (1969), *Goss v. Lopez* (1975), and *Honig v. Doe* (1988), in my office before those decisions were rendered. I wish that those of us gathered there could have made to them the same offer of, as Johnny put it, "firing-line experience." I wish that we could have convinced them to pick up the gauntlet. I am convinced that if we had been successful, their decisions in each of these cases would have then been different. It would have become clear to them that to attempt to carry out what they were considering in all but elitist boarding schools, some private schools, or some exceedingly well-funded, highly structured charter schools would be insane. The sheer weight of work that was ultimately added to the already underfunded and understaffed American schools in order to deal just with subsequent discipline matters resulting from those decisions was incomprehensible. It is clear that those who made the decisions could not possibly have understood the enormous burden they were creating.

Let us address these decisions separately. What were the crippling consequences of *Tinker* v. *Des Moines*? What are some of the consequences of declaring that only speech that materially and substantially disrupts school activities may be controlled? The Court seemed sadly unaware of the need to preserve a high level of civility and order in schools if teachers were to create protected and secure classroom learning environments. They seemed further unaware of what those who worked there did on a daily basis to preserve order. Teachers and administrators were not confused. They had always understood that their charge was to teach not only academics but civility and proper conduct to the youth of the nation.

Carrying out this charge had always been best accomplished in a setting where such values were stressed. Consequently, school days were filled with continuous reminders to young people from their teachers and school administrators such as, "Matthew, tuck in that shirt. I'm sure your parents would prefer that you look neat in school," or, "Jeffrey, Timothy, I don't believe that such gutter language is what your parents would approve of your using in a hallway at school," or "Margaret, was that a disrespectful comment you just made? Do you believe that to be proper behavior?" These and countless other teaching moments took place in school classrooms, hallways, cafeterias, and student gathering places throughout each teaching day. That kind of teaching was always going on, and most children responded respectfully with a "Yes, ma'am," or "Yes, sir. Sorry, won't do it again." Rarely did children challenge such teaching. They accepted such teaching since most students understood that such teaching was being done in their best interest. They certainly knew such teaching was expected and supported by their parents. At some level, they sensed its value to their future lives as parents, future employees, and productive, engaged members of their communities.

We have included below an excerpt from the dissenting opinion of Justice Black who foresaw the consequences of this *Tinker* decision. His emotion-filled and focused opinion is worth reading in its entirety. Tragically, while schools were having their most difficult early trials with the consequences of this decision, many were suggesting that implementation was causing no substantial problems. Such opinions must have been coming from observers who were viewing schools and classrooms from a distance or from bureaucrats analyzing and reviewing meaningless statistical data. The information was not coming from classrooms and schools. It certainly was not coming from the firing-lines where teachers were wrestling with the most difficult teaching assignments.

In an earlier section of this book, "Assistant Principals' Meeting," we spoke of Judge Melvin Perry's decision to hold in contempt, fine, and imprison for six days an observer in his court who "gave the finger" to the D.A. When he did this, the observer was neither loud nor boisterous, nor even spoke a word. The judge obviously believed that a high level of order and civility was the necessary decorum for his courtroom. He did not find it necessary to wait until the observer performed activities that "materially and substantially" interfered with his ability to conduct the trial. He simply judged that the observer's action tampered with a sacred place and that, for him, was enough.

Since the U.S. Supreme Court's *Tinker v. Des Moines* decision of 1969, teachers throughout America have been advised that for their schools and classrooms the new, more permissive standard that must be exceeded before a significant action can be taken with respect to student speech is whether or not the activity materially and substantially interferes with school purposes. Under this new standard could Judge Perry, had he been a teacher, penalize the behaviors as he did, even imposing jail sentences? Unlikely. Could a teacher or administrator challenge the student who in the hallway elected to yell, "I don't want to get married? I just want to f---." Again, very unlikely.

The following is taken from Justice Black's dissenting opinion.

Tinker v. Des Moines School Dist., 393 U.S. 503 (1969)

> Change has been said to be truly the law of life but sometimes the old and the tried and true are worth holding. The schools of this Nation have undoubtedly contributed to giving us tranquility and to making us a more law-abiding people. Uncontrolled and uncontrollable liberty is an enemy to domestic peace. We cannot close our eyes to the fact that some of the

country's greatest problems are crimes committed by the youth, too many of school age. School discipline, like parental discipline, is an integral and important part of training our children to be good citizens— to be better citizens. Here a very small number of students have crisply and summarily [525] refused to obey a school order designed to give pupils who want to learn the opportunity to do so. One does not need to be a prophet or the son of a prophet to know that after the Court's holding today some students in Iowa schools and indeed in all schools will be ready, able, and willing to defy their teachers on practically all orders. This is the more unfortunate for the schools since groups of students all over the land are already running loose, conducting break-ins, sit-ins, lie-ins, and smash-ins. Many of these student groups, as is all too familiar to all who read the newspapers and watch the television news programs, have already engaged in rioting, property seizures, and destruction. They have picketed schools to force students not to cross their picket lines and have too often violently attacked earnest but frightened students who wanted an education that the pickets did not want them to get. Students engaged in such activities are apparently confident that they know far more about how to operate public school systems than do their parents, teachers, and elected school officials. It is no answer to say that the particular students here have not yet reached such high points in their demands to attend classes in order to exercise their political pressures. Turned loose with law suits for damages and injunctions against their teachers as they are here, it is nothing but wishful thinking to imagine that young, immature students will not soon believe it is their right to control the schools rather than the right of the States that collect the taxes to hire the teachers for the benefit of the pupils. This case, therefore, wholly without constitutional reasons in my judgment, subjects all the public schools in the country to the whims and caprices of their loudest-mouthed, but maybe not their brightest students. I, for one, am not fully persuaded that the school pupils are wise enough even with this Court's expert help from Washington, to run the 23,390 public school [526] systems [note 4] in our 50 states. I wish, therefore, wholly to disclaim any purpose on my part to hold that the Federal Constitution compels the teachers, parents, and elected school officials to surrender control of the American public school system to public school students. I dissent."[1]

The Young Boxer

From 1969 through 1975 a series of Supreme Court decisions were reached that had the effect of pitting every American teacher against the law of the land. Where once the law had been a supporter of the teacher and teacher authority, such as *in loco parentis*, it now became, as it were, an opponent. Therefore, what ensued were a number of boxing matches between the champion of our nation's system of education, the American teacher, and the opponents coming out of the Washington, D.C.-based Supreme Court Boxing Club. These opponents quickly became known to educators throughout the country as ruthless and unforgiving in their styles. They were *Tinker v. Des Moines*, *Goss v. Lopez* and *Wood v. Strickland*.

The first of the matches began in 1969 pitting *Tinker* against our champion. During the early rounds of 1970-74 *Tinker* hit with immense strength and power. Our young champion went down several times for long counts but in each case managed to get back to his feet and continue the fight. By round 1975, he was exhausted, yet his opponent was showing no signs of tiring. As he returned to his corner and sat for the brief respite, he could see two fresh opponents now joining his adversary across the ring—fresh opponents named *Goss v. Lopez* and *Wood v. Strickland*. The champion glanced up and smiled at his trainer. When the bell rang, he would go back into the ring. It was not his nature to quit, but he and his trainer and all who understood the fairness and honesty of sport knew that for this lad winning could no longer be the goal. The deck had been stacked. The rules had been changed, and as he rose and stepped forward to meet all three, he did so courageously and with the full intention of simply staying alive.

Boxing was his love. He had trained much of his young life for his moment. It was his moment to compete, to give back, and to perhaps make his family and friends proud. He understood the exhausted but honorable feeling that comes at the end of a productive, hard-fought day, but this new daily beating he was about to take might be more than even he, with his youthful pride and commitment could endure. Would friends and loved ones understand? Would anyone? Or would the inevitable daily beatings be understood only by his fellow pugilists in classrooms next to his. Would that comradeship be enough to sustain him? Would it be enough to keep him from becoming an aging, bitter, and cynical teacher?

After *Goss v Lopez* and *Wood v Strickland*, teachers and building administrators throughout the country were pleading for help. In those years and the years to follow it was as though schools were experiencing a heavy and steady barrage of hammering against their fortress walls. Coupled with the strength and power of Public Law 94-142, special education legislation, the attack would go on so long that the next generation of educators would question whether at some time in the past there had been any walls there at all.

Legitimate disciplinary referral requests from teachers were being ignored. Administrators at all levels, thoroughly overwhelmed, had scant time to handle even those of the most dangerous nature. Time for classroom observations and providing instructional strategy assistance to teachers was severely limited. Brand new, inexperienced teachers didn't stand a chance. Even some veterans crumbled. Many close to retirement left early. I recall a conversation with one of those who did so. He had throughout his career been considered an outstanding educator.

"Tom, why?"

"Ray, I've got to. If I don't leave now, I swear some day in response to the next 'f--- you, motherf---er' or 'f--- off, what ya gonna do about it,' I'll get so provoked that I'll grab one of 'em. And if I go that far, God forbid, I might want to go further. I just can't risk that. It would be devastating to my family and, further, most people would never understand—particularly my non-teacher friends."

The level of acceptable classroom and school disruptions was being ratcheted up. Control and order in many classrooms were gone. If students refused to leave hallways and come into classrooms, many teachers, as a survival tactic, did nothing. A growing feeling was "better that they be out there than in my classroom where I have little power or authority to deal with them." The circles of disruption became broader and broader, eventually enveloping whole schools. The legitimate use of bathrooms frequently gave way to drug use and acts of severe intimidation. The hall pass became a practice of a different and forgotten time. Our young and veteran boxers were not only losing the fight as could have been predicted, they were losing the fight for the lives of those children who had come to learn.

The *Goss* decision made education a property right K-12. Education was no longer a privilege. It was now a right. This change to property right obligated school officials and teachers to provide to students due process procedures even when a teacher was considering the most routine disciplinary measures. Requiring that a student leave class for disruptive behavior now required a due-process hearing. School discipline was reaching the level of insanity. Following is an excerpt from the dissenting opinion of the 1975 U.S. Supreme Court case *Goss v. Lopez* 419 U.S.(1975):

Goss v Lopez 419 U.S 565(1975)

Mr. Justice Powell, with whom the Chief Justice, Mr. Justice Blackmun, and Mr. Justice Rehnquist join, dissenting.

> The Court holds for the first time that the federal courts, rather than educational officials and state legislatures, have the authority to determine the rules applicable to routine classroom discipline of children and teenagers in the public schools. It justifies this unprecedented intrusion into the process of elementary and secondary education by identifying a new Constitutional right: the right of a student not to be suspended for as much as a single day without notice or a due process hearing either before or promptly following the suspension.....conferred as an unqualified right to education, thereby compelling the school authorities to conform to due process procedures in imposing the most routine discipline.
>
> Moreover, the Court ignores the experience of mankind, as well as the long history of our law, recognizing that there are differences which must be accommodated in determining the rights and duties of children as compared with those of adults. Few rulings would interfere more extensively in the daily functioning of schools than subjecting routine discipline to the formalities and judicial oversight of due process. It is common knowledge that maintaining

order and reasonable decorum in school buildings and classrooms is a major educational problem and one which has increased significantly in magnitude in recent years. Often the teacher, in protecting the rights of other students to an education (if not his or their safety), is compelled to rely on the power to suspend.....if hearings were required for a substantial percentage of short-term suspensions, school authorities would have time to do little else. [2]

In the same year, the *Wood v. Strickland* decision raised the personal liability standard for teachers and administrators to a higher level. After this decision, teachers, *though acting in good faith*, who unintentionally violated a student's right could be sued and held personally liable. The Court raised for teachers and administrators the standard of required knowledge. The immediate consequence to this in schools throughout the nation was dramatic. Fearful teachers backed off. After all, "Go f--- yourself," as the Ohio principal said, may be the student's way of saying good morning and, therefore, his right to say so. Does a teacher now want to challenge that comment and run the risk of being held personally liable? Insanity just went up another notch. How sad.

The following is an excerpt from the dissenting opinion which accurately describes the complex issues which would arise from this decision:

Wood v. Strickland 420 U.S. 308 (1975)

Mr. Justice Powell, with whom the Chief Justice, Mr. Justice Blackmun, and Mr. Justice Rehnquist join, concurring in part and dissenting in part.

> I join in parts I, III, and IV of the Court's opinion and agree that the judgment of the Court of Appeals should be vacated and the case remanded. I dissent from 420 U.S. which appears to impose a higher standard of care upon public school officials, sued under 1983, then that heretofore required of any other official. The holding of the Court on the immunity issue is set forth in the margin. [Footnote 2/1] It would

impose personal liability on a school official who acted sincerely and in the utmost good faith but who was found—after the fact—to have acted in "ignorance...of settled, indisputable law." Or, as the Court also puts it, the school official must be held to a standard of conduct based not only on good faith, "but also on knowledge of the basic, unquestioned Constitutional rights of his charges." Moreover ignorance of the law is explicitly equated with "actual malice." This harsh standard, requiring knowledge of what is characterized as "settled, indisputable law," leaves little substance to the doctrine of qualified immunity. The Court decision appears to rest on an unwarranted assumption as to what lay school officials know or can know about the law and Constitutional rights. These officials will now act at the peril of some judge or jury subsequently finding that a good faith belief as to the applicable law was mistaken, and hence actionable. [3]

Honig v. Doe

As if the Supreme Court decisions of *Tinker, Wood,* and *Goss* were not enough to cripple order and control in American schools and classrooms, Congress in 1975 and the Supreme Court in 1988 finished the job.

The first action took place in 1975 when Congress passed the comprehensive package of special education legislation known as Public Law 94-142. This was a package of legislative requirements so layered and complex that on any given day, despite school officials' best efforts, it is virtually impossible not to violate a myriad of legally binding obligations. Furthermore, Congress to this day has never funded 94-142 anywhere near what everyone clearly understood would be its costs.

The second action came from the Supreme Court in 1988 in the form of the decision rendered in San Francisco's *Honig v. Doe* case. This 1988 decision made it clear that the procedural protections applicable to disabled children apply as well to emotionally disturbed, even dangerous disabled children. Prior to this decision by the Court there was a lack of clarity because Public Law 94-142 passed in 1975 had been silent on the issue of disciplining special education students and the decisions of court cases rendered after the passage of 94-142 were sometimes conflicting and, thus, confusing.

Let's try to understand what *Honig* did by use of a hypothetical school incident. Suppose a fourth-grade male student enrolled as an emotionally handicapped pupil comes to school with a weapon. At a time during class when his teacher is tending to another student and has her back to him, he is able to strike the teacher with the weapon causing serious bodily harm. The teacher turns and manages to subdue him. The teacher is ultimately taken from the class in order to receive medical assistance.

Some time after this incident a meeting would take place. A primary purpose of the meeting would be to determine whether or not the act of harming the teacher could have been related to the child's handicapping condition. If that committee judged that the act was related to the handicapping condition (in this case a child whose categorical designation was emotionally handicapped), then the child could not, by law (*Honig v. Doe*), be expelled. The thinking here is that such an expulsion action against the pupil would thus be penalizing him for his handicap. In *Honig v. Doe* the San Francisco Schools appealed to the court to at least allow the inclusion of a "dangerousness" exception in the congressional law, so that such a pupil could be removed from his current educational placement in order to provide a condition of future safety to classmates and teachers. The court refused, advising plaintiffs that if Congress had intended such a "dangerousness" exception provision, they would have written it into the law.[4]

In December of 2004, sixteen years after *Honig v. Doe,* President George W. Bush signed a reauthorization of the Individuals with Disabilities Act that went into effect July 1, 2005. One of the provisions of that reauthorization was to allow school authorities to take into account unique circumstances when considering the removal of a student. Therefore, in the example which we stated above, this provision allows that where the pupil "has inflicted serious bodily injury upon another person while at school or on school premises or at a school function under the jurisdiction of an SEA or LEA," the school personnel may remove a student to an "interim" alternative education setting for not more than 45 school days.[5]

There are no provisions permitting an extension beyond the 45 days, and most importantly this exception regulation cannot be used

The Problem Isn't Teachers

in situations where the student's behaviors are of the type called "a constant disruption to the educational function."

After years of challenges to the requirements of special education law with respect to discipline options that the schools may elect to use, expulsion of a special education student cannot take place if the special education student's disruptive or even dangerous behavior can be shown to be related to his handicapping condition. Again, this includes students of all handicapping categories including behaviorally disordered or emotionally disturbed.

Notes:

1. *Tinker v. Des Moines Independent Community School District*, 393 U.S. 503 (1969). Mr. Justice Black, dissenting http://www.bc.edu/bc_org/avp/cas/comm/free_speech/Tinker.html
2. *Goss v. Lopez*, 419 U.S. 565 (1975). Mr. Justice Powell, with whom the Chief Justice, Mr. Justice Blackmun, and Mr. Justice Rehnquist join dissenting, http://caselaw.lp.findlaw.com/scripts/getcase.pl?navby=search7court=US/. .../565.h
3. *Wood v. Strickland*, 420 U.S. 308 (1975). Mr. Justice Powell, with whom the Chief Justice, Mr. Justice Blackmun, and Mr. Justice Rehnquist join, concurring in part and dissenting in part, http:// Supreme.justia.com/us/420/308/case.html.
4. *Honig v. Doe*, 484 U.S. 305 (1988), http:// Supreme.justia.com/us/484/305/.
5. IDEA- Regulations. Discipline, http://www.ideapartnership.org/index.php?option=com_content&view=acticle&id=840&0.

SECTION FOUR

THE CRITICAL IMPORTANCE OF GOOD PARENTING

Chapter 10

The Cycles of Success

In our book, *The Power of Participation*, published in 1995, we wrote that prevailing beliefs in the 1960s questioned the ability of schools to overcome the vestiges of poverty when considering student achievement. We also wrote that researchers involved in what was known as Effective Schools Movement were successful in finding schools that were making some progress—making some difference.[1] The overwhelming research of that time, however, the massive and extensive Coleman Study, would suggest otherwise:

> Student achievement is influenced more by a student's background and the school's socioeconomic circumstances than by school quality. For this study, the tests administered to children were not intended to measure intelligence, but rather the ability of children to learn and perform in the American educational environment. The study further concluded that differences in school family background showed a substantial correlation with achievement. In other words, student background and socio-economic status are much more important in determining educational outcomes than are measured differences in school resources.[2]

The impact of this study on the American educational community was so intense that the dissenters to the study's conclusions were many, for it was deeply believed and accepted as fact that, despite any circumstances, schools could make the difference. Thus, predictably, the Coleman Study's methodologies, sample selections, and expertise of the researchers themselves were repeatedly challenged and continually reviewed decade after decade. However, even after such extensive scrutiny, the results have been reaffirmed. We are left with the undisputed conclusion that the power, influence, and support of family virtually ensures the success of their children. This outcome is not the result of a casual or sporadic effort. These parents intentionally forge the kind of partnership with schools and society which demands from them a profound commitment of time and effort over an extensive period of years.

It is extremely significant to note that, though this study focused on the outcomes of black and white students, many of the same conclusions could have been drawn if the study had compared the academic achievement of children of poverty (white and black) with children of wealth (white and black). The research literature is filled with such similar comparisons focused upon the impact of poverty. Research literature will also reveal academic achievement variations between rich and poor in nations other than the U.S. We are not the only nation where the children of the poor come in as a far distant second when compared with their more affluent counterparts.

Though most of us have an understanding as to why such differences exist between the rich and the poor, we thought that interviewing some well-educated and successful middle- to upper-class American parents might serve to illustrate the specifics of child rearing that result in the kind of achievement we are referring to above. What is it that educated parents with sufficient resources do with their children that results in such a difference?

One might assume, given the current heavy American emphasis on test scores as the principal measure of a student's success, that the American parents we interviewed would be focusing their teaching in that direction. One might further assume that this teaching would be strongly tied to math, science, and verbal skills. However, if you assumed such, you would have been wrong. With those we interviewed we found that these academic areas were not being ignored, but rather that the depth and breath of the teaching was going far beyond the boundaries of any content areas. These parents were focusing on the following: fostering curiosity; getting their children to believe in themselves, instilling the joy of learning, developing a moral/ethical compass; introducing reading and sharing the love of books of all kinds; and nurturing an understanding and love of country.

Besides focusing on these overarching goals, the parents we interviewed were continuously engaging their children in new skill tasks, such as gardening, farming, food preparation, home repairs, and construction skills. Though not all of the parents stated it, one set of parents advised that they viewed parenting as their highest calling. But the breath and depth of the teachings of all of those we talked to would lead one to conclude that all these parents had the same cherished view of parenting. Without exception, these parents saw social skills, religion, love of country, kindness, respect, and communication of feelings as elements they needed to weave into all aspects of daily life.

The emphasis on music was quite intense. It included studying various musical instruments and participating in choral groups, orchestras, and bands. There were treasured family moments, times set aside for listening to and playing music together. Finally, time was made consistently for new experiences in parks, zoos, and learning labs. Opportunities to visit relatives and travel to new places were high priorities. Children were very often being trained or exposed to second and, occasionally, third languages. Significantly, all of the children were being restricted from activities seen as potentially harmful or simply unproductive, such as watching television, talking on cell phones, and going to sleep-overs. Though these children were given the capacity to make choices, parents were routinely defining the boundaries within which such choices would occur.

Some Parenting Lessons Learned

We would like to add some additional thoughts on the qualities of great parenting. Over the years, we have attempted to pull from research and from our own personal experiences as educators and parents the most important qualities and characteristics of great parenting. We offer the following list as a partial representation of what we think it takes to parent successful children. We think great parenting goes beyond providing academic preparation.

We think great parenting

- is forgiving;
- nurtures dreams;
- models lifelong learning;
- maintains an on-going partnership with the child's teachers;
- always reaffirms hope;
- continuously introduces the child to the many faces of success;
- calls upon available resources that are used to assist the child's focused progress;
- demonstrates that failure is a part of learning;
- affirms that life, though difficult, is to be cherished, loved, shared, and enjoyed;
- demonstrates that there are alternative ways to achieve goals; and
- continually creates an understanding and empathy for the feelings and life conditions of others.

This list represents the need for a commitment of parental involvement that is quite challenging. We certainly have to acknowledge that such parenting is enhanced by adequate family income, education, and the setting of high standards. We also acknowledge that poverty, instability, and ignorance make this kind of parenting extremely difficult, perhaps impossible. However, when huge numbers of people—including those who should know better—criticize teachers for failing to educate all children, we must remind those people that schools and teachers cannot alone educate the ever-growing numbers of children who are profoundly lacking the kind of parenting described above. God knows, they do try.

Notes:

1. Raymond J. Golarz and Marion J. Golarz, *The Power of Participation: Improving Schools in a Democratic Society* (Champaign, Ill.: Research Press, 1995), 2-3.
2. Debra Viadero, "Race Report's Influence Felt 40 Years Later: Legacy of Coleman Study Was New View of Equity," *Education Week,* June 21, 2006.

Chapter 11

Poverty Cripples Parenting

We live in a nation that does not want to acknowledge the fact that *there is no replacement or substitute for good parenting.* While we talk of the many negative impacts of poverty, we seem to fail to recognize that one of the most devastating effects of poverty is the inability of parents to cooperate in the education of their young children. Sadly and ironically, we even hear many of these poor parents chastise the efforts of teachers. They demand to know, "Why isn't my child reading well?" Or they may ask, "Why are you failing to teach my child?" They ask these things either because they are too ignorant to understand their obligation, or because they fully believe that schools are accountable for the education of their children and that schools are capable of doing so without help from them. Either way, they seem to fail to understand a most basic truth: *a great education can only come from a partnership of good parenting and good schooling.*

What makes this situation doubly painful and frustrating for teachers is that others in our society seem to have the same lack of understanding regarding the importance of parental involvement. So, when an article regarding a school's low test scores appears in the newspaper, it many times suggests that teachers are at fault for such failure. These allegations are often leveled by politicians, business people, academics, and a multitude of uninformed critics. These are people who have never taught in a poverty-ridden classroom for even a short period of time.

It is time that this negative and inaccurate picture of teacher failure is corrected. It is time to connect the dots that allow the accurate picture to emerge. The hard truth is that, given the current conditions of all the other social ills we face, the added burden brought

The Problem Isn't Teachers

on by massive poverty and inept child-rearing practices means that the children of the poor will not catch up if they must rely on schools alone.

We live in a nation where thousands of babies in poverty are bearing babies. Thus, it is common in many parts of America to find mothers with children only thirteen or fourteen years younger than they are. They live in all parts of our country. They are not just the children who live in the inner cities and attend the inner city schools. Further, the overwhelming numbers of these young mothers are without husbands, and their children are without the necessary presence, guidance, and support of committed fathers. The situation continues to be epidemic. Nothing has really changed since the cold winter afternoon when I knocked on the door of the young woman in desperate poverty. It has been many years since I first saw those deformed veins which appeared in the darkness to be snakes on her legs. A generation has passed since that very young mother along with several of her eight children died prematurely of "natural causes." It has been a generation since her remaining children ultimately dropped out of school and were swept into the cycle of poverty and despair.

Few Americans see these hidden poor. We are so like the business colleague of mine who, after many years, came face-to-face with a poverty he had been unaware of: children eating out of garbage cans in his old neighborhood. I can still picture him shaking as he came into my office acknowledging that he was stunned by the sight of those realities as he told me, "I don't drive down those streets anymore. I've not had cause to." But others do see these children. They are welfare workers, protective service personnel, police, and teachers. They see them up front and personal, and often ache and hurt for the things they know these children are without. So, as we said in an earlier chapter, teachers bring to them the little things; a bow for a little girl's hair and a hair brush to put in her pocket. Daily they bring just the little things.

Most upsetting to our teachers who try desperately to give all they have are the painful words of the critics who, despite their own economic and social advantages, continue to say, "We just need better teachers," or "It's the unions who are to blame," or "If they would just work harder and create more efficient and effective schools, we could close the gap and make it all better." It is significant to point out that they ignore the fact that *even if we could slowly improve the education of the child of poverty, the child of affluence is not standing still. That child is rushing ahead at lightning speed, hand-in-hand with parents providing assistance in expert and devoted fashion. So, the gap continues to widen.*

A particularly astute statement affirming our position comes from Leon Botstein's book, *Jefferson's Children*:

> Adults who take on the responsibility for parenting, for whatever reason, must be prepared to run parallel to the distance traveled by the school system... similarly, all children born in this country have a right to expect that an adult of his or her own free will [is going to] seek to nurture and sustain them, not only from K-12 but from birth to kindergarten. Without this parallel support system, no educational reform will work.[1]

The bottom line is that poverty is a nation-killer. It is the primary cause of the disintegration of families, the ineptness of child-rearing, and the fostering of the condition of babies raising babies alone without fathers. This national epidemic is crushing the potential success and stunting the future of millions of American children, generation after generation. Given this continuing condition alone, there is no inexpensive silver bullet for fixing American education, and it's time that we stop listening to those who say that there is. It is time that we as a nation grow up and face realities. It is time to stop blaming those that we have sent into the trenches to fight a war they cannot win. Haven't we done this often enough with the young enthusiastic adults of our American nation?

Note:

1. Leon Botstein, *Jefferson's Children: Education and the Promise of American Culture* (New York: Doubleday., 1997), 144.

SECTION FIVE

THE WAR OVER PURPOSE

In *The Power of Participation,* my wife and I reported on a trip to the University of Ohio where I had been invited to speak to some of the faculty. As we slowly approached the gateway structure marking the entrance to the campus, we found ourselves fixated on faded words etched in its stone front. We stopped. Marion read aloud and I sat in awe, feeling as though I were being personally introduced to my benefactors, but they were not just my benefactors. I was meeting the benefactors of all the generations of children who had been privileged to attend, to grow, and to learn in American schools.

> "Religion, morality and knowledge being necessary for good government and the happiness of mankind schools and the means of education shall forever be encouraged."[1]
>
> Ordinance of 1803

Chapter 12

Revisiting the Purpose of Public Schools

This Ohio Ordinance had its origin in the Ordinance of 1787 which was enacted by the Articles of Confederation Congress. Its language reflected the concern of the Founders of our country who wanted to ensure that there was a clear understanding as to the purpose of schools in this emerging nation. They knew this clear understanding would be critical to preserving the good government necessary for the democracy and the happiness of mankind, and they were convinced that an uninformed citizenry would lead to the eventual demise of the republic. This critical need was most urgently and eloquently expressed in the many writings of Thomas Jefferson. Merrell Peterson in his 1960 book titled *The Jefferson Image of the American Mind* elaborates on this view of the purpose of education:

> Jefferson believed the elementary school more important than the university in the plan because, as he said, it is essential to have the whole people enlightened, [rather] than a few in a high state of science or many in ignorance as exists in Europe. He had six objectives for primary education to bring about this enlightenment and which highlighted what he hoped would make every person into a productive and informed voter:
> 1. To give every citizen the information he needs for the transaction of his own business;
> 2. To enable him to calculate for himself, and to express and preserve his ideas, his contracts, and accounts, in writing;
> 3. To improve, by reading, his morals and faculties;

4. To understand his duties to his neighbors and country, and to discharge with competence the functions confided to him by either;
5. To know his rights; to exercise with order and justice those he retains; to choose with discretion the fiduciary of those he delegates; and to notice their conduct with diligence, with candor, and with judgment;
6. And, in general, to observe with intelligence and faithfulness all of the social relations under which he shall be placed.[2]

This requirement for an educated citizenry is noted also by Benjamin Barber in *Public Schooling-Education for Democracy*. Summarizing the ideas of Jefferson and Tocqueville, Barber states:

> Jefferson knew full well that liberty is acquired and that citizens are educated to a responsibility that comes to no man or woman naturally. Without citizens democracy is a hollow shell. Without public schools there can be no citizens. Tocqueville spoke movingly of the need in democracies for an "apprenticeship of liberty"—what he deemed the most arduous of all apprenticeships.[3]

Clearly, for our Founders, education was essential. If education achieved its goals then citizens would acquire, beyond the benefits to themselves personally, the following: first, the capacity to accurately judge the trustworthiness and responsible behavior of elected delegates; second, a clear understanding of their own duties to neighbors and country; third, an understanding of the obligation to provide order and justice to those employed; and fourth, the benefits that come naturally to those who are enlightened by the acquisition of a broad liberal education that includes the studies of great literature, the sciences, the arts, music, languages, the history of man, his religions, and his philosophies.

There seemed initially little doubt or confusion about the intended direction of public schools—a liberal education for the enlightenment of citizens—the kind of education the Founders themselves possessed. Jefferson's dream was to provide citizens with the skills and civility needed to participate in and contribute to the perpetuation of the American democracy, good government, and the happiness of mankind.

Confusion over the Role of Public Schools

The role of public schools was broadened over many years as the inevitable result of profound change which occurred over the evolution of this nation. Tragically, however, there was also an erosion of the original purpose of schools. This erosion came, to some extent, from outside our country as ideologies and actions of some foreign countries were perceived as threats to our very existence. But many of the changes in the purpose of public school education came from within our own country.

The purpose of public schools had remained fairly constant and had reflected much of Jefferson's curriculum until the mid-twentieth century. However, by the late fifties and early sixties, schools began to change dramatically. The rise of communism, the Cold War, and the fear of being bombed by Russia, especially throughout the Fifties, became the focus of politicians and the population as a whole. The need to be a superior atomic and nuclear power was an extremely high priority, and so the call for a better scientific education began to escalate. When the Russians placed Sputnik in orbit in 1957, the need to "catch up" and reaffirm our supremacy as the most powerful country in the world dominated political and national life. Schools became increasingly responsible for producing the scientists needed to maintain our defense. Thus, curriculum and student achievement came under intense scrutiny.

The anxiety surrounding this threat from foreign countries continued to occupy this nation well into the Reagan years. But more unrest was starting to dominate the social, political, and economic agenda so profoundly that during the decades of the Sixties, Seventies, and Eighties, the very fabric of the country seemed to be unraveling. The war in Vietnam was violently protested, and these protests spilled over into protests against the "establishment" on all levels. The authority of government and other institutions, including the armed forces and education, was challenged. The civil rights movement, which also raged during this period, brought its own measure of volatility as the battle for equal rights and access to power was waged across many fronts. Racial and gender equality, individual constitutional rights, the rights of disabled citizens, and the effort to desegregate public schools became issues which drove extraordinary change in the social and legal landscape. Schools at all levels came under attack as critics assailed the traditional curriculum and methods of teaching as racist, discriminatory, irrelevant, or ineffective. The U.S. Supreme Court in an attempt to clarify and establish the constitutionality relative to these issues, rendered decisions that affected all of our institutions. The purpose of public schools and the way in which they were to function were impacted profoundly by all of these factors.

By the beginning of the twenty-first century, schools as we had known them had drastically changed in response to legislation, the continued demand to produce superior students, and the need to address the growing severity of poverty, drug abuse, and child abuse. The emphasis on producing students who would be equipped to preserve the democracy had been pushed aside. At one time, the family and other social institutions had assumed the primary responsibility for teaching life skills, health and hygiene, ethnic history, and sex education, for example. Now public schools were assuming these responsibilities. In addition, where schools once referred students with problems to the appropriate court or social welfare agency, they were now expected to partner with, or take exclusive responsibility for functioning in many communities as medical clinics, psychological counseling services, vocational institutions, drug rehabilitation centers, outreach centers, and even shelters Here again, while these efforts were—and still are—worthwhile and admirable, to make schools mainly responsible for the resolution of these problems allows for less and less time to be allocated to the essential purpose declared by our nation's Founders.

The Business Agenda

Despite the impact on schools brought about by the challenges and events described above, the most profound change in the purpose and direction of schools has come from the steady, concerted, and powerful influence of the business/industrial community. Some of these efforts have been transparent—some downright stealthy.

Beginning right after World War II, when the rest of the industrial world was working at a feverish pace to regain an industrial foothold, major players in the U.S. business/industrial community, such as steel and car companies, took an extended leave. They sat back and leisurely sunned themselves in the pleasure of an industrial head start won on the backs of American wartime workers and the American G.I. While Japan and Germany installed new oxygen conversion steel-making furnaces, the U.S. industrialists sucked up profits by continuing to use the old open-hearth systems which had been built during the first decade of the 1900s. While all of Europe and parts of Asia began producing the most efficient and durable cars, the U.S. moved further and further into planned obsolescence which required loyal U.S. consumers to replace their cars much more frequently. By the 1960s, however, foreign cars, notably the Volkswagen Beetle, began to win the hearts, minds, and pocketbooks of a new generation of Americans who were conscious of the cost savings gained not only because of the need for less gasoline, but also because of the durability of the auto itself. Meanwhile, Japan continued to cut its manufacturing teeth by producing toys for the world market until it exploded overnight into an industrial power, utilizing America Ed Deming's Quality Management. While this was happening, U.S. companies went to war with American labor, the latest version of which has been the outsourcing of American jobs to foreign countries. This was necessary the business community claimed, because of the poorly educated American worker.

Raymond J. Golarz and Marion J. Golarz

Finding a Scapegoat

By 1980, as a consequence of the inept leadership of the American business/industrial sector which resulted in continual losses to foreign competition, a scapegoat had to be found. Who better than the American schools? The narrative that was proposed (and was eventually accepted in many quarters) was that schools were failing to adequately prepare young people for the world of the workplace. Americans were told that it was this failure that was responsible for the weakening of the national economy. Schools were blamed for the erosion of our position as the most productive and competitive country in the world. Thus, there would need to be a new direction and purpose of schools. This approach provided two major benefits for business, especially for large corporations. First, it would absolve the business/industrial community of any responsibility for the weakening economy, or for the loss of American jobs. Secondly, if the mission of schools could be refocused to train a work force, industry would no longer need to accept this responsibility or bear this cost.

A full-fledged assault was undertaken to make schools K through 12 places where a remodeled curriculum would focus on the skills deemed necessary for the world of work. This function of work preparation formerly had been reserved primarily for vocational high schools, vocational colleges, regular colleges, and universities. Most businesses and industries had invested in their own training of new employees. Apprenticeship programs were common throughout the business/industrial community. Efforts were already underway in the Seventies to promote this shift in purpose when the publication of A Nation at Risk, justified the dramatic takeover and helped to speed up the process. The following commentary is taken from Clinton Boutwell's book, *Shell Game: Corporate America's Agenda for Schools*, published in 1997. This passage highlights how and why this hijacking of purpose came about:

> In essence, America's corporate elite charged that their incompetence was not responsible for the loss of America's competitive advantage. The "real" reason

was that the United Stated did not have a highly educated, world-class work force. The schools were causing this economic decline, they claimed. And their media apologists perpetuated that charge. Interestingly none of those critics has ever defined clearly what was meant by, "world-class," so educators may have been chasing a will-o-the-wisp when they contritely responded by tooling up to produce a "world-class work force."

Opinion formulators reported that American factories and jobs were going to foreigners because American students—high school and university graduates—were not educated well enough to provide American business with the kind of workers it needed.

They pointed to the educated workforce found in countries that were successfully eating into America's advantage, such countries as Japan, Korea, Singapore, Germany, France, or whatever other country whose students appeared for the moment to have higher test scores than American students.

By placing the blame on the schools for America's economic doldrums, the decline in good jobs, and consequent rapid decrease in decent wages, business had found a potent vehicle for deflecting blame from itself. And the campaign worked. Their charges gave affluent Americans a rationale to understand business down-turns, and they gave middle-class and working Americans a target on which to focus in hopes of preventing wage slippage and unemployment. Suddenly, getting schools up to snuff became *the* American cause.[4]

The speed with which this new direction of school purpose was implemented was astounding. The manipulation of public opinion, legislation, and corporate effort was ruthless and relentless.

The principal architects of this new American direction for schooling were leaders from many professions, elected officials in both American state and federal legislative and administrative bodies, along with the American/international business community itself. This community, in particular, had come to view children as future production components. Timothy J. McMannon, in *The Public Purpose of Education* and *Schooling*, attests to this new use of American children:

> By the 1990s the rhetoric had changed. The job for which school children had to be prepared was no longer saving the nation from communist aggression, but saving the nation from Japanese economic competition. The United States had to win the battle of the market and schools were to be the boot camps.[5]

The SCANS Report

The press to move schools totally in the direction of job preparation was strongly opposed by all who fought for a liberal education and the schooling needed to educate our youth regarding the principles of how to sustain our American democracy. The anger, concern, and resentment grew quickly, and soon pressure was coming from American parents and educators. In response to this growing dissention, the following olive branch was offered in 1991 by the United States Department of Labor in the form of a letter to American parents and educators:

> We, your Secretary of Labor and members of the Secretary's Commission on Achieving Necessary Skills (SCANS), write as concerned representatives of the nation's schools, businesses, unions, and government. We have completed our initial examination of changes in the world of work and the implications of those changes for learning.
>
> We understand that schools do more than simply prepare people to make a living. They prepare people to live full lives—to participate in their communities, to raise families, and then enjoy the leisure that is the fruit of their labor. A solid education is its own reward.
>
> This report concerns only one part of that education, the part that involves how schools prepare young people for work. It does not deal with other, equally important, concerns that are also the proper responsibility of our educators. We do not want to be misinterpreted. We are not calling for a narrow work-focused education. Our future demands more.[6]

Following this letter, however, the push for work-focused education and standardized assessment did not abate. Rather, it continued relentlessly and eventually included the thoroughly unrealistic No Child Left Behind mandates. The veiled—but clearly heard—threat from the business/industrial community was emphatic: either use schools to prepare American students for the workplace and teach the curriculum they supported, or they would go to foreign shores for their employees. To demonstrate their intent, they demanded that the effectiveness of teachers be determined by the success of their students on standardized tests. Further, they advocated that employment of teachers be tied to their students' success on these tests. Support for this modified purpose of education and methods proposed to judge the effectiveness of teachers gained huge support from federal and state legislative leaders.

ALEC

Recent sources have confirmed that substantial efforts have been made over a considerable period of time to ensure that the goals discussed above are actualized. Actually, efforts to control and shape the purpose and function of public schools have been proceeding in an organized manner since at least 1973. One of these entities was noted by Diane Ravitch who on an *Education Week* blog where she recently warned about an organization known as ALEC (American Legislative Exchange Council). According to Ravitch, ALEC, which was founded in 1973 and counts among its members 2,000 conservative state legislators nationwide, has engaged in an organized effort to influence negative attitudes toward public schools and has supported the privatization of public schools. Ravitch explains:

> This outburst of anti-public school, anti-teacher legislation is no accident. It is the work of a shadowy group called the American Legislative Exchange Council, or ALEC. Its hallmark is promotion of privatization and corporate interests in every sphere, not only education, but health care, the environment, the economy, voting laws, public safety, etc. It drafts model legislation that conservative legislators take back to their states and introduce as their own "reform" ideas. ALEC is the guiding force behind state-level efforts to privatize public education and to turn teachers into at-will employees who may be fired for any reason. The ALEC agenda is today the "reform" agenda for education.[7]

Could there be a more potent threat to the purpose of education as envisioned and fashioned by the Founders? How are schools supposed to guide students with an education that will equip them to nurture and preserve the intent of this democracy if efforts like those described above are allowed to prevail?

Earlier, in this chapter we quoted from Clinton Boutwell's book, *The Shell Game: Corporate America's Agenda for Schools*. Boutwell, as you read in those quotes, stated that "America's corporate elite" placed the blame on schools for "America's economic doldrums, the decline in good jobs, and the consequent rapid decline in decent wages." [8]

Taking such a position has allowed the business community to use the mantra—the schools are to blame—to dominate for many years the conversation regarding the proper role of education. The message has not changed as they continue to propose the following: Give us an endless supply of highly qualified, highly educated, top-end standardized test takers, and we will provide America with a smooth-running, highly productive, fully-employed economy.

Paul Krugman, winner of the 2008 Noble Prize in Economics, in *End This Depression Now!* takes exception to this position. He states unequivocally that our current national economic condition reveals that the answer does not lie in simply more highly skilled workers:

> There are no major occupations or skill groups doing well. Between 2007 and 2010 unemployment roughly doubled in just about every category—blue-collar and white-collar, manufacturing and services, highly educated and uneducated. Nobody was getting big wage increases; in fact, as we saw in chapter 1, highly educated graduates were taking unusually large pay cuts, because they were forced to accept jobs that made no use of their education.
>
> The bottom line is that if we had mass unemployment because of too many workers lacking the right stuff, we should be able to find a significant number of workers who do have that stuff prospering—and we can't. What we see instead is impoverishment all around, which is what happens when the economy suffers from inadequate demand.[9]

This year I was asked to keynote a conference of school superintendents in one of our northern states. In order to prepare properly, I asked those bringing me to the conference to send information regarding recent legislative educational efforts and considerations in their state and surrounding region. Some of these were as follows:

1. Art and music curriculum courses shall no longer be considered core.
2. Tenure of teachers shall discontinue, except for those who are already on tenure and have over 20 years of experience.
3. The compensation of teachers and administrators will be tied to standardized test scores of students on state proficiency exams.
4. Obligations of administrators to meet regularly with representatives of teacher unions in order to discuss contemplated new practices or programs will stop.
5. The bargaining rights of teachers will be curtailed.

The war on public schools is being waged all around us, daily creating more and more pockets of disheartened teachers while a nation stands flat-footed and inept in the distance.

As we move to close this chapter we have chosen to share a quote from Timothy J. McMannon's book *The Changing Purposes of Education and Schooling*. We find it particularly appropriate to our discussion:

> To the uneducated mind, music may be mere noise, art work simply agglomerations of media, books merely so much paper and ink, and conversations just the sounds of voices. Education, however, allows a person to perceive meaning in musical tones, in visual stimuli, and in the spoken and written word. In short, education enables one to participate more fully in the human conversation. [10]

The purposes of schooling crafted by this nation's Founders had been carefully and patiently thought out, discussed, debated, and finally set to pen. A vibrant democracy of free thinking and astute future Americans was their dream, for they understood that an uninformed and ignorant citizenry would lead to the demise of the republic. They placed their hopes in schools—schools that would be sacred places where, with each new generation, young Americans would be sent forth into the forums of liberty. As we now stand flat-footed and inept, we can see before our eyes that dream now fading along with the slow erosion of the treasured vision.

As a young school child, I sketched a picture of Christ. The image that I chose to recreate with my yet unschooled young hand was from a picture of an angry Lord. This image rather baffled and confused me. He appeared angry and the picture revealed people who were running from him. I was perplexed. When I finished my sketch I showed it to my teacher. She looked at it, smiled, and then complimented me.

Then, she said, "Raymond, you look confused, why?"

"Sister, he looks so angry."

She explained, "He's chasing them out of a sacred place, Raymond, for they were using the place for their own purposes and not for the special reasons for which it was made. His anger is called a 'just anger.' Do you understand?"

"I'm not sure, Sister. I think so. We shouldn't violate sacred places."

"That's right, Raymond. Ours is the responsibility to preserve sacred places—to protect sacred places for the purposes they were made."

I reflect on her words so often today and ask myself. Is it our time for "just anger"? Is it our time to rid schools of dysfunctional purposes? Is it time to return schools to the purposes intended by our Founders? If they are allowed to continue along the current path, what will happen to the effectiveness of the democracy envisioned so long age?

To build on these thoughts and Sister's wise advice, consider the challenge articulated in the following passage from Carne Ross in his recently published book, *The Leaderless Revolution.*

> It is pathetic to witness the injustice of the status quo and yet do nothing, however slight, to amend it. Above all, this inaction in the face of inequality and looming crises is to render ourselves less than we are.[11]

Notes:

1. "Ordinance of 1787," *West's Encyclopedia of American Law*, pp. 2-6, http://www.answers.com/topic/northwest-ordinance. http://www.u-s-history.com/pages/h365.html.
2. Merrell D. Peterson, *The Jefferson Image of the American Mind* (New York: Oxford University Press, 1960), 239.
3. Benjamin R. Barber, "Public Schooling: Education for Democracy," in *The Public Purpose of Education*, John I. Goodlad and Timothy J. McMannon, eds. (San Francisco: Jossey-Bass, 1997), 27.
4. Clinton E. Boutwell, *Shell Game: Corporate America's Agenda for Schools*, (Bloomington, Ind.: Phi Delta Kappa Educational Foundation, 1997), 86-87.
5. Timothy J. McMannon, "Introduction: The Changing Purposes of Education and Schooling," in *The Public Purpose of Education*, John I. Goodlad and Timothy J. McMannon, eds, (San Francisco: Jossey-Bass, 1997), 9.
6. United States Department of Labor, Secretary's Commission on Achieving Necessary Skills (SCANS), What Work Requires of Schools: A SCANS Report for America 2000 (Washington, D.C.: 1991).
7. Diane Ravitch, "What You Need to Know About ALEC," Bridging Differences, *Education Week*, May 1, 2012, http://blogs.edweek.org/edweek/Bridging-Differences/2012/05/dear_deborah... 5/3/2012.
8. Clinton Boutwell, 86-87.
9. Paul Krugman, *End This Depression Now!* (New York: W.W. Norton, 2012), 37-38.
10. Timothy J. McMannon , "The Changing Purposes of Education and Schooling," in *The Public Purpose of Education and Schooling*, John I. Goodman and Timothy J. McMannon, eds, (San Francisco: Jossey-Bass, 1997) 9.
11. Carne Ross, *The Leaderless Revolution: How Ordinary People Will Take Power and Change Politics in the 21st. Century* (New York: Blue Rider Press, Penguin Group, 2011), 214.

Chapter 13

A Bus Ride with a Purpose

When I started school, the purpose of education was clear. Children went to school to learn what they needed to know to become productive people who would be responsible citizens. The choice for many parents meant deciding the type of school. Would it be public, parochial, private, home, or some combination of these? In terms of fundamental curriculum there was little variation. For my parents, particularly my father, a Polish Catholic education would meet a deep need for it would reinforce his language and cultural traditions. This need was so important that I was sent by bus across town to St. Mary's, a Polish school staffed by Polish nuns. It was where my parents had completed their elementary school education a generation earlier. They believed that in addition to being immersed in an environment that set high standards for behavior and academic achievement, I would also be immersed in the traditions and language of my elders. Just as importantly, my parents were profoundly convinced that my education should prepare me to participate in the democracy that allowed their immigrant parents, family, and neighbors to live in this free country which had given them so many opportunities. Therefore, as a 5-year-old little boy, I began my education with a bus ride—a bus ride with a purpose.

It was 5:50 in the morning on a day in late August. I was five years old and walking with my father in that early predawn to the bus stop on Kennedy Avenue, some two blocks from our house. When the No. 2 bus came, we would board and take the long journey along the outskirts of the city. We would eventually get to the other side of town, a direct distance of only three or four miles but twice as far on the bus that circumvented the city. When we got to our destination on Merrill Street, we would get off and walk the two blocks to St. Mary's Polish Catholic grade school. The school was located in the city's Polish ghetto. I had been born in that ethnic community, as had my father, though we now lived a distance away.

On the long bus trip that early morning he had pointed out many stores and landmarks that would help me become familiar with the route, for today's trip was the trial run. Next week's trip, I would be on my own.

When we finally arrived at St. Mary's with its clapboard, unpainted exterior, large gravel playground area, and four classrooms, I looked up at him and said, "Kind of old, isn't it?" He replied, "Yeah, son, it is, but it's a fine school. It's a school where you'll learn things no school in our newer part of town could teach you. I went to school here myself, son. I went here myself." I looked up at him while he spoke, and I could see that he had a warm smile on his face and was clearly focused on the school. He was smiling at an old friend that I, as yet, could only see as a run-down, old, Polish Catholic school, in an equally run-down, old, Polish Catholic neighborhood.

There were many bus rides after that day—bus rides that took me around the city, back and forth between two very different cultures. I didn't understand at the time just how different they were, nor did I comprehend their core of sameness. I was only five.

Many days there would be no bus rides at all, as I would walk the five blocks after school to Busia's (my grandmother's) house to stay with her. She still lived in the old neighborhood. Most of my birth-to-5 years had been spent with her in that house as my parents, uncles, and aunts were all engaged in various war efforts, some of them serving in the Pacific and European theatres. It was the house where I sat on the living room floor and listened to Busia read to me in Polish the letters from her son, my Uncle John, serving on the Destroyer USS Ramsay in the Aleutians. It was where my dad, though quite choked-up, tried to explain to me that my Godfather, his kid brother Andy, had survived Omaha Beach on D Day.

Busia's house was on the street where on evening walks with her to the OK Bakery for a donut, I saw in the living room windows of neighbors the Blue Stars proudly displayed to show that a family member was serving in the war. Busia explained that when they were sewn over and then displayed in gold, a young Polish American soldier would not be coming home. Over the years, I can remember this making me very sad, for I knew some of them. They had, with my uncles, played with me. Some days as we walked back from the bakery and approached her house, I can remember not wanting to look up at her front porch window where her Blue Star was displayed. I wasn't sure how or when they got sewn over, and it made me afraid.

My stays with Busia became more extended, the bus rides less numerous. My Polish language became better and my experiences with ancient foreign customs and an ancient people became more the norm. I ate ethnic foods more often and somewhere they became what I preferred. At school we pledged allegiance each morning. Sometimes we pledged in English, sometimes in Polish. But every day we pledged. Boys fought on the way to school, never at recess, and then picked up the remainder of the fights on the way home. We fought until everyone knew who could beat whom, and then the fighting tapered off. But it never stopped.

When I reached the fifth grade, I transferred to a newly constructed Catholic school in our part of town. The bus rides stopped. The Catholicism continued. The Polish waned. The long, quiet peaceful evenings shared with Busia became long, quiet moments alone. My early immersion years would impact my entire life. Some impacts would be good, some not so. In the year 2010, my wife Marion and I published a book titled, *Sweet Land of Liberty*. Much of the book focused on American immigration and only when it was finished did I understand the gift given to a little boy put on an early morning bus.

I had learned very early that despite the variations of language and culture in America, there is a magnificent core of sameness. There were Blue and Gold Stars in my new neighborhood too. And in my new school each morning we said the pledge to the same country and flag. In truth though, sometimes I'd whisper it in Polish, just for old time's sake.

Still today, whenever I think of those times, my mind returns to that first bus ride that I took alone, a short week after the trial run with my father:

It was 5:50 a.m. Tuesday, the day after Labor Day. I stood alone waiting on the corner of Kennedy Avenue and Cleveland Street for the No. 2 bus. Across the dark street preparing to board his bus on its way north to Lake Michigan and Inland Steel Corporation was my father.

As his bus approached, he waved, smiled, and then he boarded. He seemed a bit nervous but happy. I watched as his bus faded into the northern dark. I continued to watch until the only faint light visible to me in that direction became the headlights of my own approaching No. 2 bus. Though I did not know it at the time, that approaching bus, once boarded, would alter the rest of my life. My formal education as a young American was to begin with a variation determined by my father. I believe, despite the variation, that the Founders of our nation would have heartily approved.

SECTION SIX

THE PRICE OF PREJUDICE

There is a commercial on T.V. these days that advertises a treatment for COPD (chronic obstructive pulmonary disease). The image of an elephant is used symbolically to show the impact of this condition on the daily lives of people who must cope with this health issue. We watch as the elephant constantly makes his presence felt. Sometimes he sits directly on the victim, or he hovers over him, occasionally nudging him with his trunk. Mostly, like Mary's little lamb, he just follows him everywhere he goes.

In schools throughout this country, there is another kind of elephant and, like his T.V. cousin, he constantly makes his presence felt. This elephant truly is like the proverbial elephant that can be found in the middle of the room—you know—the one no one wants to talk about. But we need to talk about him because he is in our classrooms, cafeterias, hallways, locker rooms, and playing fields. He is not real in the physical sense, of course. But he does embody the reality of social and legal changes that have caused teachers to be unsure of their proper role in teaching civility. They fear being sued or losing their jobs. They dread being labeled culturally insensitive, overly judgmental, old-fashioned, or racist.

The fear has caused reluctance on the part of teachers to take actions they might otherwise have considered necessary in order to correct students who are behaving inappropriately. In earlier days teachers were expected by everyone, including students and parents, to correct coarse or vulgar language, insensitive discourse and inappropriate dress, whether that dress was too sexually suggestive or just sloppy. Students were not given a free pass to act or speak in an uncivil manner either to each other or to their teachers. If they did cross that line, they were immediately made aware of their transgression.

Times have changed, indeed. Coarse language and sloppy, suggestive, inappropriate dress and gestures are common. It is not difficult to understand why. Our young people are inundated with such modeled behaviors via music, cartoons, videos, sit-coms, and movies. Celebrities from the entertainment and sports world are constantly and publicly demonstrating this kind of behavior—even gaining approval and notoriety for doing so. Unfortunately, lots of people, especially young people, mimic these behaviors.

Though this behavior is common among our youth in schools everywhere, it has become increasingly difficult for teachers to deal with or to correct, particularly when race is thrown into the mix. Teachers in all settings are sensitive to racial issues. But no matter where their school is located, teachers today worry about offending someone in a way that could quickly become a serious matter that must be formally addressed. They are aware that their actions could result in being sued and/or losing their jobs. So, most teachers go out of their way to avoid even the appearance of being racist or prejudiced in any way. They dread the allegation that can and sometimes does come: "He (she) is picking on me just because I am...."

Remember the defiant student we introduced you to in the first chapter? He was a black student. The assistant principal, Mr. Baker, was white. When the student responded with defiance and disrespect, how should Mr. Baker have handled that situation? Was he right to have just continued to repeat his request? Wouldn't it have been more reasonable to say to that student, "Look, Michael, that kind of talk is really not going to get you anyplace you want to go—it's just going to hurt you. We need to go to my office and have a talk." A truly constructive, appropriate response, most everyone would agree, would have been immediate and would have gone far beyond a reference to the rules in a school handbook. If the fear of being called racist played into this interaction at all, the student was not well-served, for the student would not have been taught that this kind of behavior might, at some future time, cost him his job or cause him to lose in other equally important ways. Was Mr. Baker feeling that elephant looking over his shoulder?

This kind of incident happens all the time. Recall the chapter that describes the kid running through the hallway filled with fellow students while yelling, "I don't want to get married, I just want to f---!" There were teachers in that hallway. Why didn't they respond?

An administrator later said he had asked one of those teachers, "Would you have said something to the boy had he been white?" Her response, after some reflection, was, "Yes, I'm quite sure I would have."

"What would you have done?" he continued.

"Probably would have grabbed him by the arm, pulled him over, and asked him: What is the matter with you? Have you lost your mind? Do you know where you are? Do you have the habit of making a fool of yourself in public places? What right have you to speak to a young girl that way? What would your mother think if she heard about this?"

"That's what you would have done?"

"Yes, something like that, or I would have just taken him to the principal's office."

So, what stopped this teacher from responding in a completely reasonable and appropriate way—in a way that most people, indeed most parents—would have expected and approved? What stopped her from taking this opportunity to explain the importance of civility? What makes it increasingly difficult for teachers who encounter situations such as these to respond as most responsible adults would expect? We think there are many reasons which explain such a failure to act:

First: A teacher who is accused of being racist is often placed in a very difficult position. When such an allegation is leveled, it is almost impossible to prove that it is untrue. Even if there is no formal administrative action taken, a seed of doubt can be planted in the minds, not of just an administrator, but also in the minds of other students. There are places in our country today, especially in major cities, where teachers who have been accused of acting in a racist manner have been removed from their classroom duties until a hearing is scheduled to clear them of this kind of accusation. This can take months, in some extreme cases, years. Yes, you read that correctly, "years."

Second: As we said earlier, teachers were at one time expected to set a standard of behavior and were expected to enforce that standard. When we were young, students expected and accepted corrections all the time. It was part of a teacher's responsibility to correct mistakes in grammar, point out a lack of neatness, or abruptly put an end to disrespectful behavior toward an adult or fellow student. Violent or abusive behavior of any kind would not have been tolerated. Teachers had authority to deal with these issues. Students knew it. Administrators knew it. Parents knew it. Teachers knew it. This is no longer the case.

Third: No one wants to be "culturally insensitive." No one should be. There are ways of speaking and behaving that are particular to certain cultures and are not offensive. No one, including teachers, has a right to criticize these just because they are different. No one, including teachers, has the right to demean a student even if their differences interfere with their ability to communicate. However, there are actions and words that most people would question as being acceptable. Yet teachers are often unsure as to where to draw this line, or whether or not they will be supported in doing so. Remember the administrator who told a teacher he over reacted to the student who told him to "go f--- yourself "? Her explanation to that stunned teacher was to say, "That's just his way of saying good morning." Some teachers may have reacted to this explanation by questioning themselves: What if she's correct? What if this is some kind of cultural thing? What would I know? Attitudes and advice like this coming from people in a position of authority or expertise, whether they are administrators, consultants, or policy makers, can create doubt. This is especially true for inexperienced teachers. The elephant hovers in this way too.

Fourth: There are very tough laws now that guard a student's right to free speech. When the U.S. Supreme Court affirmed this right, it created a complicated situation. For it is not always easy for teachers or any members of our society to determine where to draw the line regarding free speech. Thus, a teacher's reaction to what most people would agree is a serious breach of oral or written behavior, might be to just "let it go." This is not just a casual choice as the U.S. Supreme Court in *Wood v. Strickland* also made teachers legally vulnerable to suit if they were found guilty of violating a student's right to free speech. This legal sanction added a provision that a teacher could not claim ignorance of a student's right to free speech as a defense. Therefore, a teacher had better be absolutely sure that any attempt to correct a student's behavior is within the boundaries of the law, and that can often not be knowable. Seems like the elephant might be sitting on this teacher.

Fifth: There is another reason why these teacher/student interactions are so fraught with difficulty. Again, like the elephant we all know is there but don't talk about, this is a condition that is really not understood. Deep inside the hearts of most white Americans is a sense of helplessness over what has happened and continues to happen to American minorities, especially African Americans because of the horrific history of slavery. To live in a society where offensive or abusive acts can and do occur can make heavy the hearts of us all and often diminish our capacity to render appropriate sanctions on those we see as having already suffered unjustly. This feeling is the elephant which many, especially teachers, carry inside their souls.

In any discussion of this issue it is also extremely important to understand that some of these students are often so hostile that even though teachers try to treat them with dignity, the response they receive from these students is full of anger and distrust. Many of these students even resist being touched. As one teacher explained recently, "I put my hand on a student's shoulder the other day, and he quickly turned to me and with a burning anger in his eyes said, "You keep your f---in' hands off me. I've got rights." This kind of intense lack of trust coupled with a deep-seated resentment can cause many teachers to keep their distance when what is called for is just the opposite.

From where comes this defiance, the steel glare, the wall of resistance, the barrier to interaction, or the body language that suggests a coiled snake preparing to strike?

Chapter 14

A Set of Stories

In response to the extremely important question posed at the end of chapter 13, we offer a series of short true stories that might prove helpful. Such stories are always somewhat painful to read, for they expose partially-healed wounds that still live in the souls of angry and shamed children and adults. These stories that follow are true. However, the names of some persons and places have been changed to provide anonymity where we thought it was necessary.

Join us now for stories of a personal nature that allow us to peer into these somewhat healed wounds, and help to answer the questions: "Why are they so angry?" "How should our teachers relate to them?" There are no easy answers, for as we all know, the seeds of prejudice are buried deep and always have the potential for new growth.

Raymond J. Golarz and Marion J. Golarz

A Proud Young Navajo

It was the first day of a dream project created by Don Sims, Chief Administrator of Riverside Indian School in Oklahoma. Gaagii Nez, a student and proud 14-year-old Navajo had never been so happy. In his hands was his share of that dream—a copy of that day's *USA Today*. He hadn't yet opened the paper. His eyes were fixated on the newspaper label identifying him as the proper recipient. He was holding in his hand *his* newspaper, *his* newspaper addressed specifically to *him*. He gazed at it for a long time. He had never before seen his name on a newspaper. He was so proud. This, his first newspaper, he would save, and at Christmas when he went home to Arizona he would bring it and show it to his grandfather, Niyoi, leader of his family and tribe. It would be a moment of pride.

It was Saturday, the 18th of December. The bus ride that had begun in Oklahoma and was now making its way into Arizona had been uneventful. There would be a stop soon in Flagstaff. He would get off. He needed to go to the bathroom. As he left the bus, he carried only his treasured newspaper.

No sooner had he finished going to the bathroom and washing his hands, when two big white men came in. The bigger of the two looked down at Gaagii and said, "Hey, Indian kid, gimme that goddamn paper."

Gaagii grasped his paper tight, looked up nervously and replied, "Ah …. It is mine."

"Hey, give it here ya motherf---in' little shit—probably can't read it anyway." They then both laughed.

Gaagii, sensing the danger, tried to run and escape, but his pursuers were too big and blocked his way. In the brief fight that ensued, his newspaper was shredded. As he lay on the bathroom floor he could hear the men as they left, "Goddamn it … paper isn't even today's."

Gaagii, too weak yet to stand, crawled toward the urinal where most of his newspaper lay. He found the label with his name and picked it up. It was stained with urine and getting wet now from his own tears falling quietly from his face.

As he lay there on that bathroom floor with the scrap of paper bearing his name held tight in his fist, his whole body filled with rage, shame, and sadness. At that moment thoughts of his grandfather filled his mind. Niyoi would have been so proud—so very proud.

Raymond J. Golarz and Marion J. Golarz

A Trip to the Bus Garage

It was August of 2000, and I was flying to the Deep South. The next day, I would be keynoting in a somewhat obscure community about 100 miles north of the Gulf of Mexico. As I flew that afternoon, I kept pushing evil segregation thoughts to the back of my mind. I continually chastised myself by repeating, "It's the year 2000, what's the matter with you?" The superintendent who would be meeting me was a good friend and an exceptional educator. He had taken this job just six months earlier so he was new to the community. Upon landing, I had almost completely cleared my mind of the evil thoughts. I felt ready. I got off the plane, came through security, and greeted my friend. He smiled, grabbed me by my shoulders and said, "Welcome Ray. Now remember, you're in the Deep South."

We left the airport, got into his car, and began the 60 mile ride, mostly on country roads, to his district. We talked as we drove of families, health, education, and the usual things. We touched on the future, but he seemed reluctant to go there. He had just taken the job, but he wasn't sure how long he wanted to stay.

I was hungry, so we stopped at a roadside café and had supper. We talked more and he told me of the things he hoped I'd cover the next day in my address, such as the ability of all children to learn and also how children cannot achieve unless they first believe they can. These were topics that he and I had discussed often. We finished dinner and then continued our journey. It was getting dark now, and I was getting very tired. Time for a shower, comfortable bed, and sleep.

But, as we approached town, he said, "Ray, want to show you my bus garage."

I was tired, but he hadn't said it casually—more like "I've got something under this blanket I want you to look at."

So, I said after a momentary hesitation, "Sure."

We then drove the remainder of the way without speaking. When we arrived, he drove slowly past row, after row, after row of buses. Finally, I looked over at him and said, "I didn't think your district had this many children."

He looked back at me and said, "We don't. We don't bus the black kids with the whites."

Dr. Hernandez

It was my senior year at St. Joseph's College in East Chicago. It had been a great run, and I had been privileged to have some outstanding professors. They had taught me a lot. There would never really be a way to properly thank them. A favorite of mine was Dr. Hernandez. He had always been so patient with my off-the-wall questions. Therefore, on a very cold day in February, after what I knew was his final Friday class, I stood near his classroom door at 11:15 a.m. waiting for his last students to leave. He saw me and spoke.

"Mr. Golarz."

"Dr. Hernandez. I know I should have made arrangements with you earlier, but you're always so busy. Well, would you let me take you to lunch?"

He stood there for a moment, books in hand, then looked at me and said, "Why not?"

"Oh, thank you, Dr. Hernandez."

"But let me first stop at my office for a moment and drop off my books."

He did so and within minutes we had on coats, scarves, and caps and were crossing Indianapolis Boulevard. We were on our way to a restaurant a short distance from the college, me talking incessantly all the way. We went in, took a booth, and set our winter clothing aside. We then continued our conversation. We talked and talked. Finally, I looked up and around, and then I said, "Doesn't look that busy and we've been waiting a long time."

He cautioned me with his raised hand, a gesture meaning, "Be patient, wait." I did for awhile. After an additional ten minutes I said to him, "Let me check. I'll be right back." He again cautioned, but I ignored his gesture and went up to the bar across the room where the bartender/owner was pouring a beer from the tap. His name was Mike and was an acquaintance—since my friends and I had been there on many occasions.

"Hey, Mike. Can we get someone to take our order? Been here quite awhile."

He stopped the tap, looked at me and said, "Soon as you get the f---in' sp-- outta here." He then took the beer to the customer down the bar.

I was stunned, then angry, and finally enraged. I screamed out, "Hey, Mike," and as I did, I felt Dr. Hernandez's hand on my shoulder. I turned. He stood there with my coat over his arm and said in a quiet, calm voice, "No, Ray, no. I don't want this. Please, Ray, no."

I was trembling, but I put on my coat, my mind filling with thoughts of hate and vengeance. He walked me back across the street. We went to his office where he shared with me his lunch to nourish my body and shared with me other things to also feed my soul.

Heartland Basketball

On January 23, 1998, a racially-mixed high school basketball team got off of the bus in a neighboring Indiana town for a scheduled season game. About a dozen students from the host community greeted the visitors with a barrage of racial slurs including, "Here come the darkies." According to *Sports Illustrated, CNN*, the following then occurred:

During the junior varsity game, several visiting players were bitten by the host players. During the varsity game a member of the all white host team elbowed a black visiting player in the stomach so brutally that the black player began vomiting—as he doubled over on the sideline, a host fan yelled, "That n-----'s spitting on the floor: get his ass off the floor." Threats such as, "You're not safe in this town," continued after the game.[1]

Raymond J. Golarz and Marion J. Golarz

"Old Friends That I Haven't Seen for Awhile"

Attending an after-school party wasn't normally my preferred way of enjoying an evening, but I had been looking forward to this one. I was quite confident that a very attractive young English teacher would be there. She and the teacher hosting the party were good friends. Once there, I found that my instincts had been right. Consequently, the party hours went by rapidly—too rapidly. I and Otto, a fellow teacher, were planning an after-party night cap and he, noticing my preoccupation, said with a full-faced grin, "C'mon, ask her. Maybe she'll join us." The gods were on my side, and this young lady who would eventually agree to be my wife got into Otto's car with us, and we were off.

The party had been near South Chicago, so we decided not to venture too far since we would need later to get our cars. We ended up in Hegewisch at a popular restaurant/bar that I had previously been to, though neither Marion nor Otto had ever been there. We found a round table and ordered our night caps. Soon we had been served and were engaged in great conversation when a husky young man, a bit older than we, tapped Otto on the shoulder, and then whispered something in his ear. The room filled with people was somewhat loud, so neither Marion nor I thought anything of his leaning over and whispering. Otto then excused himself and left with the young man. Marion and I continued our conversation, even considered a second drink, but then it struck me. "Who would Otto know here in Hegewisch? Could he have parked illegally? Would he need my help?" I explained my concerns to Marion. She insisted that I leave her for a moment and find Otto. She assured me that she would be fine.

Toward the back of the restaurant/bar complex was a dance floor that was vacant, except for a handful of men circled around a lone figure, Otto. I hastened my step. Then from behind me two more men appeared. As I approached the group I said, "Excuse me. What's going on?"

The husky man who had come to our table stepped toward me as the others, now numbering seven or eight, circled Otto and myself.

"You the one brought the n----- in here?"

Every synapse in my brain went on full alert, and I could feel my body filling with adrenaline, my heart now racing. The look on Otto's face pleaded with me for restraint.

"Look, we are teachers from Bishop Noll right here in Hammond. Just lookin' to have a drink and then go home." I thought now of Marion, sitting alone.

The husky guy was now in my face. "You Polish?"

"Yeah, I am."

He looked around at his comrades and then back at me and said, "You know, there's nothin' worse than a Polish n----- lover."

I recognized the provocation and felt in my core that it would come again. I was not a stranger to the streets, and so I was very aware of how dangerous these guys really were and of my obligation to Marion and Otto. He punched me hard, first in the chest, and then in the face. I could feel the blood trickling from my nose. He hit me in the chest several times. The blows pushed me farther and farther toward the door. He finally stopped and looked at his friends. Then turned to me and said, "Get your lady and n----- outta here. You're lucky tonight, Pollock—don't come back."

Otto and I went for Marion.

She asked, "What was that all about?"

Otto responded, "Old friends that I haven't seen for awhile."

Raymond J. Golarz and Marion J. Golarz

"Oh, Say Can You See"

An article in the *Conservative Examiner* described what happened to a young, African American teenager Shai Warfield-Cross after she sang the national anthem before a basketball game:

> Shai Warfield-Cross is a 16-year-old high school student who has sung "The Star Spangled Banner" repeatedly at sports events in Indiana's Bloomington High School North in Bloomington without any concerns expressed by the public. However, the first time she performed the song at an event (on January 20, 2011) that included a crowd from Martinsville... there were complaints. The teen was told to perform the song in a 'traditional' way which causes some persons to raise questions about the criticism. In that Warfield-Cross is a black teen and the town from which the visiting Martinsville school comes is predominantly white raced, racism is being raised as a possible reason for the criticism of her performance.[2]

Later, another media source noted that an apology had been made to this student.

"The principal of Bloomington High School North has apologized to a student, for telling her to tone down her singing of the National Anthem after a recent rendition sparked complaints."[3]

We thought, in view of the incident described above, the following information might be of interest to our readers:

According to Scott Paulson of the *Conservative Examiner* in an article dated January 30, 2011, an Indiana State Senator, Vanetta Becker, "is currently pushing for new legislation that would take strong action against those who have the nerve to deviate the national Anthem from its intended melodic rhythms."[4]

Knowing Your Audience

Following are excerpts taken from Internet articles posted in January 17, 2012. Both articles have to do with public comments and reactions to the remarks made by Newt Gingrich, a Republican presidential candidate, during a debate which was held on Martin Luther King Day, January 16, 2012, at the Myrtle Beach Convention Center:

If you want to understand why the GOP is so ill-prepared to compete in an increasingly non-white America, just look at the exchange between Fox News questioner Juan Williams and Newt Gingrich half-way through last night's Republican presidential debate. It being Martin Luther King Day, Williams asked Gingrich whether some poor and minority voters might not be insulted by his claim that poor kids lack a work ethic and that black people should be instructed to demand jobs, not food stamps. Gingrich, as is his wont, haughtily dismissed Williams' question, to wild applause. Then Williams tried again, mentioning a black woman who had taken Gingrich to task for calling Barack Obama a "food stamp" president. By this point, the overwhelmingly white crowd had begun to boo the only African American on stage. When Gingrich insisted that Obama was indeed the "food-stamp" president—because more Americans are now on food stamps—and dismissed Williams' criticism as "politically correct," the crowd began to scream with delight. [5]

The following excerpt was submitted to the *New York Times* blog by Mr. Benjamin Todd Jealous, president of the NAACP:

> It is a shame that the former speaker (Newt Gingrich) feels that these types of inaccurate, divisive statements are in any way helpful to our country. The majority of people using food stamps are not African American, and most people using food stamps have a job.[6]

Notes:

1. *SI Vault*, "Racial incidents in Indiana." February 23, 1998, http://sportsillustrated.cnn.com/vault/article/magazine/MAG1012048/2/index.htm.
2. Scott Paulson, "Non-traditional 'National Anthem' not allowed by

Martinsville, In Crowd," *Conservative Examiner*, January 30, 2011 http://www.examiner.com/conservative-in-national/anthem/non-traditional-national.
3. "School Apologizes to Student over Anthem Flap," rtv6 abc. Jan. 28, 2011 http://www.theindychannel.com/news/26648202/detail.html.
4. Josh Feldman, "This Exists: Indiana State Sen. Proposes Bill to Penalize People Who Sing National Anthem Incorrectly," *Mediaite Columnists*, Dec. 30, 2011. www.mediaite.com/online/This exists--Indiana-state-sen-proposes-bill-to-penalize-people-who-sing-national-anthem-incorrectly.
5. Peter Beinart, "Insulting Comments at Fox News Debate Show Newt Clueless on Black Americans," The Daily Beast January 17, 2012.
6. Gabriel Trip, "Gingrich Pushes Back against Charges of Racism," *The Caucus*, January 6, 2012, http//Thecaucus.blogs.nytimes.com/2012/01/06/gingrich-pushes-back-against-charges-of- racism.

Chapter 15

Pebbles into the Water

The stories that you've just read in the previous chapter are appalling and sadly represent only a handful of such stories out there. The evil that these stories reflect is thrown like pebbles into the waters of a nation's soul, provoking anger that ultimately comes into our American classrooms. These pebbles are the shame of a nation.

The story in the last chapter regarding the recent remarks of Newt Gingrich is particularly appalling because of the crowd's response to his remarks. "The crowd began to scream with delight. By the time Gingrich finished his answer, the crowd was on its feet in a standing ovation." [1]

We are the nation that voices to the world, "Give me your tired, your poor." We are the nation that pledges to one another, "We hold these truths to be self-evident, that all men are created equal." We cheer loudest when the underdog wins. From where then comes the evil spewing from Newt Gingrich's audience? From where comes the evil that leaves a Native American boy shamed and humiliated on a public bathroom floor in Flagstaff? From where comes the evil that strips a 16-year-old black girl of her gift of song and the singing of our country's national anthem in her own American hometown? From where comes the evil found in all of the stories told here, and in the ones we didn't have the time to tell?

In his book, *Racist America: Roots, Current Realities and Future Reparations*, published in 2000, Joe Feagin, the former President of the American Sociological Association, argues that the United States can be characterized as a "total racist society." [2] Is that possible? Are the powerful and noble words espousing our honor just platitudes mouthed by us but not meant? Were they meant only by those before us who left us a task to complete that we have set aside? Or is Joe Feagin wrong? Are we rather a great society that has not yet completed our work of convincing all who live here of our nation's vision, that vision being, "All men are created equal." Deep human suffering comes to us when the pain we are given is inflicted by someone we had assumed to be a friend, brother, or fellow countryman. However, this suffering, this most profound shame, is deepest when inflicted in a place we assumed was safe and secure—a place we thought to be, as Sir Walter Scott says in his poem, *"Patriotism"*, our native land.[3]

It is this deep-seated shame that causes the greatest anger and potential hate to rise to the surface in fellow Americans. It rises to the surface when you, a black child, know that you are still sitting in the back of a segregated school bus 40 years after Rosa Parks. It shows itself when you're a young player lying injured and vomiting on a basketball court and hear from the stands, "That n-----'s spitting on the floor. Get his ass off the floor."

Racism and prejudice die slowly. In their living form they are particularly painful in a society that espouses equality and fair play. The greatest indignation they engender does not come from the remembered and resurrected pains of dead slave ancestors. These, though a painful memory, are not the greatest pain. The greatest pain comes from yesterday or this morning, and all too often schools are among the first to experience their ripple effects.

This new pain comes through schoolhouse doors in many different forms. It comes in the form of a black teacher still wincing from the embarrassment of being denied service as a consequence of his race while out to dinner last night with his wife and son. It comes in the form of a gay adolescent who just suffered a weekend's worth of Internet abuses regarding his sexuality. It lives in the soul of our proud Navaho boy who still keeps the urine-stained scrap of newspaper in his top dresser drawer to remind him to never again trust whites. It simmers in the heart of a girl who spent until early dawn calming and consoling a mother who used food stamps only to be met by the hostility of fellow customers at her neighborhood grocery store.

These and so many others who are hurting come daily through the school house door. They come with their anger, their defiance, and their shame. Pebbles of racism and discrimination have been thrown into the waters of American life and have then rippled into the smaller ponds that are our American schools and classrooms.

These ripples will again inevitably impact an additional unsuspecting teacher, as they did our Mrs. Wilson from chapter 7. And another teacher, as did Mrs. Wilson, will ask a student to sit in her own seat. This student, possibly having spent the whole night calming and consoling a mother who met hostility for using food stamps, will explode. And she in a vicious rage directed at life itself will scream out, "F--- you, bitch. Don't have to move if the seat is empty and it's empty. So quit botherin' me, bitch, and just teach." These new ripples of rage will engulf another classroom. The bedlam will reach out into new hallways and classrooms. And once more there will be another teacher who sits trembling and wondering how she can ever return to her classroom with any comfort and dignity. Following all of this there will be yet another discussion at another assistant principals' meeting where honest people will try again to resolve a continuing problem—a problem they neither created nor had the capacity to resolve.

Many miles and days away in an auditorium, a political candidate asks of an aide "How did it go?" The aide responds, "Great, you really had the audience with you, particularly when you insisted that Obama was the 'food stamp' president. Couldn't you tell by the standing ovation?"

Words to the Wounded and Abused

Schools are not the enemy. They are not the places we come to vent our anger and pain. They are not where we come to kick in a locker, intimidate and steal from a more frightened, younger self in a school bathroom or where we scream out loud, "F--- you," and disrupt the fragile learning environment of a classroom.

Schools and those who serve within them are the sanctuary. They are potentially the best friends we will ever have. They are the way out of the cycle, for within their womb they are entrusted with the only weapon that the rest of society will recognize. They hold the weapon called knowledge. It is the weapon feared by racists, by those who spew hate, and by those who intentionally provoke fights between the brothers named ignorance and poverty. Knowledge is the weapon of choice of all past great leaders and great peoples. It must become the weapon of choice of all who have, because of racism and prejudice, been wounded and abused.

So if you are one who has been injured in this way, wait no longer. Enter this place called school and take advantage of what it has to offer. Earn your weapon of knowledge and then take your part in the war against ignorance and prejudice, for until this war is won, no one is safe. No one will ever be safe.

The last two stories in this section of the book are favorites because they reach back to friends that I had the good fortune to stand with for a moment. How much of the enemy we slew, I do not know. I know only that, though we did not win the war, we fought well.

A Tree Grows in Chicago

From 1986 through 1994 I periodically worked for the CANAL Project of the Chicago schools-Creating A New Approach to Learning. My work involved providing training for teachers and parents in the 110 inner-city Chicago schools, only one-sixth of the total district. Often, I'd go to the school itself. Other times I would work with the staffs and parents from several schools at one time at CANAL Project headquarters at 51st Street on the South Side of Chicago. During the time that I worked with the project, I came to know and become friends with Dr. Phedonia Johnson, the director of this project. She was a tireless and sensitive educator whose heart was always with her schools and her children.

One late afternoon I was passing her door on my way to my car in the parking lot and saw that she was alone. I had heard something disheartening that afternoon and wanted to talk to her about it. When she saw me, she motioned me in. As I entered, she said,

"Ray, sit down, please."

"You know, Phedonia, sometimes you think you've heard and seen most everything, and then you get smacked on the side of your head with a new depth of sadness."

She waited for me to continue.

"Today some teachers and volunteers took a busload of first-grade children from Dunbar Elementary on their first field trip. They went to the Planetarium near the loop on Lake Michigan. I knew of the trip. The principal had told me about it. I had pictured them being so excited as they watched the Planetarium's program of viewing planets and stars.

"I just learned that as the bus approached its destination a number of children got giddy, giggly, and intensely excited as they pointed out the bus windows. The bus was moving down a tree-lined street and many of them had never seen real trees. Their neighborhood is an area made up of a twelve square-blocks, the limits of which are gang boundaries. They had never, for safety reasons, been out of their neighborhood and in their neighborhood there are no trees."

As I looked at Phedonia, I could see her eyes filling with tears. She then looked at me and said, "Ray, there are so, so many things they do not know of."

I Met a Nice Man

I had spent much of Saturday morning working with parents and teachers at Dumas Elementary School on Chicago's South Side. Sylvia Peters was the principal and an exceptional educator. Over time she had begged, borrowed, cajoled, and shamed the surrounding community business owners and anyone else who could help into buying musical instruments for her school so that the children of that school could have an orchestra. She also had asked her faculty to create instructional units around the lives and music of the world's great composers. The instructional program of her school was magical. I left her building about 11:15 a.m. that morning and went to Carver Middle School, where I had been invited by the principal to have lunch with a small group of middle school children in the second floor library.

As I sat talking and eating lunch with the children, eight in number, I noticed that a very pretty sixth-grade girl named Tanya couldn't seem to take her eyes off of me. We continued to eat and talk. Finally, as we were finishing our time together, I looked at her and winked. She smiled and shyly dropped her head. Then I said as she raised her eyes, "I noticed you've been watching me very closely."

She nodded and volunteered the following, "I've had two white lady teachers but I've never seen a white man in person. Just on T.V. I'm glad you're nice."

On my drive home that day I asked myself, "What price does our nation pay for its continued segregation and poverty? What price?"

Notes:

1. Peter Beinart, "Insulting Comments at Fox News Debate Show Newt Clueless on Black Americans," *Election Beast Blog, 01/17/2012.* http://www.thedailybeast.com/articles/2012/01/17/insulting-comments-at-fox-news-debate
2. Joe R. Feagin. *Racist America: Roots, Current Realities and Future Reparations* (New York: Routedge, 2000), 26.
3. Sir Walter Scott, *"Patriotism", The Oxford Book of English Verse, 1250-1900,* Arthur Quiller-Couch, ed. London: Clarendon, 1918.

SECTION SEVEN

THE EVOLUTION AND NEED FOR UNIONS

Chapter 16

Together We Stand

The following first short story is taken from our recently published book, *Sweet Land of Liberty*. The story describes a part of the pain that laboring people in our country endured in the formation of their unions. These were unions they believed necessary in order to secure for themselves a living wage and safe and humane working conditions.

The setting of this book is a small immigrant neighborhood in America immediately after World War I. We see the story as the foundation for the unions that followed, including unions for teachers.

The stories that follow this introductory story are the author's early personal memories of work without unions and memories of some of the pioneer teachers who initiated and nurtured the early growth of teacher unions near Chicago. The chapter concludes with more recent examples of courageous and visionary teacher leadership.

Raymond J. Golarz and Marion J. Golarz

"Sweet Land of Liberty"

In August of 1919, thousands of steel workers across the United States voted to strike the steel companies and steel-related companies of America.

It was Sunday, September 7, 1919, in the early afternoon at the company houses in Hammond, Indiana, adjacent to Standard Steel Car Manufacturing Company, later to become Pullman Standard. It was a hot day in early fall. The temperature by mid-afternoon would reach a high of 89 degrees. Most residents of the company houses, some 7,000, being Polish and Catholic, had attended one of the four masses that morning at St. Mary's Church, located on the northwest corner of Merrill and Tapper. The walk from the company houses was anywhere from six to ten blocks, depending upon the location of your company house.

That morning Joe and Mary Golarz decided to attend the 8:30 a.m. mass with their four children. Even for this earlier mass, the streets were alive with fellow walkers, for few had cars and the trolley that took you to downtown Hammond came down Conkey Street to Columbia where it turned around and went back.

Sunday afternoon at the company houses was tense. Few seemed to want to be inside and despite prohibition, there was a great deal of drinking going on. Men seemed to be clustered everywhere in small groups. Talk filled with frustration and anger could be heard. The children who normally ran and horse-played outside on such days seemed to sense the extreme tension and were subdued. As evening approached, the talk of the men grew louder, the suppers prepared by wives were ignored, and it became obvious, even to the young children, that many of the men now clustering with their fathers, uncles, and adult older brothers were not residents of the company houses. Some wore uniforms decorated with their military rank and honors won while fighting in Europe. Others were simply fellow workers from other neighborhoods who had walked to the company houses. By early evening, mothers had gathered their young children indoors. The one-room residences with a large blanket or sheet nailed to create two rooms was the safer place this evening for their young children.

The light, in some cases a candle, would be put out early tonight, and young ears would go to sleep to the sound of loud talk outside which would fade and eventually be gone without incident by 2 a.m.

Morning sounds around the company houses came early on Monday, September 8th of 1919. And these sounds were uncommon, for they were the sounds of men. They were the sounds of men who would normally be on their way to work. By mid-morning, thousands had gathered. Their numbers stretched on Columbia Avenue as far south as Highland Street. By 1 p.m. the workers began to walk slowly south on Columbia Avenue toward the plant entrance. With them marched a number of returning uniformed veterans from the war. Those other than war veterans marching were primarily Poles, Jews, and other Eastern European immigrants. They marched behind their American flag carried by an honor guard of vets. Those in the lead, notably veterans in uniform, knew that they would be marching into a heavily armed force of company guards and uniformed Hammond police. The marchers were unarmed. As leading marchers looked back they could see what appeared to be a very nervous group behind them. And then spontaneously, as is often common with such tension, the workmen and vets began to sing—to sing a hymn of honor or courage—some tune that would quiet their inner fears, something they all had occasion to know. So, with mouths too dry to spit, they began the very popular marching song known to all Poles of that day, " Jeszcze Polska Nie Zginela," the song sung by General Dabrowski's legions as they marched from Italy to Poland in 1797. Before long, those in front could hear the echo of the song resounding all around them as the entire group of nearly 1,800 marching workmen and vets began to sing. The pace of their step quickened, and the heavy tension began to drain from their faces. The song had the intended consequences, but was too short and ended before the march to the gates had concluded.

Then there was a momentary pause of quiet marching followed by the sound of a lone, but strong yet mellow tenor voice—the voice of Peter, revered cantor of St. Mary's Men's Choir before he went to war. From somewhere near the front of the marching workmen, he began to slowly and powerfully sing, "My Country, 'Tis of Thee, Sweet Land of Liberty…"

Within moments all had joined in, young and old. And the sound of their song, even in its broken English, became a potent melody drowning out all other sounds of that day, including the sound of their marching workmen's heavy shoes. This modern day strike of a wave of new immigrants challenging for better living conditions and recognition of their union had begun. Then the unthinkable occurred. No sooner had they reached the entrance to the plant when shots rang out.

The following is taken from the *American Federationist*, the official written correspondence of the AFL-CIO, American Federation of Labor:

> On the eighth day of September, 1919, in Hammond, Indiana, four Steel Car Workers (one of whom wore the uniform of an American overseas soldier and had just returned from patriotic service to his country) who were striving to better their condition in life, economically, morally, and physically through the agency of a strike, were shot down and killed by armed policemen employed by the City of Hammond and armed guards employed by the Standard Steel Car Company, and at the same time and place, by the same parties, many other workmen seeking to obtain the same ends were shot down and seriously wounded.

Eye witness accounts of that day reported that the slaughter went on for nearly half an hour as workers and veterans ran and attempted to carry fallen comrades to safety. In the end, four workers, including a uniformed and decorated American soldier, had been killed, and the number of severely wounded workers and soldiers exceeded sixty. Further accounts of that day observed that nearly all of those killed and severely wounded had been shot in the back.

Meanwhile in the company houses, responding to the sounds of gunfire and fleeing workers, mothers had gathered their children indoors. Years later, Lefty, this author's father, recounting these events said, "Ma gathered the four of us around an old crate in the middle of the room and had us all get on our knees with her as she pulled out her rosary and began to pray. As she prayed, her eyes filled with tears, and she tried to hold tight to all of us as she trembled. It was one of my very first childhood memories and would later often wake me at night for years to come."

The mortar that would bind these working immigrant Americans to one another and their union had been laced with the blood of friends and neighbors. East Hammond and other American communities like these that suffered such tragedy would never again be the same. These immigrants had not taken the long, hard journey to America with its promise and commitment simply to return to what many had left in foreign lands. A new day would dawn, and they vowed that they and their children would own that new day.[1]

Raymond J. Golarz and Marion J. Golarz

"Lift That Bale"

Many years had come and gone since that strike. I was in my late teens. The steel companies across America and around the south end of Lake Michigan had been running 24 hours a day and stockpiling steel orders in anticipation of another national steel strike predicted to be of extraordinary proportions. I was attending St. Joseph's College, a community college in East Chicago, but I understood that my college days might soon come to an abrupt end. My father was a steel worker. Soon all family resources would need to be focused on food, heat, and essential bills. When the strike finally did start, it hit like a sledge hammer. Virtually everything stopped except for the essentials. Though people could drive their cars to the grocery store, they walked. Everything slowed down. Everyone seemed to know that it would be a long, bitter strike. Any money that people had, they were hoarding and only using for essentials. All of those who were able to work but now without a job were looking for work of any kind.

The third week into the strike I got lucky. While walking from plant to plant near Whiting, Indiana, the South Side of Chicago, and north Hammond, I landed a job. Junior Toy Steel Corporation, some four miles from my home, was looking for two laborers. I filled out the application in their employment office and turned it in.

"You didn't fill out when you could start, kid."

"When do you need me?"

"Now!"

"Then I'm ready."

They let me make a quick phone call home. I took off my tie, rolled up the sleeves of my white shirt, and hit the slippery, greased-soaked floor of the plant running. I had a job.

I had worked lots of part time jobs before, even worked at Standard Forge in East Chicago, but this would be a new level of experience and occasional terror. I would soon find a lack of any plant safety standards, press machines repaired but not replaced since the Great Depression, grease and dirt everywhere, and huge rats. The intense noise from the massive presses never stopped except when they crushed a worker's hand or arm. Workers on piece work (pay for the quantity produced) were constantly attempting to beat the odds for a few more dollars. Those were the most frightening of all moments as you helped or watched the effort made to create a makeshift tourniquet in order to stop the spraying blood. There was no way to stop the screaming. Your prayer always was that he would soon pass out or be taken to a waiting vehicle and rushed to the hospital.

Junior Toy Steel Corporation was my first non-union experience, and I was rapidly learning what that meant. On my third day of work, we had been on a dead run since 7 a.m. It was now noon. The temperature in the plant was near 105 degrees. The lunch whistle blew, and the kid next to me dropped to his knees then wiped his brow with his work glove.

The foreman came over to him and said. "You. Get back on your feet. You guys aren't done."

The kid said. "The lunch bell."

"There ain't no lunch today. You're behind. You work faster tomorrow, you eat. Today you work till you catch up."

The kid got up, looked at the foreman and said, "Bullshit. I'm gonna eat."

The foreman then pointed at him and said, "You're fired. Outta here."

From noon till 1:30 p.m., I worked alone. By 1:30 a new kid had been hired. There were always six or seven guys waiting on an old wooden bench in the sun outside of the employment office hoping for a break. I felt bad for the guy who got fired, also for the new kid in the white shirt with the rolled-up sleeves. He'd never get the grease out of that shirt—had one hanging in my closet just like it at home.

The non-union experience was incongruent with my nature. I suspect it's incongruent with the nature of all of us. I was the only one in our family working so we needed the job. I found myself taking a lot of abuse for fear of losing the job. It wasn't a good feeling.

The worst came during my second month of work. The temperature in the plant that day exceeded 120 degrees on the upper floor near the tin roof where steel was stored in large bins and needed to be shoveled into large wooden boxes below. I was up there shoveling alone. I had been shoveling for about an hour. I was beginning to cramp and was soaked. Even the insides of my shoes were soaked from the sweat running down my legs. They would be coming for the loaded boxes in 15 minutes. I knew I could finish filling the boxes in ten minutes then catch a five minute break, or I could use the five minutes to run to the bathroom near the locker room and urinate—something I had been holding off doing, but couldn't anymore. We got no bathroom breaks, only the ones we might manage if we worked faster. I chose civility. Then with my arms alone, I moved my shaking legs down the wooden ladder but began to cramp badly in both legs. Finally, I just hung there and almost without my consent I began to urinate. I hung onto that ladder, urinating, cramping, and weeping at the same time. Anger was filling my whole soul while shame waited its turn.

Five minutes later I was again shoveling, filling the next empty boxes. I vowed to myself that I would fill those boxes until I dropped. I was distancing myself from those I worked for. My anger was turning to bitterness and hate. I began to understand how camaraderie and good feelings between employees and employers could be crushed, and as importantly, I was learning how easily it could have been preserved.

The Growth Years of Teacher Unions

I was doing my student teaching. I had already taught on emergency licenses, but was now taking appropriate coursework and attempting to professionalize my license. I had been assigned by the college to do my student teaching at Hammond Technical Vocational High School. I would be teaching economics. My students would be primarily seniors, and my supervising teacher would be a very proper Mr. Henry Callantine. He was about five feet, nine inches tall, a tad stout, balding, wore wire-rimmed glasses, and was always impeccably dressed down to his shoes that looked to have a Marine Corps spit shine. He occasionally sported a cane that gave him a rather dapper look.

As I worked under his tutelage, I found that his best friend and colleague was another teacher of his vintage, a Mr. Gerald Kackley. After school, at a long table in the back of Mr. Callantine's room, the two of them would work for hours on potential contract language for the Hammond Federation of Teachers. They would discuss and debate various concepts such as working conditions, benefits, tenure, and a host of others. I found their discussions absolutely intriguing. Sometimes they would let me pull up a student desk and simply listen. On rarer occasions, Mr. Callantine would actually take me aside at day's dusk, and we would talk till dark—me with my questions, he with his patient, fatherly answers.

"You see, Mr. Golarz, teacher unions or associations are here for much, much more than the bargaining of wages. One of our primary focuses has to do with working conditions. Across the United States we still have teachers who work without a break from the time they enter the building until they leave. They are engaged in either supervision or teaching young people every minute of every work day. To use the bathroom, they need to find someone to cover their assignment. Their lunch is reduced to a piece of fruit eaten while walking through the cafeteria and supervising young people who are eating their lunches. You understand?"

"Yes, sir. I believe that I do."

"Mr. Golarz, some day you may be a master teacher supervising other teachers or you may opt to be an administrator. Whichever you do, show your colleagues respect and preserve their dignity, and they will give you back a hundred fold. The leader who preserves their dignity will hold in his hand their hearts, and they will spend their days of teaching in harmony with you."

Union Leadership with Courage and Vision

Over the years I became quite good at securing grant monies for the school district, so the then superintendent, Dr. Frank Sanders, sent me to Indianapolis in the dead of post-Christmas winter to get some money. I made contact with Dr. Dean Evans, the State Superintendent of Public Instruction. He invited me to drive down, but advised me that he would need me to bring a complement of Hammond leadership that extended beyond the schools. Dr. Sanders complied with the request and the entourage included business people as well as two school board members.

When we arrived in Indianapolis, we were hosted by Drs. Gary Phillips, Gil Johnson, John Paden, and John Boehner, representatives of the Eli Lilly Foundation, Kettering Foundation, IDEA, and State Department. We didn't know at that point that they were selling an innovative approach to school governance and had decided that we were to be their principal customer. Only later did we learn that they had developed a new school improvement concept that they wanted to launch in a near perfect environment. For them that environment needed to be an urban school district with significant pockets of poverty and racial diversity—not too big (Chicago) and not too small. We were perfect. Within four days and during an unanticipated Indianapolis blizzard, they had convinced us to become a national pilot for the Kettering/Lilly school improvement project.

All professional development and community training would be paid for by the foundations. I remember calling Dr. Sanders on day four and explaining the extraordinary excitement of the entire group he had sent. I must say he seemed less than ecstatic. He had sent forth his grant-securing wizard to purchase a cow, and I was telling him how excited he would be about the handful of beans we were bringing back home.

Raymond J. Golarz and Marion J. Golarz

Planting the Beans

The first in the Hammond community to embrace this new exploratory educational effort was the Hammond Federation of Teachers under the direction of their president, Mr. Pat O'Rourke. Pat, with his leadership people and the involvement of Al Shanker, national President of the American Federation of Teachers, saw the potential in this new concept for improving schools. Even though the concept was not without peril to teacher organizations because of its design of shared power, the AFT stepped forward as the primary leadership component.

The pilot began with three schools. Each had outstanding leaders who, in addition to union support, were the persons most instrumental in the success of this effort. They were Dr. Elizabeth Ennis at Hammond High School, Dr. Jane Kendrick at Eggers Middle School, and Mr. Mike Hriso at Spohn Middle School. Within four years, primarily due to the successes at these three schools, all of the schools in the district became involved. Teams of parents, teachers, administrators, support staff, students, and community persons were designing and implementing improvement plans in each school that were unique to their needs. There were struggles, of course. There were no district-wide models anywhere in the country to study and learn from. The greatest praise in years to come that could be given to the Hammond effort was its continued commitment to its consensus design. Where Chicago's parents in later years went to war with administrators and teachers, where San Diego decided to battle teachers from the top, Hammond stayed true to its original design of shared leadership. This was unquestionably due to the continued commitment that was spearheaded by its teachers and their union leadership. Without that continued leadership the concept would have crumbled as well as the benefits that came to students in those years.

Note:

1. Raymond J. Golarz and Marion J. Golarz, *Sweet Land of Liberty* (Bloomington, Ind.: AuthorHouse, 2011), 7-12.

Chapter 17

Southern Indiana

Marion and I were considering taking a different superintendency located in beautiful Southern Indiana. The community was racially, economically, and ethnically diverse. Within its boundaries it had neighborhoods in the older part of town, newer suburban areas, and farms. It had a great Indiana high school basketball team, two colleges, and great doctors. Most importantly, it had an absolutely astute school board. What else could a superintendent ask for? The only negative was its reputation for a hostile teachers' union. During my first year on the job, that reputation seemed accurate. We couldn't seem to keep high school principals. There was always a rash of grievances. Bargaining a contract was brutal and never agreed to for more than one year. Required meetings were always tense and filled with anger, and trust in administrators was minimal.

The eventual break and movement toward trust with union leadership came with two strategies. The first was the hiring of a new assistant superintendent for finance, Dr. Anthony Broadwell. Tony was a life long friend who had worked with me when we were young teachers working the streets of poverty neighborhoods. Tony had moved his way up the finance side of school business and had a reputation as a no-nonsense, straight-shooter who hid nothing from constituents, school boards, or teacher union leadership. He was known as the guy who would always "tell it like it is." He was the critical breath of fresh air that we had to have.

The second strategy was a simple directive from me and the school board to all administrators. "Never fight back." In my youth I had learned that a good boxing match or a good street fight took two. To stop a fight someone has to stop fighting, so as difficult as the teachers' union might be, we would not fight back.

Several months after initiating this strategy, I remember coming out of a monthly meeting with union leadership and having a frustrated young administrator stop me in the hall and angrily challenge the strategy: "Dr. Golarz, you can't let them disrespect you that way. You're the superintendent. Their comments were demeaning." I could feel his frustration, but knew things he wasn't aware of. Union leadership was trusting Tony, grievances were declining, and we seemed slowly to be moving toward an uneasy calm.

The next month we had a turning-point meeting. During the early part of the meeting, it was as if evil were having its final death-throes. The anger and viciousness went on for nearly an hour. Somehow the time seemed right, so without a script, simply acting on gut instinct alone, I blurted out for all to hear, "I don't know who you were married to before, but I am not that person." The room got silent. Then there was muffled laughter, finally open laughter. More open laugher. Then silence again.

At this point, Stu Thomas, the revered emeritus leader of the union who always sat near the end of the table but seldom spoke, looked up and with tears of laughter still filling his eyes, he said, "It's time. It's time." As he spoke, he maneuvered his wallet out of his back pocket, reached into it and pulled out a tattered and worn two week pay stub of $2.47 that he had received as a teacher at the end of a brutal teachers' strike from many years earlier. He had kept the stub to remind himself to never again trust school board members and administrators. He then in the presence of all at the table tore up the stub and repeated, "It's time."

It's so very difficult to explain what happened after that. When the nature and climate of an organization changes, it's somewhat like watching the lights on a Christmas tree when they're set to flash randomly. Changes are occurring, but you just can't predict when and where the next will be. Tony and I got invited to a "teachers only" bar for an after-work beer—we went. A few days later I was invited to Stu's classroom during his prep period. We talked. I mostly listened. He told me of the superintendent who had preceded me. As he and that superintendent were signing the agreement to a negotiated teachers' contract, the superintendent said to the union leadership and Stu in front of a gathered group of teachers: "If you were so damn smart, you'd have known that I had a full percentage point yet to give when you gave in and agreed to settle." He told me of other abuses that had come from other administrators and superintendents—a long history of unprofessional, belittling, and evil incidents.

Marion hosted several house parties that included school board administrators and teacher leadership. Someone began wine and cheese gatherings at the Radisson on Friday evenings for members from these same groups. The culture of the organization was changing, but changing while still respecting and protecting the natural and necessary boundaries of both the board and teachers' association. It was sort of an instinctive protection that we somehow afforded one another because the bond of trust we were forging was too important to risk losing. We all fell into this mutual bond of protection, whether school board members, teacher leadership, or administrators. An example of how this had impacted me occurred one late afternoon at the administration center. I was walking to my office and encountered a newly hired young math teacher coming the other way. He spoke first.

"Good afternoon, Dr. Golarz."

"Michael, isn't it?"

"Yes sir."

"Aren't you going to the teachers' meeting at the high school across the parking lot, Michael? Think it started about ten minutes ago."

"Well, I'm not going, sir. I don't believe in that unprofessional stuff. I'm for kids—kids and the school district."

I thought to myself, "Should I?" I was not really not permitted to involve myself in the decisions of teachers regarding their involvement or choice not to be involved in their professional organizations, but he looked so young and naïve. I thought of past teacher association leaders that I had known: Pat O'Rourke, Mr. Henry Callentine, Vidal Lopez and then I said, "Michael, sit here with me for a moment. Your first year teaching?"

"Yes, sir. I'm really excited."

"Michael."

"Yes, sir."

"Michael, do you know where my primary allegiances need to be as I carry out my job as superintendent?"

He looked puzzled.

"To the children of the district, to teachers, and to a balanced budget."

He sat silently and nodded.

"Do you know where the primary obligation of the teachers association is and will continue to be?"

He again looked puzzled.

"Their primary purpose is the education of children and your protection, including the protection of your job. If things in this district ever get really bad financially for whatever reason, and my key administrators advise me that we must cut positions including teacher positions like yours to balance the budget, I would have to make that recommendation to the school board. Who do you think would be fighting that recommendation with all of the wisdom, creativity, and charisma they could muster?"

He sat there silent and then responded, "Nobody ever explained it that way."

I looked back at him and said, "Your call, Michael. Your call."

We parted company in the hallway, and I went to my office. Several minutes later I saw a tall, lanky young math teacher at a quick pace crossing the parking lot. I said to myself, "Good call, Michael. Good call."

A Union Comes Through

It was a cold, late afternoon near the Christmas holidays. I had a great deal of paperwork so was in my office late. Ruthie poked her head in and said, "Dr. Golarz, there are two young teachers out here who would like a moment of your time."

"Send them in, Ruthie."

I set aside my papers in a disorganized pile, stood up, and greeted my two young colleagues, Sam Thomas and Dar Haywood.

"Sam, Dar, what can I do for you?"

Sam began. "Well, you know, Dr. Golarz, how you and the board are always asking us to think outside the box, be bold, don't be afraid to try new things?"

I nodded.

"Well, Dar and I and some others would like to start a new school."

For the next three hours, I listened to the enthusiastic dream of two teachers. They had many more questions than they had answers. Our lengthy conversation produced more logistical negatives than positives, and their chances of success in a time of financial constraints didn't appear good. What they did have was boundless enthusiasm, immense energy, and a belief that they could, if given a chance, create something that would be truly exciting for kids and for a community in need of hope. How could anyone say no? So I cautiously advised them that I would take their idea to the board and leadership people in our organization. I would attempt to get them conditional approval, but I warned them that if I were successful, the work for them would be immense. I watched them as they floated out of my office. Through the window I could see them near the parking lot engaging one another in excited conversation. Their saga of creation but mostly hard work was just beginning.

For the next year they were tireless, speaking to an endless number of teacher groups, making school board presentations, state department visits, holding parent meetings, designing and redesigning, doing cost factor analysis, and working on location considerations. They were building a dream, a dream of a new school. At a school board meeting in November, Sam and Dar made a presentation. They concluded their presentation by reading Dr. Seuss's book, *Oh, the Places You'll Go.*[1] Soon afterwards in response to that presentation, the new school would have a name—"Discovery."

It was right about that time that I got a late afternoon visit in my office from Bill Fish, the president of the teachers' association.

"Bill, please come in. What brings you out on this wintry December afternoon?" He sat, looked up and said, "Ray, had you asked me a year ago if these young teachers could create their own school, I'd have bet against it."

"Truthfully, Bill, I didn't know that they would pull it off either—all of the logistics, groups they had to convince, paperwork, monetary considerations—it's been mind boggling."

Then he looked up soberly and said, "Ray, we have a problem."

I nodded and encouraged him to continue.

"Ray, if this school gets approved by the state and the school board, and that looks now as if it will occur, then one of the next steps will be a determination as to the kind of licensed teaching staff that will be needed for the new school. Immediately afterwards the following will need to occur: posting of such positions, allowing six weeks for those interested to bid on the new vacancies, and then selection of staff based almost exclusively upon the applicants' district seniority. Ray, I'm confident that there are teachers in this district with more seniority than those designing and creating this school who will bid on these new positions. Our own agreement with the board will keep these young teachers from teaching in the school they created."

A hush filled the room. After a long silence, I said, "Got any ideas?"

"Yeah, Ray, I do, but let me call you about it later tonight. Right now I have an association leadership meeting I need to go to."

He left. Ruthie and I turned out the lights, set the night alarm, and I drove the long way home. I got a phone call later that evening around 9:30 p.m.

"Ray?"

"Yeah, Bill."

"Need to see you tomorrow with some teacher association leadership. We think we have a solution."

"What time, Bill?"

The Problem Isn't Teachers

"About 4 p.m., your office. Have a couple of school board members there if you want to. See you then."

The next afternoon at 4 p.m., Bill and three association leadership members walked into my office. I had been waiting with the school board members. Once everyone was settled, Bill and the association members made the association's position clear. Together they informed us of their resolution. The following summarizes what they said:

> The teachers' association has never been in the business of stifling the creative energies of our members. We have, as you have, watched these young teachers dream and create for over a year now. We didn't think they would come this far. But they have, and now their own district teachers' contract may be in their way. We, the association leadership, will not let this happen. The association of teachers is going to forge contract language unique to this situation and preclude the seniority clauses of our contract from causing them to not get the teaching assignments that they designed. Once we have done so, we would request that you, the superintendent, and school board, sign off on the addendum language so that the dreams and plans of these teachers can move forward.

The bold and unprecedented move by the teachers' association was one that we believe would happen more frequently everywhere if associations were treated with trust and respect. It is the atmosphere of tension and antagonism that stops such positive actions from occurring. Creative visioning seldom occurs in hostile environments

The next fall after many logistical meetings and hard work, the Discovery School began. A stratified lottery was used to select the 160 K-6 grade students. The enrollment included boys and girls, blacks and whites, rich and poor, special education and regular education. There were no exceptions made to the results of the lottery. Even Sam's son, whose name had been placed by Sam and his wife into the lottery, never attended the Discovery School. His name had not been drawn, and Sam's commitment to fair play would not allow anyone to change the rules so that his son could attend. For over ten years, until the Discovery School merged with the Elizabeth Starr Academy, it had a waiting list of from 80 to 100 families.

The language adopted by the teachers' association had designated that the superintendent and president of the teachers' association were to select the first two teachers to serve as faculty at the new school. Those two teachers, in accordance with the newly adopted contract language, would then choose the remaining staff.

The clearest understanding of community involvement and commitment to participation that I ever heard came to me one day when I asked Sam and Dar, "What will this new school be like beyond the vision prescribed for all American schools?" I recall that they looked at one another and then back at me and said, "Dr. Golarz, we don't really know. We haven't yet met with the parents."

Collaborative Bargaining

I had just come back from lunch when Ruthie came in and advised me that Bill Fish had called and requested that I come to his classroom after school. At 3:30 p.m. I walked into Bill's classroom. He was finishing with two after-class students and motioned for me to take a desk. Soon the students left. Then Bill grabbed a desk and scooted it along the floor so that it was next to mine.

"Ray?"

"Yeah, Bill."

"Stu wants to do collaborative bargaining."

"Collaborative bargaining?"

"Yeah. You know. Win—Win. That sort of thing."

"Well, Bill. I have to talk to the board first, but I'm sure they're going to agree."

"Well, you talk to the board. Stu wants to take this a step at a time, so let the board know that our talk this afternoon was simply preliminary. If the board is agreeable, then Stu would like to meet with you at Earlham College here in town, take a walk in the woods adjoining the campus, and talk it through."

"Agreed, Bill. I'll ask the board to call an executive session (a special meeting not open to the public held for discussion of specific topics that can legally be discussed in private), and then I'll get back to you in a week or so."

As I walked the two flights down to the main floor exit, I kept saying to myself, "I don't believe it. I don't believe it. Hope we can pull it off."

The school board was perfect—supportive, excited, but cautious. We were taking a step into new territory, and we all knew it. It could go wrong. These things sometimes do. Was the trust level high enough? Could we suffer the bumps that any bargaining session can bring? Dr. Broadwell, all of the board members, and I had been together for nearly six years. We knew each other quite well. If there was a time to try this, it was probably now.

Toward the end of the executive session, I was told to have that walk with Stu and cautioned and reminded that the walk itself was a bargaining session—so, "don't give away the store." That comment was followed by some smiles, winks, pats on the back, and a final, "but don't give away the store." We all laughed. I then got momentarily pensive and remembered a torn-up pay stub and the words, "It's time. It's time."

Agreeing to Guidelines

Earlham is a quiet little college in the southwest corner of Richmond, Indiana. The campus has an adjoining section of wooded acres and winding paths that take you through the mature and maturing oaks, maples, chestnuts, and various kinds of pines. Fifty yards into the woods, the quiet of a rural southern Indiana campus wraps its arms around you, and you can usually then cast aside any of the day's concerns and problems and allow the masterful work of the Creator to take over and fill all of your senses. It's not an experience you soon forget.

We had walked slowly that early afternoon, enjoying the rays of sunlight slicing through the trees now in winter, naked of their clothing of leaves. We had talked so far only of the simple things like families and friends that are the cherished memories we each keep stored in our hearts. We were enjoying the real treasures of one another and in so doing becoming better friends, as it was intended that we do.

When it was time, we found a bench in those woods, then sat down and together fashioned the things we believed necessary for the success of this planned venture.

Stu began. "I will do this thing and preside as chair for our teachers only if you agree to chair for the board and sit with me at all sessions," I smiled as we clasped one another's hands. The rest of what we agreed to was easy and is as follows:
- We would seek, find, then mutually agree to a facilitator who would be with us throughout and carry us through the process.
- Our leadership people would participate in the process. This was to include a majority of the board members.
- Dr. Broadwell, trusted associate superintendent, would be at all sessions.
- We would hold the sessions on the campus of Earlham College

in the retreat center adjacent to the meadow where horses grazed.
- Our sessions would begin at 8:30 in the morning with a joint breakfast. At noon we would lunch together, and we would conclude each day when we agreed that further work for that day would be fruitless.
- Teachers participating in the bargaining would be paid their regular pay for that work, and the district would provide substitutes for their classes in their absence.
- The focus of our work would be the contract language, and it would be our goal to create contract language that would enhance the dignity of teachers and the school district.
- We would do as much small-group work as possible using the extensive wooded grounds as places to sit, gather, and work.
- We would invite to our sessions any of our extended membership who felt a strong need to be present for a specific topic we were planning to discuss.
- We would press our membership to complete all sessions by early summer for the needs of being with our families would then be upon us and to lose sight of that obligation would be incongruent to what we were about.
- Finally, if we missed anything in these items agreed to, we would jointly create the missing pieces.

The sessions, once under way, went smoothly. This success was in no small measure a credit to the skills of the facilitator we chose, Bob Cambridge, an attorney from Bloomington, Indiana. Bob had come to us with highest recommendations from another trusted attorney, Pete Goerges of the Bose, McKinney and Evans law firm in Indianapolis. From our first joint preliminary meeting with Bob, it was clear to all that he was masterful. He had done this sort of thing before, and he brought all of his past experiences to bear on his intention to assist our success. What he was most skilled at was preserving his personal commitment to maintaining neutrality. Never, despite our testing, did he allow us to corner him into either supporting or chastising either side. For him the process was always sacred.

New Beginnings

On day one we began, each with a complete copy of the current contract before us. Our task was to create a contract language that would enhance the dignity of teachers and the school district. As we pored over the document, it began to become very clear to all of us that in this first year we would probably not be able to complete the task because of the obvious need for profound changes in virtually every section of the contract. The document before us had been written for a different age and for what appeared to be people at war. Section after section had been written in a heavy, legalistic, demeaning, and threatening language.

I thought back to my first superintendency. I was scampering to perform opening school duties when my secretary Pat raced into my office and placed in front of me on my desk a letter for my signature.

"Dr. Golarz, I'm sorry. This is late. Can you please sign it?"

"Sure, Pat."

I grabbed my pen as she waited and then positioned the paper for signing. As I did, I noticed several words and phrases in the body of the letter that bothered me. I read further. Then I looked up at Pat and said, "Who gets this letter?"

She responded, "It's the opening-of-school letter from the superintendent to all teachers. Dr. Jackson worked hard on it over the years, so I just retyped the one from last year and put your name at the bottom. It's late."

"Pat, thanks so much for your efficiency and recognition of timeliness, but let me take this home and look it over. I'll have something for you tomorrow. I promise."

On the way home that afternoon I thought, "I'm sure that teachers need to know that their pay will be docked if they miss a significant part of any work day, *but in a welcome back to school letter?*"

Several days later I got a visit from Vidal Lopez, president of the teachers' association. He popped his head into my office door and said, "See you changed the letter."

I just looked up and smiled. He then said, "Come to my classroom sometime. Let's have coffee."

Language of the Heart

The task before us in the retreat center at Earlham College would take some time, but we all knew it was doable, for we were of like minds. The days of creating and rewriting would drift by, as would the small-group discussions under the trees. Eventually, there would be an end to the shared meals, the moments of disagreements and arguments, and the times of pensive reflective thinking, but the pride that came with the joy of having worked together to create a new language would never end.

It was our twelfth day of bargaining now, and the days of leaning over wooden pasture fences and watching horses feed while the sun dropped below the distant tree lines would soon be over. We had saved one contract language piece for the end. We did not clearly know why. It was as if we understood that it would, in its difficulty, present for us a final gift. So on that last day after breakfast, we addressed a section titled, "Bereavement." It read as all such provisions of that nature read:

> When a parent, spouse, child, or grandparent dies, a teacher will receive five days paid leave to attend the funeral. Uncles, aunts, nephews and nieces—two days. Death of other relatives or a friend requires the use of personal business days not to exceed two. Usage beyond such limits will be unpaid.
>
> The language fashioned under the trees that late afternoon to replace that bereavement language read as follows: *When a loved one dies, and you define who a loved one is, take the time you need.*

Our collaborative bargaining session was over. It had lasted twelve days. It was the shortest successful bargaining session the district had ever had. It had taken only a third of the time of the previous shortest session. Its total cost in money was less than what we had ever spent. Its total savings in probable frustration, bitterness, anger, and resentment—not measureable. Did we, "give away the store"? Actually, I did not work for a school board that felt that we really owned it.

Five years after leaving that superintendency, I was keynoting a conference for the American Southern Schools in Charlotte, North Carolina. As I walked up the stairs that morning to check the microphone on the podium, I noticed five teachers and an administrator from the Richmond schools. I walked to the edge of the stage, knelt on one knee and motioned them over.

"What are you doing here? You're not from the South."

We saw that you were speaking and wanted to come to hear your speech, so we paid our own way. Dr. Golarz, will you please tell them the story of the bereavement language?"

"Well, sure. I'd love to, but why?"

"Well, in the last five years since you left no teacher has ever taken more than five days."

Somewhat surprised, I replied, "But they can. If they need to, they can."

"No, Dr. Golarz, no. We will never give a future leadership cause to take from us something that we fashioned with our hearts."

It was difficult to tell their story as I keynoted that morning and looked into their smiling, proud faces—just kind of difficult. They were so sincere and made me so proud.

When Stu Thomas passed away, Marion and I went to his funeral. First, we stood outside in a light rain. Then we waited in the snake-like inside line for three hours. When finally we got to his coffin and Stu's family, his mother looked up and said, "Oh, Dr. Golarz, have you seen his obituary? He so wanted you to know. He so wanted you to see it. He was always so proud. In his obituary he wanted it noted that he was the teacher association's bargaining chair and spokesperson for the first collaborative bargaining effort. He was always so proud of that, so very proud."

As Marion and I drove back home that night, my mind moved from union leader to union leader: first, Stu Thomas and Bill Fish; then Vidal Lopez, Pat O'Rourke, and Al Shanker; then, Mr. Jerald Kackley and Mr. Henry Callantine. Finally, I recalled Mr. Callantine's words from so long ago, "Show your colleagues respect and preserve their dignity and they will give you back a hundred fold. Preserve their dignity, and you will hold in your hands their hearts, and they will spend their days of teaching in harmony with you."

Note:

1. Dr. Seuss, *Oh, The Places You'll Go!* (New York: Random House Children's Books, 1960).

SECTION EIGHT

FOR EXTRA CREDIT

Marion and I have noticed that with each book we have written we are compelled to write several pieces that go beyond the major theme of the book but are essential to it. In the writing of The *Power of Participation* we used a building construction metaphor throughout the book. Thus, the last chapters that opened new issues and questions in that book were put into a final section titled, "Some Blocks Left Over." With this book, *The Problem Isn't Teachers,* the principal writing fits into stories and discussions that are focused on problems outside of the control of teachers: *problems that our country must address, for they are the nation's problems, not the problems of teachers.*

Having completed that part of the book which focused directly on those problems, we now have several chapters that we believe are essential to the whole story—chapters that go beyond problems and complete the painting of the still partially-naked canvas. These are chapters that we think may be most enjoyed after reading the sections of the book dealing with the nation's problems. Thus, the last major section of the book is titled, "For Extra Credit." The issues we included here are meant to function just like the follow-up discussion sections that so often follow textbook chapters. Like those sections, these stories are intended to provoke a deeper analysis or inspire conversations which express different points of view.

Chapter 18

Thoughts from the Trenches

Over the past 20 years, I have had the rare privilege of working in school districts and educational conferences all over this country and in most of Canada. During these times Marion and I have had many conversations with school administrators and teachers, and we have made a habit of asking them about their work. We have found, whether in Seattle, Boone, North Carolina, Miami, or Regina, Saskatchewan, that what they told to us had significant commonalities. In addition, we found teachers and administrators everywhere daily giving it their best shot. The question heard most often from them was, "Why the hell are people so mad at us?" It's a question we've really had no good answer for and a question that, in part, prompted the writing of this book. Marion and I, over the years, have talked of these conversations with teachers and grappled with ideas as to how to take these thoughts and put them into some compelling format in the book. We have found that simply using charts or graphs filled with statistics or even quoting heavily from scholarly research is oftentimes ineffective, so we use this kind of approach sparingly. Then, recently on a trip out east, we met and had a conversation with a teacher who had the capacity to bluntly describe what teachers have to struggle with and how they cope. He didn't beat around the bush, just told his story straight out. He had been teaching for fifteen years and had been everywhere. He had taught in both wealthy schools and poor schools in various parts of our country. I remember thinking, "What a delightful guy to be with," and then we asked him the question, "Would you do an interview?" He responded, "Sure, why not, but don't buckle me down too tight. When I talk, I tend to bounce all over the place. " Then he asked, "By the way, what's the interview for?"

"A book."

He hesitated for a moment, looked at us and said, "Been around a bit, let's say we make it anonymous—okay with you?"

We responded. "No problem."

What follows is that interview. We tried to focus the questions in the interview on the ideas, concerns, and issues we've been hearing about from teachers all over the country.

A Glimpse Inside Our Classrooms

Question: Can you talk about how a typical day goes? When is it easiest? When hardest?

Response: It's never easiest. Now if you mean when do you need to dig into your bag of tricks less frequently to make it through the period, then we're talkin' first period. Many of the students aren't even awake yet. The day gets more complex and difficult as you move closer to lunch. The period just before lunch is typically the most difficult of the morning, but the period right after lunch is the most difficult of the day. For that period you better have your skates on and buckled tight, especially if the cafeteria had a lot of sugar choices or if the kids were heavy into those damn vending machines. In that case, you might soon be peeling some of your students off the ceiling. Sixth or seventh period, the last period, is the second most difficult. By the way, you can kiss off this whole definition of difficulty if your school is on block scheduling and you are teaching remedial, basic, or special ed.

Question: What do you mean?

Response: Block scheduling, you know, ninety-minute periods?

Question: Can you explain?

Response: Okay. Well, with adolescents, if you're good and really know your stuff, you can keep 'em engaged and learning for maybe 45 minutes, unless you're talking about advanced placement kids, or physics or chemistry, but for my kind of kid, you're doing really great if you can do 45 minutes. Now, after lunch and during the last period of the day, you can keep them really engaged for maybe half an hour, but you better be moving. Keep in mind, regardless of how good you are, problem behavior begins to occur the closer you get to the end of any period, assuming you're trying to keep them engaged in learning. Oh, if your objective is just to keep them quiet, you can do that. Just give them a work sheet. But if you're really trying to teach—then half an hour to 45 minutes. Now, let's throw some things into the mix that will take down even the best of teachers. Make the periods 90 minutes long. Make the students a combination of special education, remedial, and basic. Be alone in the room with no aide and, finally, make it right after lunch. Getting the picture? At the end of the day with experiences like that, you are absolutely raw meat. Make it a poverty inner city school, and when it's over you'll just want to sit there without moving and stare at a blank wall for about three hours.

Question: How do you handle disruptive kids?

Response: Do you mean disruptive, or really disruptive?

Question: I mean how you handle *really* disruptive kids.

Response: Well, when you're new and young and don't know any better, you send them to the office. You know, get on the phone, ask someone to come down to your room to escort 'em. Hang up. Wait 15 or 20 minutes for them to arrive while this kid further disrupts and makes a total shambles of any dignity and order left in your room. Watch other students get into the fray because you appear now to be inept. Finally, somebody picks up the kid. Then you try to regain control of your class. Twenty minutes later, the kid comes back into your room with a note advising you that he's been talked to and that you should follow up with a parent conference. Now, on the other hand, if you've been around for a while, you buy a life-time pass into the "let's share" teacher network.

Question: What's that? How's that work?

Response: Okay, look. You don't want to keep sending kids to the office—get's you on the administrative "can't teach" list. Not good for your continuing good mental health or your career. People will now be sent to your room suggesting various instructional strategy conferences; no administrator will be willing to approve your temporary teaching license. You know, bad stuff. So, if you're lucky, at some point, some older, relaxed-looking teacher will see you in the lounge, shaking while you're trying to pour your coffee, and he will invite you into the life-time "let's share" club. Works like this: Next time you have a really bad situation, you know, a kid's really tearing up your room, bad language, screamin,' won't sit, smackin' other kids, you know, the whole nine yards. Now, you just grab the phone, call the big relaxed guy that you met in the teachers' lounge. He comes from his classroom and gets the kid. He then takes the kid to another classroom filled with students in, say, Advanced Placement

English—you know, not a particularly comfortable environment for this kid. They sit him in the back of this room with his book, paper and pencil, and then tell him to shut up. Works every time. Problem's gone for the remainder of the period. Your name begins to fade off of the administrative "can't teach" list. People stop coming and suggesting conferences and new strategies. Eventually you become the recipient of some other teacher's "bad-ass" for the day. Get the idea?

Question: But what about the principal, what does he or she say?

Response: You got to be kiddin'! You think the principal's stupid? You ever seen that three-monkey thing? You know. One monkey has his hands covering his eyes, the second...

Question: See no evil, hear no evil, speak no evil?

Response: You got it. Like they say...if it ain't broke, don't fix it.

Question: Tell me about textbooks. How important are textbooks?

Response: They're critical if you have a book that has been carefully selected by teachers for those kids, and the book is designed to complement the teaching strategies that teachers find most effective for these kids.

Question: You gave me a lot of qualifiers for my question. Is there a story here?

Response: Damn right.

Question: Want to tell me about it?

Response: Sure, why not. Let's see, where do we start? Well, been in schools where it's been done right and schools where it's not. Let's start with done right. Lots of good textbooks out there. First thing you do is find one that fits where your students are and has the potential to take them further. That's what good schools do. What they don't do is base the selection of the textbook on where you want kids to be on some damn standardized test, or select the book based upon where you want the public to think your students are—like giving algebra books to kids still struggling with multiplication and division. Talk about setting the stage for disruptive behavior and chastising teachers for not getting the job done! The other thing to remember is that different texts complement different teaching styles and strategies. Don't decide for teachers their teaching styles or strategies. Don't even presume to make these choices for them, not if you want good teaching and learning to occur. Always respect the teacher. Been in places where districts have attempted to force inappropriate texts on teachers. When that happens, you will find teachers at Target or Walmart buying reams of paper and then going to Kinko's or Staples to run off what they need to teach. Oh, and while we're at it, always have a set of books for the classroom in addition to the ones the kids take home. Remember, these are kids that we're dealing with and sometimes, through no one's fault, they don't bring their books back and forth everyday.

Question: Do teachers need prep periods?

Response: Need them? Are you out of your mind? They are absolutely essential. You couldn't pay me enough to give up my prep period. It's so difficult to explain how hard a good teacher works in a day: the countless emotion-filled interactions with human beings not yet fully mature; the never-ending effort to help them focus and refocus; the continual observations needed to keep everyone on task or prevent fights. You are looking and listening so intently you feel as though you need additional sets of eyes and ears. To ask teachers who move in this highly-charged mode, period after period, to give up their prep period would be like saying to the marathoner crossing the finish line, "Great job, now do another one."

Question: When's the best period to have a prep?

Response: Right after lunch. Need I say more?

Question: When's the worst?

Response: First period of the day. Some fellow teacher is always late because of a family illness, or a flat tire, or a sub didn't show up, and then there's the principal in your doorway with that please-help-me look on his face.

Question: Yeah, but you can say no. It's your prep period. Right?

Response: You really want to do that? I mean, you really want to say no? You learn quickly that schools are one of those kinds of places where people really need to depend on each other. I help you now. You help me when I need it. And guess what? At some time everybody needs help. So, as I said, "you really want to do that?"

Question: Any thoughts on standardized tests?

Response: Not any good ones. I've got a couple of logistical suggestions though. I worked in a plant some years ago where workers had to perform jobs that didn't permit them to leave the work-station. So, they had people who came around periodically to spell them and give them a chance to go to the bathroom. You might want to consider doing that for teacher-proctors. For some reason, in schools almost everywhere, someone in charge forgets these folks need a break. Also, in every school there is a handful of kids who are predictably disruptive in these settings. You know exactly what they are going to do when you sit them in front of a two-or-three hour test they can't successfully complete. If you were a student who needed a high score on that standardized test, how would you like to be seated next to that kid? There's got to be a dozen ways to be preventative in that situation. Just pick one and do it.

Question: What do you think of charter schools?

Response: Don't get me started on this. You give me a classroom of kids whose parents not only chose this school, but had to be part of a lottery to get into my class. Give me parents who further committed to stay in touch and interact with me—parents who also had to sign on the dotted line that they would support their kid at home. Give me a school where firm standards are set for classroom behavior and are supported by the administration and where, if schools do take special education kids, the state often gives them four to five times as much money per pupil. Like I said, "Don't get me started.

Question: Can I ask you kind of a personal question?

Response: Sure, go ahead. If it's not too personal, I'll probably answer it.

Question: When you're with your fellow teachers and you have a moment to talk—say after school or over a beer, where's the conversation go?

Response: I thought you'd have a tough question. Most often if we've let our guard down and are relaxed, the conversation drifts to talk of early retirement. On the other hand, if you're a teacher who's still young enough, it's talk of leaving and doing something else for a living.

Question: Really?

Response: Well, it wasn't always like this, but it is now. I know almost no teachers who don't give it all they have every day. They'd never boast about it, they just do it. And as corny as this sounds, they're giving it all because of the kids. But these days there's a hell of a lot of depression our there. Lots of teachers feeling alone and pretty beat up.

Question: Any final thoughts?

Response: No, not really.

Question: We'd like to put all this in the book. Okay?

Response: Great. Hope it makes a difference. Hope it helps people understand. It gets pretty tough out here.

Chapter 19

Good Teacher? Bad Teacher?

This chapter has two parts. The first part is a series of short stories intended to give a hard rap on the knuckles of those people who endorse the current erroneous position that good teaching or bad teaching can be judged by how well students do on standardized tests. We hope that the stories, at least partially, cause you to question such beliefs.

The second part of the chapter steps back and, with the help of Dr. Seuss and Peter Drucker, asks under what kind of leadership would teachers of today best succeed. Seventy years of research, beginning with the Hawthorn Studies in Chicago, overwhelmingly directs us to practices of leadership that enhance human dignity.[1] So what are the questions that we all need to begin to ask if we want to provoke this truly artistic and effective teaching.

The Class from Hell

One of the stories I often tell when doing a keynote address is the story that I title for humorous purposes, "The Class from Hell." If you've taught for any time at all, you come to know that each group of students has, so to speak, its own soul. Whether it's a grade-level grouping, or a content-based group, such as Algebra I, each group has its own personality. Some classes have a very slow quality. From the time they enter and throughout the entire period they just move slowly. Even when students in such classes raise their hands—that is, if they should do so—they do it slowly and deliberately. On the other hand, there are classes that come in with the speed of Jim Carey in the movie *Mask*. You need to hold tight to the papers on your desk to keep them from being caught up in the tornado of energy that has just entered. You find yourself pushed into high gear, despite your best efforts to slow the pace. Within ten minutes even your speaking voice has gone up nearly an entire octave.

Then there's the class that is made up of "gremlins" like those creatures in the movie of the same name that have all been hit by the powerful water of a fire hose that turns them from cute, cuddly little things into intensely destructive, impossible-to-contain little hellions—the class from hell.

As I tell the story during a keynote address, I speak of a sixth-grade teacher named Sandy who is aware that one of these classes is now in the third grade in her school. But, she doesn't worry, nor does she spend too much time thinking about them, for it will be years before they will reach her in her sixth grade. Then one day, two years later, in the spring of the year when Sandy is trying to relax for a moment in the faculty lounge with a cup of coffee, in comes the fifth-grade teacher Martha. "But," she wonders, "Is it Martha?" She looks so gaunt, so frail, so exhausted. Her gait is slow, almost labored. Even her head is bowed, eyes focused on the floor in front of her as if raising her head would itself be extremely painful. She stops just in front of Sandy. Martha looks up and their eyes lock. Now from deep inside of Sandy comes a rush of awareness coupled with terror. My God, it is Martha—she has that class.

Their locked gaze continues. Then an ever-so-faint smile comes over Martha's face as she leans in close to Sandy and says in almost a whisper, "I passed them all."

At this point, the audience normally fills the auditorium with uncontrolled laughter. It's a laughter that comes from a collective knowing. It is a response to a shared understanding of one of the fundamental truths understood by all of those who have taught: There really are classes from hell, and if you stay in teaching long enough, you will get your fair share. If you're a secondary teacher with four, five, or six classes a day, you could conceivably get several of these in the same year.

Can you get such a class as early as kindergarten? Absolutely! Just this morning we were talking to an extremely effective substitute teacher who works in the state of Illinois. She has been substituting for several years in all kinds of classes, including some very challenging special education classes. The requests for her services come often because of her maturity and her ability to relate so effectively to all children, including those who have special needs.

Yesterday, however, was for her a new experience—the kindergarten class from hell. Prior to even entering the classroom, several teachers and the assistant principal came to her and said, "If there's anything you need today—anything at all, please let us know. And don't feel bad about the day, regardless of how it goes. We've not found anyone who can handle this group of youngsters. We would really appreciate your coming back if it does go well, for we very often need a substitute."

The day did not go well. In fact, it was, by far, her worst teaching experience. Even an attempted trip to the library, with the principal and librarian present and focused on helping her, ended miserably. There was no controlling this group. The behaviors of some of them were frightening. Eventually her primary purpose was no longer teaching but rather, "How do I keep them from hurting themselves or one another?" After the day was over, she went to other teachers asking, "Was I doing something wrong?" Everyone, including veteran teachers with outstanding reputations, advised her that it was nothing she had done or had not done. They told her that they have not been able to find anyone who's been able to handle this group. Then she did something that she never thought she'd do. She told the principal never to call her back for this class.

What do you do when you're the teacher assigned to this class and you can't say, "Don't ever call me back?" What do you do? How do you now view yourself? How do others view you? Are you a good teacher? Are you a bad teacher? What does it mean when no one has been able to handle this group? Are they all bad teachers?

Same Classes—Different Outcomes

Living near Chicago was always a treat in so many ways, especially because of the proximity to so many colleges and universities. Once Marion and I completed our advanced degrees, we periodically agreed to teach an occasional evening course. The college/university atmosphere was always exciting, and we enjoyed the challenges that came from undergraduates.

One year in mid-July, I received a call from one of the universities asking me to teach a Thursday night course in child psychology. This was a course I loved to teach, so I accepted immediately. An additional benefit was that I was familiar with the text that was being used. It had recently been republished as a third edition, and I had already taught from the book in the spring when it had first come out. I was looking forward to the fall experience.

Nearly a month later, I got a second phone call to teach. This call came from the academic dean at another university, an educator I had known for many years

"Ray?"

"Yes, Jack."

"Ray, we are kind of in a bind here. You know Dr. Frank Wilson?"

"Certainly I do. Fine educator."

"Well, he has had a heart attack, so we need to reassign the classes he was to teach this semester. Those classes begin next week. I know this is short notice, but is there any chance that you could handle child psychology for us beginning next Tuesday night?"

"Jack, I'm already committed to teaching on Thursday night and I try to avoid two commitments, but given your situation, I'll do it. Tell Frank that I'll try to do a good job for him."

I had never before had the experience of teaching the same course at two different universities in the same semester. Frank, before his heart attack, had selected the same text that I was preparing to use on the other side of the city. When I walked into Frank's class that first Tuesday night I found 36 ready-to-learn undergraduates—a good sized class. On Thursday night my class had 38 students. Many of the students that I had in both universities were evening students. These students do not often take daytime classes because of other commitments, primarily work. Often they are a little older and paying their own way, so they are usually highly motivated.

The content obligations to be covered by teaching staff in each university were established by their respective psychology departments, and for these two universities, the child psychology courses, with respect to content, were virtually identical. During the semester, I created four exams which I had never given before. Each was weighted equally and each contained sections of true/false, multiple choice, short answer, and essay. I corrected all exams by myself. I liked to do that as it helped me to get to know my students better.

After completing the corrections of the second exam from

both classes, I determined a condition I could not account for. One university group was performing, as a group, a full standard deviation, or a full letter grade, above the other university group. I remember asking myself about the lower-achieving class: *Is it me? Am I somehow not as available? Am I not being as clear with my in-class explanations? Have I not communicated sufficiently the necessity of the class readings?* I was asking the kinds of questions that teachers always ask of themselves when students don't seem to be getting it.

Over the next several weeks, I attempted in every way I could think of to correct any deficiencies that might be mine, even coming in earlier, staying later and extending office hours. Then I gave the third exam. I covered the names of all students from both classes and mixed the exams. I corrected them. I removed the temporary name coverings, sorted the exams again, and tallied. The difference between the group scores was a standard deviation of 1.1. The students from one university continued to do better. The final exam resulted again in the same break-down. When I put both university groups together, after computing final grades, the total group scores resulted in a nearly perfect bell-curve. When I separated the groups, I found again a difference of one full standard deviation between them. On average, the difference was a full letter grade for the semester.

So, what kind of a job did I do that semester? Was I effective or ineffective? Given the tenor of the current times, would I get a raise at one university? Would I get a decrease in pay at the other? Might I not be asked to teach another course? Was I a good teacher? Was I a bad teacher?

He's an Outstanding Teacher...Really?

When I was a superintendent, I recall being advised as to the excellent teaching skills of one of our high school algebra math teachers. His students consistently scored significantly higher than students in other algebra classes. Comments about his excellence came to me even from school board members, some of whose children had been students in his algebra class in past years.

Some months later as a part of my normal classroom visitations, I was able to observe this teacher as he taught. I also had the opportunity to observe the others in that building who also taught algebra. I've never considered myself an expert in capturing all of the nuances that collectively make one teacher a "touch better" than another, but I do know good teaching when I see it. Frankly, all these teachers looked good to me.

As I was leaving, I inadvertently strayed into the guidance department and had a chance encounter with the lead counselor who oversaw scheduling with one of the assistant principals.

"Sandy."

"Hello, Dr. Golarz."

"I had another wonderful opportunity today to see more of your teachers in action. Quite impressive."

"We have a great staff here."

"Also saw the gentleman who does so well teaching your morning algebra class."

"Oh, Jack Morehouse. He's multiply licensed. We need him in the afternoons to teach English."

"Well, I am impressed. Sandy, I watched all of your algebra teachers today. What gives this Jack Morehouse the edge?"

She responded in a matter-of-fact manner. "He has all the band kids."

"What?"

"He has the kids who play in the band—the band kids."

I remember being confused. "Sandy, I don't understand."

She then explained, "We can't schedule many band kids in the afternoon algebra classes. Just won't work out. So, almost all of the band kids end up taking morning algebra. You know, the band kids, orchestra kids, the Advanced Placement types. C'mon, Doc. You've been spendin' too much time in the administration center. Band kids just don't get low grades...remember?"

Good teacher? Bad teacher?

Can You Act, Dance, Sing?

Clarity as to what makes the difference between a good teacher and a bad teacher continues to evade us, particularly if you're using student grades to judge. The reviewing of standardized test score results that measure some narrow band of academic content is certainly not a valid way to judge. A recently published book, written by Harris, Smith, and Harris, expertly illustrates the truth of this statement, so we highly recommend reading *The Myths of Standardized Tests.* [2]

Furthermore, as a consequence of the continuing negative impacts of Supreme Court decisions on classroom order and civility, it is ludicrous to use classroom order and civility as benchmarks when judging a teacher's effectiveness. The variables and ever-moving conditions of the teaching profession itself, coupled with the minute-by-minute obligatory human interactions, make capturing a clear distinction between good and bad teaching virtually impossible. A powerful read on this topic of classroom dynamics is *The Classroom Crucible* by Edward Pauly.[3]

Possibly, before we firm up teaching assignments, we should directly inquire of teachers: Are you good with this type of student? How about this type? How about a combination of these types? Or, maybe we should probe into this area: What is your most effective instructional strategy? Under what conditions does this work best? With what content do you best succeed? With whom do you best succeed? What time of day?

How are we doing? Wrong approach? Wrong questions? Then possibly we should head in this direction: Are you good with special education students? Gifted? Minorities? Which minorities? Or, how about this: Can you motivate? Do you excite? Do you provoke curiosity? Do you send disruptive students to the office? Do you get completed forms in on time? Are you always assisting in supervision of the halls between classes?

Can you act? Dance? Sing? Juggle? Juggle while singing? Gets complex, doesn't it? Are we, like the Grinch before his epiphany, simply on the wrong path?

> Then the Grinch thought of something he hadn't before.
> What if Christmas (good teaching) he thought,
> Doesn't come from a store (assessments or strategies or content)
> What if Christmas, perhaps, means a little bit more? [4]

Maybe we should ask the questions we should have started with—the questions that target the heart of the profession. Maybe we need to ask questions that by-pass the ever-changing variables and moving conditions. Perhaps we could think *of something we hadn't before.*

Maybe we simply ask instead: Do you love what you teach? Do you love those you teach? If the answers to these questions are still "yes," the next and final question needs to be. Then how can we help? Before you answer, remember to consider some hard facts: Given the fact that no one has relieved teachers of the great numbers of America's poor children daily coming into their classrooms, that there has been no significant work done to curb the American epidemic of abused children, that the necessary and promised funding for the handicapped has never been properly appropriated, that an answer to drug abuse and meth labs with their crippling impact on children has not been forthcoming, that the will to address American racism and its adverse impacts on schools has been put on hold, that there's been no response to pleas for court decisions or legislation to provide safe and orderly classrooms—given all of these things and more, then the question should be a deeply apologetic, *"How can we help?"*

Start by Saying Thanks

Once as a newly hired superintendent, I asked my veteran secretary Ruthie for advice regarding what she thought I should do to get to know and understand the community she had lived and worked in for so long. She looked up at me, smiled and said, "Well, the Chamber of Commerce called and would love for you to come over. The administrators from the universities would like a meeting and lunch, and the mayor's office called and said that the door is open anytime."

She then hesitated. So I probed. "Yes, Ruthie, what else?"

"Well, if it were me, I'd visit schools. The teachers and kids just love it when you visit."

Following Ruthie's suggestion, I ventured forth. I spent that entire morning visiting classrooms at an elementary school nestled among the trees in a forest outside of town. All of the classrooms had outside views. It was a sunny and brisk, fall day, and I found that although the outside views were extraordinary, the teaching was even more so.

Once on a trip to Paris, I spent the entire day on the West Bank across from Notre Dame watching artists paint. On this day, in like manner, I could have sat forever and watched these artists perform in their classrooms. But now it was near noon, and I needed to leave them and the elementary school nestled in the woods.

That late afternoon, as I sat at my desk, I couldn't get the morning experience out of my mind, so I decided to write some thank-you notes to the teachers I had visited, complimenting them on something special that I had seen each do for a student. The letter writing didn't take but a moment, and it gave me immense pleasure.

A week later, I had just finished a meeting and was preparing to do some wrap-up-the-day paper work when Ruthie came into my office and half-closed the door behind her. I looked up.

"There's a teacher here in the outer office who would like to see you. She is one of those you sent a note to last week. Dr. Golarz, she seems upset."

"Well, Ruthie, please have her come in."

Ruthie brought her in immediately and gave her a handful of fresh

Kleenex. I recognized her and asked her to sit. She looked up and began to speak. She got only a couple of words out before breaking into a sob.

"Oh, Dr. Golarz, I didn't mean to break down like this. I'm so sorry. You sent me a note."

Assuming I had offended her, I stammered, "I'm so sorry."

Then she interrupted, "No. No. You don't understand. Dr, Golarz, I've been teaching for 13 years. No one has ever sent me a note like that before—no one. I had it framed and it's hanging on the wall near my desk in my classroom."

She stopped for a moment, regained some composure, and continued.

"Dr. Golarz, you'll never know how much I needed that note. This last year, particularly, I've been so tired at the end of each day, so very tired. I know that I've let my students down this year. For some reason the joy has been gone. Then I received your note." She stopped again. I waited. She took a deep breath and then continued, now with a bit of a smile pushing its way through her tears and ruined mascara.

"I just wanted to come in and thank you. Really didn't mean to break down like that. I'm so sorry. Please come and see me again, I'll show you some real fire in the belly."

I promised that I would. And I told her that I'd come if for no other reason than to check my note on her wall to make sure I hadn't misspelled anything. She chuckled a bit, sniffled, and again wiped her face. We then sat together for a while and watched the blue sky over the trees in the distance turn its evening oranges that so exquisitely precede dark.

That evening, I sat in my office quite late thinking of many things: of Marion's fourth-period class, of the teachers who have asked me, "Why are they so angry at us?" and, finally, of Ruthie and her wisdom, "Go visit schools. The teachers and kids just love it when you visit."

The Definitive Drucker

I have a truckload of favorite authors when it comes to the topics of moral leadership, the importance of respecting human dignity, and effective mechanisms and strategies to organizational improvement. As I reshuffle the messages of these various authors in my mind, the one that continually floats back to the top is Peter Drucker and most particularly his definition and formula for organizational greatness. In his book, *The Definitive Drucker*, he suggests:

> The test of an organization's potential for greatness is as follows: Can every person in the organization answer yes to the following three questions every day?
> (1) Are you treated every day with dignity and respect by everyone you encounter?
> (2) Are you given things you need—education, training, encouragement, and support so that you can make a contribution?
> (3) Do people notice that you did it? [5]

Is this the answer to the question, "Good teacher? Bad teacher?"

Do we get off of the road we're on and take a different road to make good teaching better? Is it really that simple?

But then, if we do, what becomes of our quest to find the evildoers, to seek out and destroy the bad teachers, to crush the ones who are tired and have, for the moment, given up? What then would we do with our instruments of standardized measurement? What then would become of us?

Maybe, just maybe, what would happen to us is what happened to the Grinch at the end of that wonderful story. Remember?

> In Who-ville they say
> That the Grinch's small heart
> Grew three sizes that day![6]

Notes:

1. Baker Library, "The Hawthorne Effect, – The Human Relations Movement," Bloomberg, http://www.library.hbs.edu/hc.hawthorne/09.html.
2. Phillip Harris, Bruce Smith, and Joan Harris, *The Myths of Standardized Tests* (Lanham, Md.: Rowman and Littlefield, 2011).
3. Edward Pauly, *The Classroom Crucible* (New York: Basic Books, 1991).
4. Dr. Seuss, *How the Grinch Stole Christmas* (New York: Random House 1957).
5. Elizabeth Hass Edersheim, *The Definitive Drucker: Challenges for Tomorrow's Executives* (New York: McGraw-Hill, 2007), 166.
6. Dr. Seuss, *How the Grinch Stole Christmas,* (New York: Random House 1957).

Chapter 20

You Don't Really Know Us

The thought behind the title of this chapter was prompted by a theme from the movie *Gosford Park*. The movie reveals the total lack of understanding that a group of the very rich in England had of their personal servants, despite the fact that they lived together in very close settings. The similarity of insensitivity demonstrated by the wealthy of their society and our own is striking.

Critics of all kinds, particularly those who are wealthy and influential, berate our schools and teachers for failing to educate all students to a level where they can win when competing on a narrow band of standardized international tests. Many of the most formidable of these critics have never attended the public schools they berate, nor do they send their children to public schools. Besides not understanding our schools, they seem to have even less appreciation for what this country is, what it is capable of, who its real people are, or the core values that these real people rely on for their inner strength and purpose.

As they berate us, they hold up foreign countries as models for us to emulate. They showcase developed and developing countries throughout the world, where the only way out of poverty and deprivation is to do exceptionally well in school and on tests. In these countries the number one national priority is for very young children to post very high achievement scores. This childhood attainment is used to decide which lifetime opportunities will be open to students and which closed. Second chances that could assuredly impact one's life are rarely built into their systems. In addition, these countries focus on educating only those who they believe can be the most competitive. They will very often exclude the kinds of children we embrace. Our student Tony, introduced in chapter 2 of this book, would likely not ever have been allowed to sit in Mr. Nelson's class. Is this really the vision they believe we will embrace?

The vision we have for our children is so much more. And the lives that we Americans want for our children are lives filled with an array of richness and growth in a multitude of areas. We recognize that our children must be well educated. However, we also want them to taste and enjoy and grow from much more. We want them to lie in a grassy field on a summer day and read a novel for pleasure, to know the sound of Bach, to enjoy rap, and to share the satisfaction that can come from the caring of an elder grandparent. We want them to enjoy and be proud of their capacity to repair a car, to play in a football game, to run a race. We want them to gain skills with the many tools that they find in their family garage and kitchen. We want them to take pride in and understand the history of their own race and ethnicity, to sense and then to respond to the needs of their fellow man, to know the thrill of hitting a home run, and to glory in the skill of controlling a soccer ball, knee-to-knee-to-toe-to-knee. We want them to babysit a neighbor's child, work in a fast-food establishment, deliver newspapers—earn their own dollar. We want them get a little choked-up when they hear the playing of their own national anthem and to waste away an afternoon playing basketball with friends in a park. We want for our children all of these things and more. *If that means some nation with less freedom and less true breadth and depth of knowing outscores us on some artificial measure of greatness, then so be it.*

If we, as individuals or as a nation, find we need to compete at the highest levels for something we really want or need, we will do so. We always have. And when we are permitted to compete on a fair and level playing field, we will win, or finish honorably. Give us half a fighting chance, and we'll come the rest of the way. No. We'll come all the way.

To those who don't believe this and to those who have forgotten what we are, we say, *"You don't really know us."*

Note:

1. *Gosford Park,* Dir. Robert Altman, DVD USA Films, Capital Films, January 2002.

Epilogue:

A War worth Waging

In my young adulthood, I worked in steel production plants. I worked most often as a member of a labor gang. On some days, when we lacked a full complement of workers, we might be required to work in a gang of two or three, rather than the normal five. Those were the most difficult of days, for the task of shoveling tons of manganese or other steel ingredients did not diminish because we lacked needed workers.

As new young employees, we knew on these days that we must work harder and faster to get the job done. So, though the temperature in the plant might reach 120 degrees by noon, though we would weaken from the continuous heat of the open hearth furnaces on our backs as we shoveled, though water was often unavailable, we worked. We would work at a feverish pace, even through our lunch breaks, in order to stay on task. By early afternoon the cramping would begin. Then, despite the rescue of water and salt, our bodies would give way and the more intense cramping would take over. We would often work through the pain, but success was now judged by completing the day, not the job assigned.

When the plant whistle blew marking the end of the shift, we would drop our shovels and just sit and stare into empty space. Eventually, we would move, but not with the quick step of winners but rather the shuffling steps of the shackled. We had finished the day but had not won. As young and strong as we were, we were learning one of life's most important lessons. We were learning that you are given some jobs which, despite your best efforts, are beyond your ability to complete.

Throughout my years as a school superintendent, I often saw this overwhelmed look on the faces of teachers and building administrators as I walked the halls of their schools at day's end. I stopped momentarily in their open doorways and, often without their knowing, observed them as they sat and stared exhausted into empty space. During earlier parts of those same days, I saw them in their rooms and offices working harder and faster to complete the ever-evasive task. I observed as they skipped their lunch break.

Did they shovel, heavily perspire, and cramp? No, but in a way, their work was harder. You see, when the job is to shovel, you can always look up at the remaining pile and know how much of the manganese is left. It may not be a task you can complete, but you can at least see that you have made progress, and this affirms your effort and gives some hope. In the role of teacher or school administrator there is no smaller pile as the end of the day nears. You learn quickly in today's schools that, despite your best efforts, the job is beyond your ability to complete, and you're often unsure that you have made any progress at all. You do what you can. You help as many as you can.

Several years ago, I was asked to keynote the administrative retreat of one of the largest school districts in Texas. A colleague of mine had just assumed the superintendency of that district. At dinner the night before I was scheduled to present, I asked his permission to begin my presentation to his entire administrative staff with this statement: "As we begin this session, let's start with this clear understanding: The task that you and your teachers have been asked to perform cannot be done." He not only agreed, he concurred. The next afternoon, after all of the administrators had gathered, I began my keynote address with those words.

For the next full minute, neither I nor the conference coordinators could stop the spontaneous standing ovation. The statement had struck a raw nerve with the hundreds of administrators present. And they were all experiencing a sense of immense liberation and relief as a consequence of hearing the truth spoken out loud. Once in a while, we all just need to hear the truth said out loud. Does it mean that tomorrow we will walk into work and refuse to pick up our shovel? No, not at all. If anything, we will probably shovel with more intensity. Why? Because finally someone has affirmed what we all knew. The job under these conditions can't get done. With that affirmation, we can work with pride. We can work with pride and honor—not doubt or shame.

Anyone who has been in the profession of education for any significant time knows through experience that there is no magic bullet that will get the job done. There is no miraculous curricular program. There is no permanent or long-lasting fix.

Yet, year after year, new programs or revised old programs with new names are brought forth which claim to be that magic bullet. The landscape of educational history is filled with these. Young teachers are particularly vulnerable to jumping on board as they've not seen the train before. Seasoned veterans are a little more cautious. If you study the history of new programs directed at education, you will find that most have, at their center, the goal of either improving teachers or modifying how or what they teach. They are not directed at resolving the problems exposed in this book.

Few teachers, nonetheless, would ever suggest to you that they can't get better at what they do. Nor would we make such a suggestion. Improvement in any profession is always a primary goal. But, as we have said countless times in this book, the problem isn't teachers. Furthermore, organizational research that comes from a multitude of disciplines is filled with an endless number of studies that attest to the fact that programs imposed on an organization from the top have little chance at success. Unfortunately, much of our educational history is filled with these. The one currently biting the dust is No Child Left Behind.

If we really intend to move toward completing the essential task of schools, then we must go far beyond anything we have yet had the will or courage to consider. We must supplement the efforts of our teachers with truly meaningful change. It is immoral of us to ask of these teachers that they continue, day after day, to go back into environments where they cannot win. Do we, as fair-minded citizens, really want to chastise and humiliate another group of young Americans for failing to complete an undoable task?

Our new vision for public education must have the muscle, the power, and the authority that we have rarely mustered for any national effort. The elements of that vision must be capable of eliminating the national problems that cause the real plight of American education. They must be profoundly bold, and they must begin soon.

As a consequence of the conditions that we, as a nation, have neglected to address, more and more young Americans are leaving this profession of education, and growing numbers are refusing to even consider teaching as a career. Most importantly, the millions of our American teachers who have remained are exhausted and are losing hope while millions more of America's children are losing an opportunity that will soon not be retrievable. The following is what we believe must happen if the job is to get done:

(1) The federal government of the United States needs to declare this nation's first War on Poverty of the twenty-first century. Its goal should not be to simply add programs of charity, such as food stamps, but rather programs of justice and dignity, as should be the heritage of all Americans. To truly wipe out poverty, we must have empowerment programs, such as the G.I. Bill enacted at the conclusion of WWII. This congressional action ultimately expanded the nation's middle class, thus jump-starting a period of economic prosperity unparalleled in our history. If this new war on poverty is to have any chance at success, it must be grounded on a solid foundation—a trust in the potential of the American people.

(2) The Congress of the United States must reaffirm that the primary purpose of K-12 education in this country is the same purpose dreamed by the Founders. This purpose was written of by Thomas Jefferson, making it clear to the nation that schools and the means of education were "necessary for Good Government." [1] Congress should further affirm that such an education requires, as the Founders had envisioned, the inclusion of the arts, music, literature, languages, the sciences, and the thousands of years of man's philosophic thinking. A broad liberal education is essential to an enlightened citizenry. It must be made clear that the essential purpose of our schools is to prepare our youth with the skills and civility needed to participate in and contribute to the perpetuation of the American democracy.

(3) *Goss v. Lopez* needs to be overturned. The U.S. Supreme Court must study the devastating consequences of that decision. To have declared education to be a property right for those still too young to understand the obligations which accompany that right was a decision that was ill-advised. That decision, along with the other decisions discussed and cited in this book, have all but destroyed countless numbers of American classrooms. Education needs to again become a privilege if the system is to survive.

While this is being accomplished, any teacher (K-12) who declares that he or she must have assistance in order to maintain a classroom of reasonable civility will be given such federally-funded help. This help will be in the form and nature of a classroom bailiff empowered to remove disruptive students, either temporarily or permanently, as is the decision of the teacher. The classrooms of American teachers being held hostage by these court decisions must have immediate relief. Only teachers, their administrators, and the parents of the children who have been, or currently are the collateral damage in one of these classrooms can understand this urgency.

(4) The business/industrial communities must redirect their work preparation efforts for new and existing employees toward the post high school technical-vocational schools and centers across this country, not the American K-12 system. State legislative bodies need further to view these technical centers as their first priority when considering post high school educational funding.

(5) State legislative bodies need to cease their interference with and manipulation of the affairs of local school districts. The American model of local control has served this nation well for over 200 years. State legislative bodies and governors need to restrict their involvement to the asking of one question, "How can we help?"

(6) The federal government and Congress must reaffirm to the states the importance of organized unions and their strength and necessity for this nation. This reminder should come in the form of legislation that affords unions of public employees in America the same benefits and protections now afforded to the membership of unions of private employers. The work of President Franklin Delano Roosevelt should be completed and the National Labor Relations Act modified accordingly by an act of Congress.

(7) All Americans must recommit themselves to the ideals Dr. Martin Luther King so eloquently expressed in his speech, "I Have a Dream," for until we have the first generation of Americans who, without reservation, view one another as equals, we will continue to have an imperfect place called school.

(8) The Congress of the United States needs to appropriately fund its special education mandates so that schools across the country can effectively serve these children in the manner intended by the legislation.

(9) The nation must create a set of strategies that would quadruple both federal and state efforts in dealing with the American epidemics of child abuse and drug abuse. Each state legislature should establish a permanent committee to oversee its state's prevention and intervention efforts. Such committees should report publicly every six months to the citizens of their state as to their success in bringing these epidemics under control.

Let us say up front that we agree with those of you who have little confidence that our current political system can be coaxed to act quickly, for as we all know, the system is filled with many who have neither the will nor the understanding of the necessity to deal with these or any such parallel actions. Yet, the manganese needs to be shoveled. The nation's dream needs to become a reality. What hangs in the balance is the potential loss of the democracy itself.

In the Author's Preface, we said that a young boxer was in the ring fighting virtually alone. We now ask you, as we told you we would, to consider stepping into the ring with him. He can no longer continue without help. As you take that last cautious step forward, join us for a final sip of courage from these words in Carne Ross's recently published book, *The Leaderless Revolution*.

> There is thrill in the fight, even if there must be fear. As Spartacus gloriously put it in the eponymous movie, "I'd rather be here, a free man among brothers, facing a long march and a hard fight, than be the richest citizen in Rome, fat with food he didn't work for, and surrounded by slaves."[2]

Here, let us hold the ring ropes apart for you. Step in. You'll join a nation's war worth waging.

Notes:

1. "Ordinance of 1787," *West Encyclopedia of American Law*, 2-6 http://www.answers.com/topic/northwest-ordinance.
2. Carne Ross, *The Leaderless Revolution: How Ordinary People Will Take Power and Change Politics in the 21st Century* (New York: Blue Rider Press, Penguin Group. 2011), 215.

Suggested Readings

Adler, Mortimer. *Reforming Education*. New York: Collier Books, MacMillan Publishing Co., 1977.

Barth, Roland. *Improving Schools from Within*. San Francisco: Jossey-Bass Publishers, 1990.

Boutwell, Clinton. *Shell Game: Corporate America's Agenda for School*. Bloomington, Ind,: Phi Delta Kappa Educational Foundation, 1997.

Botstein, Leon. *Jefferson's Children*. New York: Bantam Doubleday Dell Publishing Group, Inc., 1997.

Bracey, Gerald. *Final Exam*. Bloomington, Ind,: Technos Press,1995.

Broom, Leonard and Philip Selznick. *Sociology*. New York: Harper and Row Publishing Co., 1977.

Bruer, John T. *The Myth of the First Three Years*. New York: The Free Press, Simon and Schuster, Inc., 1999.

Clark, David and Terry Astuto. *Roots of Reform*. Bloomington, Ind.: Phi Delta Kappa Educational Foundation. 1994.

Evert, Thomas and Amy Van Deuren. *Making External Experts Work*. New York: Rowman and Littlefield Publishers, Inc., 2012.

Fiske, Edward B. *Smart Schools, Smart Kids*. New York: Simon and Schuster, Inc., 1991.

Galbraith, John Kenneth, *The Culture of Contentment*. Boston: Houghton Mifflin Company, 1992.

Gatto, John Taylor. *Dumbing Us Down*. Vancouver,Canada: New Society Publishers, 2000.

Gladwell, Malcolm. *What the Dog Saw*. New York: Back Bay Books, Little, Brown and Co., 2010.

Golarz, Raymond and Marion Golarz.. *Sweet Land of Liberty*. Bloomington, Ind.: AuthorHouse Publishing Co., 2011.

———. *The Power of Participation*. Champaign-Urbana, Ill.: Research Press Publishing Co., 1995.

Golarz, Raymond J. *When the Yellow Jackets Played*. Bloomington, Ind.: AuthorHouse Publishing Co., 2009.

Goleman, Daniel. *Emotional Intelligence*. New York: Bantam Books, 1995.

Gould, Stephen Jay. *The Mismeasure of Man*. New York: W.W. Norton Publishing Co., 1993.

Hacker, Jacob and Paul Pierson. *Winner-Take-All Politics*. New York: Simon and Schuster Publishing Co., 2010.

Hall, Philip and Nancy Hall. *Educating Oppositional and Defiant Children*. Alexandria, Va.: Association for Supervision and Curriculum Development, 2003.

Harris, Phillip, Bruce Smith, and Joan Harris. *The Myths of Standardized Tests*. Lanham, Md.: Rowman and Littlefield Publishers, Inc., 2011.

Hart, Leslie. *The Human Brain and Human Learning*. White Plains, N.Y. Longman, Inc.1983.

Hirsch, E.D. *Cultural Literacy*. New York: Random Books, 1988.

Kohn, Alfie. *Punished by Rewards: The Trouble with Gold Stars, Incentive Plans, A's, Praise, and Other Bribes.* New York: Houghton Mifflin, 1999.

Kozol, Jonathan. *Amazing Grace.* New York: Crown Publishers, Inc. 1995.

———. *Savage Inequalities.* New York: Harper Collins Books, Crown Publishers, Inc. 1991.

Krugman, Paul. *End This Depression Now!* New York: W.W. Norton and Co., 2012.

Lewis, James, Raymond Golarz, and Richard Neil. *Restructuring Schools for Excellence through Teacher Empowerment.* Westburg, N.Y: Wilkerson Publishing Co., 1991.

McWhorter, John H. *Losing the Race.* New York: The Free Press, Simon and Schuster, Inc., 2000.

Myrdal, Gunnar. *An American Dilemma.* New York: Harper and Brothers Publishers, 1944.

Pauly, Edward. *The Classroom Crucible.* New York: Basic Books, 1991.

Payne, Ruby. *A Framework for Understanding Poverty.* Highlands, Tex.: aha! Process Inc., 2005.

Phillips, Kevin. *Wealth and Democracy.* New York: Broadway Books, Random House, Inc., 2000.

Ravitch, Diane. *The Death and Life of the Great American School System.* New York: Basic Books, 2010.

Ross, Carne. *The Leaderless Revolution.* London: Penguin Books Ltd., 2011.

Rothstein, Richard. *The Way We Were?* N.Y: The Century Foundation Press, 1998.

Sacks, Peter. *Standardized Minds.* New York: Perseus Books, HarperCollins Publishers, Inc., 1999.

Senge, Peter. *The Dance of Change.* New York: Doubleday, Random House, Inc., 1999.

Steinberg, Laurence. *Beyond the Classroom.* New York: Simon and Schuster, Inc., 1996.

Stiglitz, Joseph, E. *The Price of Inequality.* New York: W.W. Norton and Co., 2012.

Thoreau, Lester. *The Future of Capitalism.* New York: Penguin Books, Inc., 1997.

Yevtushenko, Yevgeny. *A Precocious Autobiography.* Middlesex, England: Penguin Books Ltd., 1965.

About The Authors

Marion J. Golarz received a B.S. in English Language Arts Education and an M.S. in Education with a certification in reading from Indiana University at Bloomington. She has taught high school English, and she was a Title I reading teacher for elementary, middle school, and high school students. She also taught reading and social studies to special education students. She taught at Purdue University Calumet, Indiana University Northwest, and Indiana University East as a guest lecturer in composition. While at Purdue University Calumet, she tutored students in the writing lab. Her educational experiences have also included presenting workshops to teachers, parents, and administrators regarding research relevant to educational topics. With her husband, Raymond, she co-authored *The Power of Participation,* an in-depth discussion regarding shared decision-making processes in schools, and also co-authored *Sweet Land of Liberty*, a touching story of immigration to the United States in the early twentieth century.

She and her husband Raymond have six children: Tanya Scherschel, Michael Golarz, Scott Golarz, Jocelyn Golarz, Daniel Golarz, and Thomas Golarz. They presently have five grandchildren. She currently resides in Bloomington, Indiana, with her husband Raymond, their youngest son Thomas, who is completing postgraduate studies, their two cats Lucky and Patches, and Tom's boxer pup Conan. Life remains full. Their e-mail address is mjgolarz@live.com.

Raymond J. Golarz holds a B.A. degree in Sociology and a B.S. degree in Education from St. Joseph's College in Indiana. He received his master's degree and his doctorate in Education from Indiana University. He taught as a middle school and high school teacher, and then served as the Director of Child Welfare Services, where he supervised delinquency prevention and intervention programs and worked with delinquent gangs. He taught psychology at St. Joseph's College, Purdue Calumet, Indiana University Northwest, and City College in Seattle. In addition, he taught Psychology for Law

Enforcement to Chicago area law enforcement officers for nearly 10 years. He has been an assistant superintendent and superintendent of schools. He enjoys keynoting and has keynoted for school districts and major conferences in virtually every state in the United States. In addition, he has keynoted in most Canadian Provinces. He is the co-author of *Restructuring Schools for Excellence through Teacher Empowerment.* He co-authored with his wife Marion *The Power of Participation* and *Sweet Land of Liberty.* In addition, he is the author of *Yellow Jacket Football in Hard Times and Good* and a companion book, *When the Yellow Jackets Played.* These two books, using the backdrop of rugged American sandlot semi-pro football near Chicago, focus on the strengths of the early immigrants who came to America and with their children lived the challenges of the Great Depression.

All of his life, Ray has enjoyed sketching and oil painting. He now resides with his wife Marion and their two cats in Bloomington, Indiana. He will miss his son Thomas when he completes his second college degree and moves on. And, of course, he and the cats will also miss Tom's pup Conan. Who will there be to sneak in and eat the cats' food when he's gone?